europan 15 produktive städte 2 ergebnisse results

europan deutschland

europan 15
produktive
städte 2
ergebnisse
results

Inhalt

Vorwort 7
Produktive Städte 2 9
Europäische Standorte 13

Zur Aktualität der Produktiven Stadt 15
in Zeiten der Pandemie
Dieter Läpple

Die Produktive Stadt 27
Stefan Werrer

Ergebnisse in Deutschland und Polen 33

Bergische Kooperation 34
Bergisch Plugin 36
The Productive Region 40

Selb 44
Scherben bringen Glück 46
Selbstgemacht 50

Warschau 54
Feedback Placemaking 56
NEW neighborHUT 60
Volcano 64

Weil wir suchen … (und finden) 69
Peter Stubbe

Regionale Quartiersentwicklung 71
Uta Schneider

Bergische Kooperation 72
Irene Wiese-von Ofen

Deutsche Preisträger und Preisträgerinnen 75
im Ausland

Hyvinkää (FI) 76
The Green Ring 78

Tuusula (FI) 82
60°North 84

Romainville (FR) 88
Bridging Productivities 90

Guovdageaidnu (NO) 94
Catalogue of Ideas 96

Borås (SE) 100
P2P–Plugin 2 Produce 102
RE:MEDIATE 106

Halmstad (SE) 110
Walking Halmstad 112

Uddevalla (SE) 116
Wake „BU-HOV-BERG" up! 118

Appendix 123
Jurys 125
Bildnachweis 126
Impressum 128

Content

Preface
Productive Cities 2
European Sites

On the Significance of the Productive City
in the Pandemic Era
Dieter Läpple

Productive Cities
Stefan Werrer

Results in Germany and Poland

Bergische Kooperation
Bergisch Plugin
The Productive Region

Selb
Scherben bringen Glück
Selbstgemacht

Warschau
Feedback Placemaking
NEW neighborHUT
Volcano

Because We Seek… (and Find)
Peter Stubbe

Regional Neighbourhood Development
Uta Schneider

Bergische Kooperation
Irene Wiese-von Ofen

German Award-Winners
Abroad

Hyvinkää (FI)
The Green Ring

Tuusula (FI)
60°North

Romainville (FR)
Bridging Productivities

Guovdageaidnu (NO)
Catalogue of Ideas

Borås (SE)
P2P–Plugin 2 Produce
RE:MEDIATE

Halmstad (SE)
Walking Halmstad

Uddevalla (SE)
Wake "BU-HOV-BERG" up!

Appendix
Juries
Credits
Imprint

Vorwort

Karin Sandeck
Vorstandsvorsitzende Europan Deutschland e.V.

Kaye Geipel
Mitglied des Vorstands von Europan Deutschland e.V.

Europan 15 behandelt ein einfaches Thema: die Zukunft der Arbeit als Motor des Städtischen. Wie sehr die Stadt von den Räumen der Arbeit in ihrem Innersten zusammengehalten wird, wird in diesen außergewöhnlichen Tagen wie unter einem Vergrößerungsglas klar. In vielen Ländern der Welt hat die Corona-Krise große wie kleine Städte in ihren entscheidenden Funktionen stillgelegt. Wir sehen, was es tatsächlich bedeutet, wenn sich die öffentlichen Räume in de-Chirico-artige Bühnenbilder transformieren, wenn alle Restaurants geschlossen, die Büros ins digitale Home-Office ausgelagert sind und die Wohnung zum Universalraum wird. Der Lebensraum Stadt, die Verbindung von Innen und Außen, von privat, halböffentlich und öffentlich als gesellschaftlicher Lebensraum, scheint selbst von einem Virus betroffen.

Wir sehen in diesen Monaten aber auch, wie entscheidend es sein wird, dass Architektinnen und Architekten, Stadt- und Landschaftsplanerinnen und -planer die enormen Veränderungen im Arbeitsleben, die in den letzten Jahren stattgefunden haben, in neue räumliche, architektonische und städtebauliche Vorstellungen übersetzen und dabei die Vision einer „Stadt für alle" im Blick behalten. Die Räume der Arbeit sind nicht nur wegen der Digitalisierung in einem nie gekannten Umbruch begriffen. Fragen der Solidarität sind ein eminenter Teil der Gestaltung von Architektur – städtische und ländliche Nachbarschaften, die immer auf der Verknüpfung von Wohnen und Arbeiten basieren, müssen erst einmal konzipiert werden, sonst werden sie nicht gebaut.

Der Europan 15-Wettbewerb hat mit der Fortführung des Themas der „Produktiven Stadt" eine europaweite Pionierarbeit geleistet – der innovative Rechercheansatz von Europan 14 zur Produktiven Stadt wurde bei E 15 um das Nachdenken über Ressourcen, Mobilität, sozialen Ausgleich und unterschiedliche urbane Maßstabsebenen erweitert.

Insgesamt 901 Teams haben zu diesem Thema in Europa Lösungen entwickelt. An 47 Standorten und in 12 Ländern wurden sie von jungen Architektinnen und Architekten, Stadt- und Landschaftsplanerinnen und -planern eingereicht.

Die deutschen Standorte Selb und Bergische Kooperation, Hilden, Ratingen, Solingen und Wülfrath-Düssel haben ganz außergewöhnliche Ergebnisse erzielt, die dieser Band dokumentiert. Die vorliegende Publikation ergänzt diese Projekte um die notwendige Debatte, die die Autorinnen und Autoren Irene Wiese-von Ofen, Uta Schneider, Dieter Läpple, Stefan Werrer und Peter Stubbe beisteuern. Präsentiert werden außerdem die Vorschläge für den assoziierten Standort Warschau-Bielany. Dazu kommen die Beiträge der bei der Europan 15-Runde besonders erfolgreichen jungen Architektinnen und Architekten aus Deutschland an acht weiteren Standorten in den Nachbarländern.

2020 ist Europa mit der Coronakrise in eine Bewährungsprobe eingetreten, deren Auswirkungen die Umbrüche und Krisen der vergangenen Jahrzehnte wohl noch über-

Preface

Karin Sandeck
President of Europan Deutschland e.V.

Kaye Geipel
Member of the Board of Europan Deutschland e.V.

Europan 15 deals with a simple topic: the future of work as an engine for urban development. The extent to which the city is held together by the spaces used for work within it is becoming as clear during this strange time as if seen through a magnifying glass. The Corona crisis has shut down the crucial functions of cities both big and small in many nations in the world. We can see what it actually means when public spaces are transformed into De-Chirico-like stage sets, when all restaurants are closed, digital work from home has replaced offices, and homes are becoming a universal space with no way out. The city as a living space, the connection between inside and outside, between the private, the semi-public, and the public as well as social living space seems itself to be affected by a virus.

We have also seen in these months how crucial it will be for architects and urban and landscape planners to translate the huge changes in working life that have taken place in recent years into new spatial, architectural, and urban development ideas, and to bear in mind the notion of a 'city for everyone' in doing so. Spaces for work are in a state of never-before-seen upheaval. Questions of solidarity are a significant part of designing architecture – urban and rural neighbourhoods, which are always based on interconnecting living and working, must first be conceived or they will never be constructed.

With its continuing focus on the topic of the 'productive city', the Europan 15 competition has achieved pioneering work throughout Europe – Europan 14's innovative research approach to the productive city was expanded in E 15 to include thinking about resources, mobility, social balance, and a wide range of urban scales.

A total of 901 teams developed solutions for Europe in connection with this topic. They were submitted by young architects and urban and landscape planners for forty-seven sites in twelve countries.

The German sites, Selb and the Bergische Kooperation, Hilden, Ratingen, Solingen, and Wülfrath-Düssel, produced outstanding results, which are documented in this book. This publication supplements these projects by incorporating the relevant debates, which were contributed by the authors Irene Wiese-von Ofen, Uta Schneider, Dieter Läpple, Stefan Werrer, and Peter Stubbe. The book also presents the proposals for the associated site of Warsaw-Bielany. The book also includes contributions by young architects from Germany who were particularly successful in the Europan 15 competition for eight other sites in neighbouring countries.

In 2020, the Corona crisis is presenting Europe with an acid test whose effects will probably even exceed the impacts of the upheavals and crises of the past decades. Europan – as a unique model for cooperation between planners that transcends borders – has never before been so important as a space for thinking about and designing a European city of the future. It is thus a European model that might take the place of the 'quarantine urbanism' frequently being discussed at this time, in which 'every

treffen werden. Noch nie war Europan als Denk- und Gestaltungsraum einer europäischen Stadt der Zukunft so wichtig – als einzigartiges Modell der Kooperation von Planerinnen und Planern über die Grenzen hinweg. Es geht dabei um ein europäisches Modell, das an die Stelle eines in diesen Tagen häufig diskutierten „Quarantäne-urbanismus" tritt, bei dem das „Jeder-für-sich" zum Maß der Dinge werden könnte, die Idee einer Stadt des Ausgleichs sozialer und ökologischer Ressourcen stellt und diese in beispielhaften Projekten umsetzt.

man for himself' might become the measure of all things. It also provides an idea of a city that balances social and ecological resources and implements this idea in exemplary projects.

Produktive Städte 2

Das Verfahren Europan 15 beschäftigte sich angesichts der weiterhin massiv voranschreitenden Entmischung der europäischen Städte und des damit drohenden Verlustes ihrer Identität als gleichwertige und gleichzeitige Lebens- und Arbeitswelten nach Europan 14 erneut mit der „Produktiven Stadt" und erweiterte das Thema um die dringliche Fragestellung der ökologischen Dimensionen einer „Produktiven Stadt der Zukunft".

Eine ökologisch gedachte, produktive Transformation setzt auf Synergien anstatt auf Gegensätze. Wenn man Synergien zwischen Ökosystemen, Menschen und der gebauten Umwelt ernst nimmt, dann impliziert dies die Entwicklung neuer, nicht sektoraler, gemeinschaftlicher Lösungsansätze. Ein solches Vorgehen forderte sowohl von den am Wettbewerb teilnehmenden Architektinnen, Architekten, Planerinnen und Planern als auch von den Entscheidungsträgerinnen und Entscheidungsträgern das Bekenntnis, die ihnen anvertraute Verantwortung für die städtische Umwelt wahrzunehmen und voranzutreiben.

Für das Verfahren Europan 15 wurden im Sinne solcher nicht sektoraler, gemeinschaftlicher Lösungsansätze für eine produktive Stadt drei Themenbereiche definiert:

Ressourcen – Mobilität – Fairness.

Ressourcen

Wie können der Verbrauch und die Verschmutzung von Ressourcen minimiert werden (Wasser, Luft, Boden, Energie usw.)? Wie können Ressourcen besser geteilt werden? Welche Vorstellungen sozialer, technischer, architektonischer und stadtplanerischer Neuerungen sind in diesem Zusammenhang zu entwickeln?

Mobilität

Wie können neue Formen der Mobilität und allgemein die möglichst schwellenlose und offene Zugänglichkeit zu und innerhalb der produktiven Stadtviertel umgesetzt werden?

Fairness

Was kann die Idee einer räumlichen Gleichheit zu sozialer Gerechtigkeit beitragen? Wie lassen sich räumliche und soziale Bedingungen besser miteinander verknüpfen? Wie kann man eine gute Balance zwischen verschiedenen Stadtvierteln mit ihren unterschiedlichen Formen der Produktivität herstellen, wie die Differenzen und Konflikte zwischen Stadt und Land, zwischen Arm und Reich im städtebaulichen Kontext ausgleichen?

Die Integration der drei Themenbereiche in die konkreten Aufgabenstellungen der 47 teilnehmenden Standorte des Wettbewerbs Europan 15 wurde über die Definition von Strategien zur Entwicklung von Prozessen und Projekten erreicht. Diesen lauteten wie folgt und waren den Standorten (siehe Karte auf S. 13) zugeordnet:

Productive Cities 2

Following Europan 14: The Productive City, the Europan 15 competitions process once again occupied itself with the ongoing, inexorably progressing demixing of European cities and the consequently impending loss of their identity as balanced worlds for both living and working, and, by extension, with the topic of the urgent question of the ecological dimensions of a 'Productive City of the Future'.

An ecologically conceived, productive transformation focuses on synergies rather than contrasts. If one takes the synergies between the ecosystem, people, and the built environment seriously, then this implies developing new, non-sector-based, collaborative approaches to solutions. This kind of approach put demands not only on the architects, planners, and decision-makers involved in the competition, but also on the commitment of decision-makers to recognizing their responsibility to foster the urban environment entrusted to them.

For the Europan 15 process, three topic areas were defined in line with such non-sector-based, collaborative approaches to solutions for a productive city:

Resources – Mobility – Fairness

Resources

How can the consumption and contamination of resources (water, air, ground, energy, and so on) be minimized? How can resources be allocated better? What ideas for social, technical, architectural, and urban planning innovations have to be developed within this context?

Mobility

How can new forms of mobility and, in general, optimal barrier-free and open access to and within the productive city district be realized?

Fairness

What can the idea of spatial equality contribute to social fairness? How can spatial and social conditions be interlinked with one another more optimally? How can a good balance be achieved between various city districts with their various forms of productivity, and how can the contrasts and conflicts between the city and the countryside, between the poor and the rich be counterbalanced in the urban development context?

The incorporation of the three topic areas into the concrete tasks posed by the 47 sites that participated in the Europan 15 competition was achieved by defining strategies for developing processes and projects. These strategies were as follows and were assigned to the sites listed (see the map on p. 13):

Einbetten

Damit Städte sowohl produktiv als auch nachhaltig sein können, müssen Ressourcen, Mobilität und räumliche Fairness so miteinander verbunden werden, dass neue Dynamiken in Bezug auf zwei Aspekte entstehen: produktive Milieus und produktive Nutzungen.

Produktive Milieus

Hier ist das Einbetten oder auch Revitalisieren eines natürlichen, sozialen oder ökonomischen Umfeldes gemeint, das im Gegensatz zur technischen Stadtplanung und den objekthaften Architekturen steht und Synergien zwischen Natur und Kultur erzeugt.

Produktive Nutzungen

Als Reaktion auf eine Situation, in der jegliche Dynamik abhandengekommen ist, kann das Schaffen von neuen produktiven Nutzungen eine neue Dynamik des Wandels unterstützen, die die Umgebung mit einem zuverlässigen Programm transformiert.

Nähe schaffen

Im physischen Stadtraum, auf der temporären Ebene und der Ebene der Agierenden, geht es hier um die Schaffung von Nähe zwischen Leben und Arbeiten innerhalb von Wohngebieten sowie zwischen Wohngebieten und monofunktionalen Produktionsbereichen. Zudem wird das Thema des Übergangs zwischen der schnellen Mobilität der Metropolen und der langsameren Mobilität der Nachbarschaften behandelt.

Der dritte Raum dazwischen

Der dritte Raum wird zwischen Wohnen und der Produktion eingesetzt und könnte als Katalysator die Transformation bestehender Produktionszyklen unterstützen, indem Synergien mit städtischen Bereichen und dem alltäglichen Leben erzeugt werden. Er kann auf Restflächen innerhalb der Quartiere oder zwischen bestehenden monofunktionalen Zonen platziert werden sowie aus wiederverwendeten urbanen Strukturen entstehen.

Schnittstellen und kurze Zyklen

Die Schaffung von Schnittstellen trägt zur Veränderung von Mobilitäts-Infrastrukturen, Logistik, kommerziellen oder anderen Dienstleistungen bei, indem Produktionszyklen beschleunigt werden. Es werden neue Arten von Beziehungen zwischen Wohngebieten und landwirtschaftlich genutzten Bereichen, zwischen Wohnen und Dienstleistungen oder zwischen Raum und Gemeinschaften geschaffen. Die Schnittstelle ist ein fließendes Kontinuum in stufenweisen und adaptiven Prozessen, bei dem keine vordefinierten Masterpläne eingesetzt werden.

Veränderung des Metabolismus

Ein neues Gleichgewicht zwischen den Beziehungen, Prozessen, Strömungen und verschiedenen Kräften derjenigen Standorte, die große Flächen umfassen und

Embedding

To ensure that cities are both productive and sustainable, they have to interlink resources, various forms of mobility, and conditions of fairness in order to create new dynamics based on two aspects: productive milieus and productive uses.

Productive Milieus

This is the level where a natural, cultural, social, or economic environment is embedded or revitalised symbiotically by contrast with the architecture of objects or the urbanism of technocracy. It is therefore necessary to activate human and nonhuman resources and an ecosystem of partners, while paying attention to values that integrate nature and culture.

Productive Uses

Uses can become productive if they go beyond their own functional limitations: productive uses act as a trigger that can initiate dynamics of change in a way that transforms the surrounding environment. They are a response to a situation in which an absence of dynamics has led to a powerful 'use ambition', the demand for a credible program and a catalyst for change that fits smoothly into the existing context.

Creating Proximities

In the physical space of the city and on the temporal and stakeholder-related scales alike, it is about establishing proximities between living and working both within residential areas and between residential areas and monofunctional production zones. It is also about rethinking the transition between high-speed metropolitan mobility and the slower speed of neighbourhoods.

Third Spaces in Between

A third space is a new space inserted between housing and production areas that can catalyse the transformation of current production cycles by creating synergies with urban areas and day-to-day life. This third space can be located in residual areas within neighbourhoods or between existing mono-functional zones, or emerge from the recycled urban fabric.

Interfaces and Short Cycles

The creation of interfaces contributes to the transformation of infrastructures for mobility, logistics, commerce, or general services by shortening production cycles, and also generates new kinds of relationships between residential and farming activities, housing and services, and spaces and communities. An interface is a fluid space based on incremental and adaptive processes and rejects predefined master plans.

Altering the Metabolism

A new balance must be found between the relationships, processes, flows, and multiple forces of the sites, which are large and involve a variety of protagonists (human

eine Vielzahl von Protagonisten (menschliche und nicht menschliche) einbeziehen sowie langfristige und kurzfristige Kreisläufe aufweisen, sollte gefunden werden. Dieses Gleichgewicht sollte weitreichende positive ökologische, ökonomische und territoriale Auswirkungen haben.

Von der linearen zur Kreislaufökonomie

Diejenigen Standorte, die von einer linearen, obsoleten oder monofunktionalen Ökonomie bestimmt werden, suchen danach, andere Ressourcen und Nutzungen einzubeziehen, die Synergien und neue Potenziale für Interaktion schaffen können. Ziel ist es, ein Kreislaufsystem zu erzeugen, das neue Strömungen und Prozesse auf eine integrative Art und Weise anstoßen kann.

Vervielfachende und verbindende Vermittler

Durch die Definition und Verbindung von zukünftigen Vermittlerinnen und Vermittlern in Bezug auf Luft, Wasser, Erde, Überflutungen, Programme, Aktivitäten sowie Nutzende und neue Funktionsebenen kann es zu einem ausgewogenen Wachstum an diesen Strandorten kommen. Der letztendliche Entwurf wird dann mehr sein als die Summe der einzelnen städtischen Kreislaufökonomien.

and nonhuman), and have long- and short-term cycles and far-reaching ecological, economic, and territorial implications.

From a Linear to Circular Economy

Sites that are characterized by a 'linear', obsolete, or mono-functional economic approach aspire to incorporate other resources and to use the synergies and new potentials for interaction thus generated in order to create a circular system that catalyses flows and processes in a more integrative and efficient way.

Multiplying and Interlinking Mediators

Defining and interlinking future providers significant to air, water, soil, flood, programs, activities and users, and new layers of functions can lead to balanced growth at these sites. The final design will be something more than the sum of circular urban economies.

Einbetten – produktive Milieus
Embedding – Productive Milieus
1 Barcelona (ES), 2 Bergische Kooperation (DE),
3 Helsingborg (SE), 4 Palma (ES), 5 Raufoss (NO),
6 Rotterdam Visserijplein (NL), 7 Saint-Omer (FR),
8 Tuusula (FI)

Einbetten – produktive Nutzungen
Embedding – Productive Uses
9 Innsbruck (AT), 10 Oliva (ES), 11 Pays de Dreux (FR),
12 Rotterdam Groot IJsselmonde (NL), 13 Uddevalla (SE),
14 Verbania (IT), 15 Visby (SE), 16 Wien (AT)

Nähe schaffen – der dritte Raum dazwischen
Creating Proximities – The Third Space in Between
17 Hyvinkää (FI), 18 La Louvière (BE), 19 Lasarte-Oria
(ES), 20 Madrid – La Arboleda (ES), 21 Rødberg (NO),
22 Rotterdam Kop Dakpark (NL), 23 Sant Climent de
Llobregat (ES), 24 Villach (AT)

Nähe schaffen – Schnittstellen und kurze Zyklen
Creating Proximities – Interfaces and Short Cycles
25 Auby (FR), 26 Casar de Cáceres (ES), 27 Floirac (FR),
28 Halmstad (SE), 29 Romainville (FR), 30 Rotterdam
Brainpark I (NL), 31 Selb (DE)

**Veränderung des Metabolismus – von der linearen
zur Kreislaufökonomie**
Altering the Metabolism – From a Linear to a Circular
Economy
32 Charleroi (BE), 33 Enköping (SE), 34 Graz (AT),
35 Karlovac (HR), 36 Laterza (IT), 37 Port-Jérôme-sur-
Seine (FR), 38 Rochefort Océan (FR), 39 Warszawa (PL)

**Veränderung des Metabolismus – vervielfachende und
verbindende Vermittler**
Altering the Metabolism – Multiplying and Interlinking
Mediators
40 Borås (SE), 41 Champigny-sur-Marne (FR),
42 Guovdageaidnu (NO), 43 Marseille (FR), 44 Nin (HR),
45 Rotterdam Vierhavensblok (NL), 46 Täby (SE),
47 Weiz (AT)

12

Europäische Standorte
European Sites

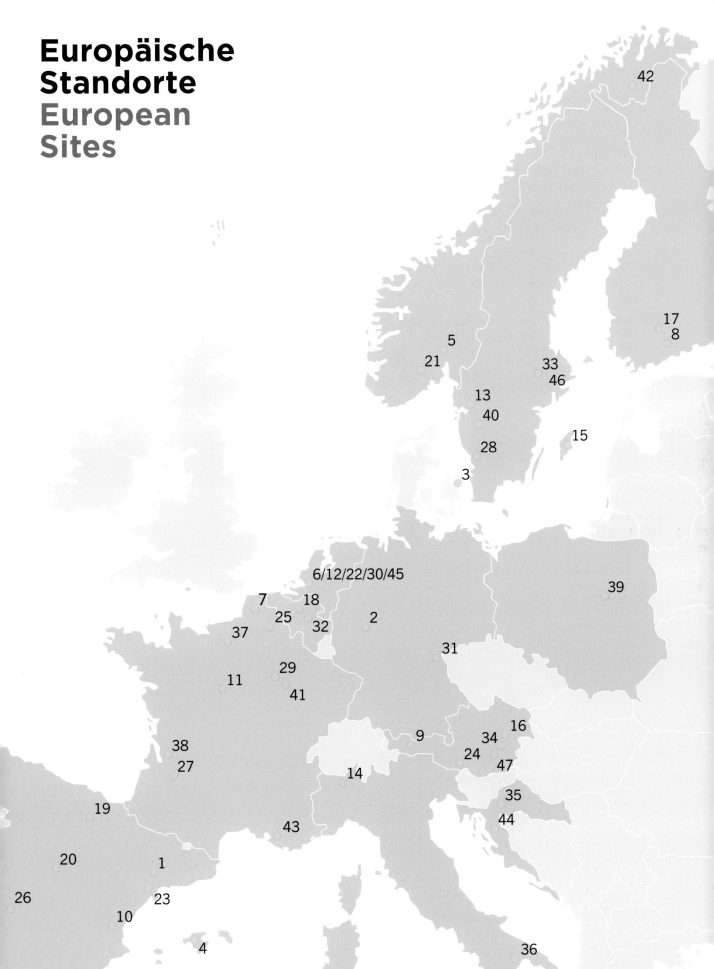

Zur Aktualität der Produktiven Stadt in Zeiten der Pandemie

Lehren aus der Corona-Pandemie

Dieter Läpple, Dr. rer. pol., emeritierter Professor für Internationale Stadtforschung an der HafenCity Universität Hamburg, langjähriger Leiter des Instituts für Stadt- und Regionalökonomie an der Technischen Universität Hamburg

Die wohl elementarste Erfahrung aus der Pandemie war und ist unsere Verletzlichkeit, als Menschen und als Gesellschaft, und damit verbunden das Gefühl einer existenziellen Unsicherheit. Diese Unsicherheitsgefühle beziehen sich nicht nur auf die Gefahren für Leib und Leben, sondern auch auf die ökonomischen, sozialen und politischen Folgen dieser Pandemie und insbesondere die Folgen für unsere Städte.

Der Wirtschaftshistoriker Adam Tooze konstatiert, dass sich die Weltwirtschaft derzeit nahezu im freien Fall befindet. Mitte März konnte nur mit massiven Finanzinterventionen der Notenbanken ein Zusammenbruch des Weltfinanzsystems verhindert werden. Die Staatsschulden sind auf Rekordhöhen gestiegen und werden weiter steigen. Die globale Krise hat nicht nur den Finanzsektor und die Exportindustrien erfasst, sondern auch den größten Teil der Dienstleistungen. Nach einem jahrelangen Beschäftigungsboom droht nun auch in Deutschland wieder das Gespenst einer Massenarbeitslosigkeit.

Der stationäre Einzelhandel, die Gastronomie und das Unterhaltungsgewerbe sind von dem Lockdown und der Verunsicherung der Verbraucherinnen und Verbraucher besonders stark betroffen und haben die Handelsimmobilien in eine Ab- wärtsspirale gezogen. *Der Spiegel* (21/2020: 64) titelte: „Totentanz in der City" und konstatiert den Beginn einer gigantischen Krise, durch die die Innenstädte in ihrer Substanz getroffen werden könnten. Das mit dem Lockdown gestartete, historisch einmalige Realexperiment zum Home-Office, das erstaunlich erfolgreich verlief, wird auf absehbarer Zeit zu einem signifikanten Rückgang des Bedarfs an Büroflächen führen, was Auswirkungen auf den Büromarkt haben wird.

Die Folgen dieser vielfältigen Krisenerscheinungen sind ebenso wenig absehbar wie Zeitpunkt und Verlaufsformen einer möglichen Erholung: „So viel Wissen über unser Nichtwissen und über den Zwang, unter Unsicherheit handeln und leben zu müssen, gab es noch nie." Mit diesen Worten charakterisiert Jürgen Habermas (2020) in einem Zeitungsinterview die aktuelle Situation.

Trotz aller Unsicherheit lassen sich aus der bisherigen Entwicklung die folgenden vorläufigen Lehren ziehen: Der „starke Staat" und die Bedeutung der „Commons": Seit Beginn der Pandemie sind wir mit einem bisher kaum denkbaren Primat der Politik und einem „starken Staat" konfrontiert. Um Leben zu retten, wurde in fast allen Ländern das soziale Leben durch Ausgangssperren und Kontaktverbote massiv eingeschränkt, wurden

---

On the Significance of the Productive City in the Pandemic Era

Lessons from the Corona Pandemic

Dieter Läpple, Dr. rer. pol. professor emeritus for international urban research at the HafenCity Universität in Hamburg, longtime director of the Institut für Stadt- und Regionalökonomie (Institute of Urban and Regional Economics) at the Technical University in Hamburg

The perhaps most elemental experience of the pandemic has been and is our vulnerability, as human beings and as society, and, consequently, a feeling of existential uncertainty. This feeling of uncertainty pertains not only to dangers to life and limb, but also to the economic, social, and political impact of this pandemic, especially the impact on cities.

The economic historian Adam Tooze states that the global economy is currently in virtual free fall (2020: 47). A collapse of the global financial system in mid-March was averted only by means of huge financial interventions by the central banks. Government debts have risen to record heights and will continue to rise. The global crisis has affected not only the financial sector and the export industries, but also most services. Following a decade-long employment boom, the spectre of mass unemployment now threatens Germany once again, along with the other nations.

Stationary retail, gastronomy, and the entertainment industry have been hit particularly hard by the lockdown and the uncertainty of consumers and have dragged commercial real estate into a downward spiral. *Der Spiegel* (21/2020: 64), under the headline 'Totentanz in der City' (Dance of Death in the City), postulated the beginning of a huge crisis that might impact the substance of city centres. The unique real life experiment of working from home that started with the lockdown – and which was surprisingly successful – will lead in the foreseeable future to a significant decline in the need for office space, which will have strongly negative impacts on the office market.

The repercussions of these multifaceted crisis phenomena, as well as the time frame and stages of a possible recovery are hardly predictable: "Never before has so much been known about what we do not know and about the pressure of having to make decisions and live under conditions of uncertainty." These are the words that Jürgen Habermas (2020) used to describe the current situation in a recent interview.

Despite all the uncertainty, the following tentative lessons can be learned from developments thus far: Firstly, a *'strong state'* and the significance of the *'commons'*. Since the beginning of the pandemic, we have been confronted with a hitherto barely conceivable *primacy of politics* and a 'strong state'. To save lives, social life was massively restricted by curfews and contact restrictions in almost all countries, fundamental basic rights like the right to travel and freedom of religion were more or less suspended, parts of the economy were put in an artificial

elementare Grundrechte wie Reisefreiheit, Versammlungsfreiheit und Religionsfreiheit mehr oder weniger außer Kraft gesetzt, Teile der Ökonomie in ein künstliches Koma versetzt und Kitas, Schulen, Universitäten und nahezu alle Kultureinrichtungen vorübergehend geschlossen. Gleichzeitig übernahmen der Staat und die staatliche Verwaltung die Rolle eines Retters in der Not. Mit spektakulären Eingriffen stützten die Zentralbanken und Regierungen die Börsen, wurden Soforthilfen und Kredite verteilt, ein zeitlich begrenzter Kündigungsschutz erlassen und billionenschwere Konjunkturprogramme vorbereitet. Länder mit mangelhaften Sozialsystemen und kaputtgesparten Gesundheitssystemen wurden während des Höhepunktes der Pandemie mit dramatischen Situationen und großem menschlichem Leid konfrontiert. Aber inzwischen bröckelt der allgemeine Konsens für einen „starken Staat" und es beginnen politische Auseinandersetzungen um eine neue Machtbalance und Aufgaben- und Verantwortungsverteilung zwischen Staat, Ökonomie, Zivilgesellschaft und Individuen. Was sehr wahrscheinlich bleiben wird ist die Einsicht der zentralen Bedeutung einer gut funktionierenden Daseinsvorsorge und sogenannter Gemeingüter („Commons"), für die der Staat die Verantwortung übernimmt. In Zeiten von Unsicherheit und Prekarität kommt solchen inklusiven Institutionen eine zentrale Rolle zu.

Die erschöpfte und störanfällige Globalisierung: Das wesentliche Merkmal unserer durch die Globalisierung geprägten Weltgesellschaft lässt sich in einem Wort zusammenfassen: Interdependenz. Die gegenseitige Abhängigkeit von Staaten und Ökonomien hat ein bedrohliches Ausmaß angenommen. Die lokale Epidemie, die in China in einer Region begann, hat sich in kürzester Zeit als Pandemie über den gesamten Globus ausgebreitet und eine Spur der ökonomischen Verwüstung und Destabilisierung nach sich gezogen. Nur langsam rückt es ins Bewusstsein: Solange die Pandemie in anderen Ländern nicht unter Kontrolle gebracht ist, sind wir gefährdet; und solange die Wirtschaft in anderen Ländern nicht wieder läuft, wird die Wirtschaftskrise auch bei uns weitergehen. Wir haben es mit systemischen Risiken einer globalisierten, interdependenten Welt zu tun, auf die Goldin und Mariathansan mit ihrem Buch *The Butterfly Defect* (2014) schon vor einigen Jahren hingewiesen haben. Dieses Buch liest sich wie ein Drehbuch der Corona-Pandemie mit ihren gesundheitlichen, sozialen und ökonomischen Gefährdungen und erinnert uns zugleich daran, dass wir zusätzlich mit einem sich verschärfenden ökologischen Risiko leben.

Mit der Corona-Pandemie zeigte sich schlagartig die enorme Störanfälligkeit einer globalisierten Ökonomie. Globale Produktionsverflechtungen und Zulieferbeziehungen sind teilweise so eng gekoppelt, dass bei einem Ausfall einer Fabrik im Krisengebiet oder bei Störungen der Transportwege ganze Wertschöpfungsketten zum Erliegen kommen. Insbesondere bei strategisch wichtigen Produkten, wie zum Beispiel Medikamenten, kann dies fatale gesellschaftliche Folgen haben.[1] Ökonominnen und Ökonomen unterschiedlichster Richtungen sind sich darin einig, dass es zu einer Neukonfiguration der internationalen Arbeitsteilung, insbesondere zu einer Neujustierung der Wertschöpfungsketten kommen muss. Allein schon aus Gründen der Versorgungssicherheit wird es in der kommenden Zeit zu einer stärkeren Re-Regionalisierung der Produktion kommen.[2] Die Alternative darf aber nicht sein: Nationalisierung statt Globalisierung, sondern es muss eine Rekonfiguration der Globalisierung stattfinden. Die Gestaltung einer

coma, and day care centres, schools, and universities and almost all cultural institutions were temporarily closed. At the same time, the state and the government administration took on the role of a knight in shining armour. The central banks and governments shored up the stock market with spectacular interventions, emergency aid and loans were handed out, a temporary protection against eviction passed, and a stimulus packet amounting to trillions prepared. Countries with inadequate social security and heavy budget cuts in their healthcare system were confronted with dramatic situations and enormous human suffering at the peak of the pandemic. However, in the meantime, the general consensus on a 'strong state' has begun to crumble, and political confrontations have begun over a new balance of power and the redistribution of tasks and responsibilities between the state, the economy, civil society, and individuals. What will most likely remain is the recognition of the key importance of a well-functioning supply of public services – so-called 'commons', for which the state assumes responsibility. At a time of uncertainty and precariousness, such inclusive institutions have been given a central role.

Exhausted, disruption-prone globalization: The key characteristic of our world's society as it is shaped by globalization can be summarized in one word: *interdependency*. The mutual dependency of states and economies has reached a quite dangerous level. A local epidemic that began in one region in China spread out as a pandemic across the entire globe in a noticeably short time period and brought a trail of economic devastations and destabilizations along with it. As we are only slowly becoming aware, as long as the pandemic has not been brought under control in other countries, we are at risk; and as long as the economy is not up and running again in other countries, the economic crisis will continue for us as well. We are living with the systemic risks of a globalized, interdependent world, previously discussed by Goldin and Mariathansan a number of years ago in their book *The Butterfly Defect*. This book reads like a script for the Corona pandemic, with its health-related, social, and economic threats. It simultaneously reminds us that we are also living with a growing threat to the ecosystem.

With the Corona pandemic, the huge susceptibility to failure that is inherent in a globalized economy has been underscored. Global production interdependencies and supply relations are in many cases so tightly coupled that the loss of a factory in a crisis region or disruptions of transport routes can bring entire value chains to a standstill. This can have fatal social effects particularly in the case of strategically important products like medications.[1] Economists with widely differing points of view agree on the fact that the international division of labour must be reconfigured and value-added chains in particular must be readjusted. A more far-reaching re-regionalization of production will take place in the near future simply for reasons of supply reliability.[2] However, the alternative cannot be nationalization in place of globalization, but must instead entail a *reconfiguration of globalization*. The shaping of a new, crisis-resistant globalization that takes environmental costs into account is a central task for the post-Corona era. The guiding principle of the productive city should become a central cornerstone of this new global economy.

The necessary transformation in materials: As a result of the current crisis, the 'consumerist' paradigm, which is particularly influential in culturalistic urban discourses and is based on the hypothesis that in the 'symbolic economy' of cities (see Zukin 1995) the organization of

neuen krisenresistenten Globalisierung unter Berücksichtigung der ökologischen Kosten ist eine zentrale Aufgabe der Post-Corona-Zeit. Das Leitbild einer produktiven Stadt sollte dabei ein zentraler Eckpfeiler dieser neuen Weltökonomie werden.

Die notwendige materielle Wende (Läpple 2018): Das vor allem in den kulturalistischen Stadtdiskursen einflussreiche „konsumistische" Paradigma, das von der These ausgeht, dass in der „symbolischen Ökonomie" der Städte (vgl. Zukin 1995) die Organisation des Konsums prägend sei für das städtische Leben, erwies sich mit der aktuellen Krise als konstruktivistische Kopfgeburt. Die unmittelbare Erfahrung der Materialität des Städtischen gehört zu den kollektiven Lernprozessen der Pandemie. Damit verbunden ist eine neue Sensibilität für die zentrale Bedeutung von Arbeit, insbesondere für die Bedeutung von bisher sozial und politisch weitgehend ausgeblendeten Tätigkeiten, die unter dem Problemdruck der Krise plötzlich als „systemrelevant" erfahren wurden, zum Beispiel die Müllbeseitigung und die Warenlogistik, die Tätigkeiten im Supermarkt oder die Pflege im Krankenhaus ebenso wie die Produktion von Schutzkleidung und Beatmungsgeräten. Es ist zu hoffen, dass durch diese Erfahrungen auch die Engführung der Stadtdiskussion auf eine postindustrielle Perspektive und eine „Kulturökonomisierung der Arbeit" aufgebrochen wird und sich die Einsicht durchsetzt, dass neben all den wichtigen kulturellen Phänomenen urbanen Lebens die *materielle Produktion*, auch in ihren industriellen und handwerklichen Formen, eine notwendige Basis für das Funktionieren einer Stadtgesellschaft und der vielgestaltigen Stoffwechselprozesse mit der Natur bleibt. Dies gilt umso mehr, da wir – auch in der Corona- und Post-Corona-Zeit – vor der zentralen Aufgabe stehen, unsere Ökonomie zu dekarbonisieren und als Kreislaufwirtschaft zu reorganisieren.

Die entscheidenden Leitprinzipien für die anstehende Transformation und Erneuerung der Ökonomie, insbesondere der Ökonomie der Städte, sind – so die Konklusion aus den Lehren der Corona-Pandemie: Versorgungssicherheit, Resilienz, Nachhaltigkeit und soziale Kohäsion.

Versorgungsengpässe bei lebenswichtigen Medikamenten und Atemmasken rückten die Frage der *Versorgungssicherheit* schlagartig ins öffentliche Bewusstsein. Mit der unmittelbaren Erfahrung systemischer Risiken einer globalisierten Ökonomie stellt sich die Frage nach robusten, adaptiven und inklusiven Strukturen. Dies ist die zentrale Fragestellung der *Resilienz* bzw. der Resilienzforschung[3]. In ihrem Buch *The Butterfly Defect* fordern Goldin und Mariathasan eine „resiliente Globalisierung", die eine inklusive und nachhaltige Entwicklung ermöglicht (2014: 31f.). Die Dringlichkeit der *Nachhaltigkeit* ist, angesichts der bedrohlichen Auswirkungen des Klimawandels, offensichtlich. Vor dem Hintergrund der sich verdichtenden Probleme auf dem Arbeitsmarkt und der Polarisierung der Gesellschaft steht das Leitprinzip der *sozialen Kohäsion* für die Aufgabe einer Stärkung der Integrations- und Aufstiegsperspektiven einer kosmopolitischen Stadtgesellschaft.

Für die bauliche Gestaltung der Stadt erfordert dies einen überfälligen Paradigmenwechsel: Das in den Köpfen verfestigte Leitbild der funktionsgetrennten Stadt muss endlich durch das einer nutzungsgemischten Stadt ersetzt werden, damit sich über eine kreative Mischung von Wohnen und Arbeiten die besondere Produktivität und die Integrationspotentiale der Stadt

consumption in particular shapes urban life, has turned out to be a constructivist brainchild. Directly experiencing the materiality of the urban environment is part of the collective learning processes during the pandemic. Connected with this is a new sensitivity to the central significance of work, and particularly the importance of activities that were previously overlooked by society and politics, but are suddenly being experienced as 'system-relevant', such as garbage collection and goods logistics, work in supermarkets, or nursing in hospitals, and likewise (for instance) the production of protective clothing, respiratory masks, and ventilation devices. Let us hope that these experiences will also break up the narrow focus of the urban discourse on a post-industrial perspective and a 'cultural economization of work' and that there is growing recognition that – besides all the important cultural phenomena of urban life – material production, including industrial and manufactural forms of material production, is a necessary basis for the functioning of an urban society and the diverse metabolic processes it applies to nature. This is all the more true since we are confronted with the central task of decarbonization and the reorganization of the urban economy as a circular economy.

To Conclude the lessons learned from the Corona pandemic, the essential guiding principles for the forthcoming transformation and renewal of the economy and the urban economy in particular are: security of supply, resilience, sustainability, and social coherence.

Difficulties in the supplying of vital medicines and protective clothing have especially highlighted public awareness for the need for *security of supply*. The immediate experience of the systemic risks of globalization raised the question of how to shape robust, adaptive, and inclusive structures. This is the key question for resilience, or resilience thinking[3]. In their book "The butterfly defect" Goldin and Mariathasan ask for "a greater focus on the idea of resilient globalization that fosters inclusivity and sustainable growth." (2014: 31) Now that we are faced with the threatening impact of climate change, the urgent need for development based on *sustainability* is obvious. And finally, considering the evolving problems on the labour market and the polarization of society, amplified by the Corona crisis, the principle of *social coherence* requires the strengthening of social *integration and advancement* opportunities.

In urban design, this necessitates an overdue paradigm shift: the guiding principle of a city of separate functions must finally be replaced by a city of mixed uses so that a creative mix of living and working can unfold the special potentials of the city with respect to productivity and integration. Notably, this implies the reintegration of material production into the urban fabric and, coupled with this, the concerns of the productive city (Läpple 2018). But is this effectively feasible?

Myth and Problems of a Post-industrial Perspective on Development[4]

In the last few decades, the economic basis of cities has changed profoundly. It seems that, today, services shape the economy of cities. Significantly as a result of an urban policy aimed primarily at an undisturbed life and the one-sided promotion of services, our cities are confronted with a problematic tendency towards a *thinning out of urban spaces* in terms of a mix of functions. More and more medium-sized and small enterprises in the manufac-

17

entfalten können. Eine Reintegration der materiellen Produktion in das städtische Gefüge ist – wie noch genauer begründet wird – dringend erforderlich und damit auch die Perspektive einer produktiven Stadt (Läpple 2018). Aber ist die produktive Stadt tatsächlich realisierbar?

Mythos und Probleme einer postindustriellen Entwicklungsperspektive[4]

In den letzten Jahrzehnten hat sich die ökonomische Basis der Städte tiefgreifend verändert. Heute – so scheint es – prägen Dienstleistungen die Ökonomie der Städte. Nicht zuletzt als Folge einer Stadtpolitik, die vor allem auf störungsfreies Wohnen und die einseitige Förderung von Dienstleistungen ausgerichtet war, sind wir in unseren Städten mit der problematischen Tendenz einer *funktionalen Ausdünnung städtischer Räume* konfrontiert. Immer mehr Mittel- und Kleinbetriebe des verarbeitenden Gewerbes, des Handwerkes oder der Migrantenökonomie wurden aus den städtischen Quartieren und der Stadt verdrängt. Das machte Stadträume zu Orten des monofunktionalen Wohnens und des Konsums, zu Standorten hochwertiger Dienstleistungen und zum Festivalplatz einer ausufernden Entertainmentbranche.

Das urbane Aufstiegsversprechen wird untergraben und der ökologische Fußabdruck wird immer größer.

Diese einseitige Ausrichtung einer postindustriellen Stadtpolitik erhöht nicht nur die Krisenanfälligkeit, sondern verschärft auch die Probleme der Integrationsfähigkeit städtischer Arbeitsmärkte. Städte, deren Ökonomie primär auf Dienstleistungen ausgerichtet ist, weisen eine stärkere Polarisierung der Einkommen und der sozialräumlichen Strukturen auf als Städte, die noch ein solides Fundament im Bereich des verarbeitenden Gewerbes – also der Industrie und der urbane Produktion – haben. Integrationskraft und Aufstiegspotenziale städtischer Arbeitsmärkte haben sich mit dem wirtschaftlichen Strukturwandel gravierend verringert. Die soziale „Rolltreppe" nach oben, die Geringqualifizierte früher bestiegen haben, als sie in die Stadt zogen, funktioniert nicht mehr. Die postindustrielle Stadt untergräbt offensichtlich das urbane Aufstiegsversprechen, also das Versprechen auf ein besseres Leben, das eines der prägenden Charakteristika der modernen Großstadt war.

Gleichzeitig haben sich die postindustriellen Städte zu gewaltigen Müll- und „Entropie"-Maschinen entwickelt. Mit der Auslagerung der materiellen Produktion wurde der Zusammenhang von Produktion und Konsumtion räumlich entkoppelt und damit auch die Verantwortung für die Probleme der Ressourcenbeschaffung, der Emissionen und der Entsorgung von Abfall ausgelagert. Die unseren urbanen Lebensstil ermöglichenden Stoffwechselprozesse sind mental ausgeblendet und auch sinnlich nicht mehr erfahrbar. Die Folge: Der *ökologische Fußabdruck* der „postindustriellen" Stadt wird immer größer. Die Müllmassen haben sich inzwischen zu einem „Paralleluniversum" unserer Warenwelt entwickelt. Es wird Zeit zu begreifen, dass Müll kein Abfall, sondern ein großes Rohstoffpotenzial ist, und dass man die bisher linear ausgerichteten Stadtökonomien zunehmend in Kreislaufökonomien transformieren muss und kann. Dies birgt ein großes Potenzial, die Stadt nicht nur als Ort des Konsums zu sehen, sondern auch als Ort einer nachhaltigen Produktion.

turing sector, crafts, or migrant economy have been forced out of urban neighbourhoods and the city. This has made urban spaces into places for mono-functional living and consumption, into locations for high-end services, and into festival grounds for a mushrooming entertainment industry.

The urban promise of advancement has been undermined and the ecological footprint is becoming ever bigger.

This one-sided orientation of a post-industrial urban policy not only increases our susceptibility to crisis, but also exacerbates the problems of inclusiveness of urban labour markets. Cities with an economy oriented primarily towards services show a greater polarization of incomes and socio-spatial structures than cities that still have a solid basis in the manufacturing sector – which suggests urban industry and urban manufacturing. The inclusiveness and the opportunities for advancement of urban labour markets have been severely eroded by the structural shift toward a service economy. The social 'escalator' that low-skilled workers used to ascend when they moved to the city in the past no longer works. The post-industrial city appears to undermine the urban promise of advancement, and thus the promise of a better life, which was once the distinctive nature of the modern metropolis.

At the same time, post-industrial cities have developed into veritable waste and 'entropy' machines. With the outsourcing of material production, the relationship between production and consumption has been spatially decoupled and responsibility for the problems of resources, emissions, and disposal of waste thus outsourced as well. The metabolic processes that facilitate our urban lifestyle have been mentally blanked out and can also no longer be experienced sensually. As a result, the *ecological footprint* of the 'post-industrial' city is becoming ever bigger. The masses of waste have meanwhile developed into a 'parallel universe' of our world of goods. It is time to understand that waste is not worthless, but a great potential source of raw material, and also that the hitherto linear-flow economy must and can be transformed into a circular-flow economy. This prospect holds great potential for the city not only as a place for consumption, but also as a place for sustainable production.

'Network of industry' – a supporting pillar of the urban economy

Fortunately, manufacturing has not yet vanished entirely from cities in Germany. There is still a critical industrial base in most cities, despite de-industrialization. The vital importance of industry is shown by the intertwining and interdependency of industry and services. Many authors regard a performative industrial base as a crucial prerequisite for the strong growth of business-oriented services. This 'service-manufacturing link', which is also called a *'network of industry'* (Eickelpasch/Behrend 2017: 639), is a supporting pillar *of economic growth and innovations in German cities*. Due to the increasing interlinking of value-added processes, in many cases services and material production can barely be differentiated from one another anymore. In the German production model, industry and urban manufacturing continue to occupy an important anchor position.

„Netzwerk Industrie" – eine tragende Säule der Stadtökonomie

Glücklicherweise ist in Deutschland das verarbeitende Gewerbe noch nicht ganz aus den Städten verschwunden. In den meisten Städten gibt es trotz Deindustrialisierung noch eine kritische industrielle Basis. Wie wichtig die Industrie ist, zeigt vor allem der Verflechtungs- und Wirkungszusammenhang von Industrie und Dienstleistungen. Viele Autorinnen und Autoren sehen eine leistungsfähige industrielle Basis als wesentliche Voraussetzung für das starke Wachstum der unternehmensorientierten Dienstleistungen. Dieser „Service-Manufacturing-Link", auch als *Netzwerk Industrie*" (Eickelpasch/Behrend 2017: 639) bezeichnet, ist eine *tragende Säule des wirtschaftlichen Wachstums und der Innovationen in deutschen Städten*. Durch eine zunehmende Verzahnung von Wertschöpfungsprozessen lassen sich Dienstleistungen und materielle Produktion vielfach kaum mehr voneinander unterscheiden. Die Industrie und urbane Produktion nehmen im deutschen Produktionsmodell nach wie vor eine wichtige Ankerposition ein.

Digitale Transformation – ein „disruptiver Jobveränderer"

Die Digitalisierung ist einer der entscheidenden Treiber der gegenwärtigen Transformation der Arbeitswelten. Künstliche Intelligenz, Robotertechnologie, additive Fertigungstechnologie (3D-Druck), die Vernetzung der digitalen und physischen Welt, Big Data und digitale Plattformen können Wertschöpfungsketten, Unternehmensstrukturen, die Organisation der Arbeit, Wettbewerbsstrukturen und das Verhältnis zwischen Produzentinnen und Produzenten und Konsumentinnen und Konsumenten tiefgreifend verändern.

Wird die Digitalisierung zum „Jobkiller" oder zum „Jobmotor"? Frey und Osborne legten bereits 2013 eine Studie vor, nach der sich 47 Prozent der US-amerikanischen und 54 Prozent der europäischen Arbeitsplätze aufgrund von Fortschritten im Bereich der KI automatisieren ließen. Allerdings relativierte Frey dieses Schreckensszenario jüngst mit der Einschätzung, dass die eigentliche Herausforderung heute im Bereich der Politik, nicht der Technologie liegen würde. Heute hätten die Beschäftigten politische Rechte und die Regierungen müssten bemüht sein, die sozialen Kosten der Automatisierung durch die Gestaltung der Technologie in den Griff zu bekommen (Frey 2019a: 11).

Galten Dienstleistungen bisher als weitgehend resistent gegen Arbeitsplatzverluste durch neue Technologien, so ist es inzwischen sehr wahrscheinlich, dass nicht nur in Fabriken, sondern auch in Büros, Banken, Versicherungen, Krankenhäusern, Anwaltskanzleien oder im Verkehr Roboter oder Algorithmen in zunehmendem Umfang Aufgaben übernehmen. Als „disruptiver Jobveränderer" wird die Digitalisierung zu einer zunehmenden Entgrenzung der Arbeit führen – zum Beispiel in der Form einer über digitale Plattformen vermittelten „Gig Economy" (vgl. Crouch 2019) – sowie zu einer Polarisierung der Einkommen und Lebenschancen.

Produktion zurück in die Stadt – eine realistische Perspektive

Die Transformation der tradierten, auf Massenproduktion ausgerichteten Industrie in eine neue, stadtverträgliche

Digital Transformation – a 'Disruptive Job Changer'

Digitization is one of the key drivers of the current transformation of working worlds. Artificial intelligence, robot technology, additive manufacturing (3D printing), the interlinking of the digital and physical world, big data, and digital platforms can profoundly change value chains, business structures, the organization of work, competition structures, and the relationship between producers and consumers.

Will digitization become a 'job killer' or a 'job creator'? In 2013, Frey/Osborne presented a study according to which 47 % of American and 54 % or European jobs could be automated thanks to progress in artificial intelligence. Frey, however, recently relativized this horror scenario, stating that today the real challenge shall be sought in the field of policymaking and not in the field of technology. Today, employees would have political rights, and, as a result, government could be obliged to reduce the social costs of automation by shaping the application conditions of technology (Frey 2019a: 11).

While services have long been regarded as being largely resistant to job losses as a result of labor-replacing technologies, it is currently highly probable that robots or algorithms will take over tasks to an increasing extent not only in factories, but also in offices, banks, insurance companies, hospitals, law firms, or transport.

As a 'disruptive job changer', digitization is increasingly blurring the boundaries of work – for instance in the form of a 'gig economy' (see Crouch 2019) via digital platforms – and this is leading to a polarization of income and opportunities in life.

Bringing Production Back to the City – a Realistic Perspective

The transformation of traditional mass production manufacturing into a new, city-compatible network of production is far from finished. Digital production technologies, some of which bear the label Industry 4.0, offer important shaping options. Digitization has hitherto been primarily discussed in the character of a 'replacing technology'. Replacing technologies render jobs and skills redundant. Here, in contrast, we will explore digitization as an *'enabling technology'*, and thus a technology that makes people more productive in their existing tasks or creates entirely new jobs for them (Frey 2019b: 13). With its great potential for flexibility, digitization can – so goes the argument – open up new corridors for development and fundamentally alter the growth and location patterns of material production.

Further deliberation concentrates on the question of whether the return of production to the city is a realistic option (see et el. Läpple 2016 and 2018; Gärtner 2019; Juraschek, Thiede, Herrmann 2018). A strengthening of the productive basis of cities could be achieved not only through the enabling potentials of digitization, but also – as will be explained in what follows – by changes in the global economy, a change in society's values, and the ever more urgent need to decarbonize the economy.

19

Netzwerkökonomie ist längst nicht abgeschlossen. Die digitalen Produktionstechnologien, die teilweise das Label „Industrie 4.0" tragen, bieten wichtige Gestaltungsoptionen. Bisher wird die Digitalisierung primär unter der Perspektive einer „Replacing Technology" diskutiert, also einer Technologie, die Jobs und Qualifikationen überflüssig macht. Hier sollen die Potenziale der Digitalisierung als *„Enabling Technology"* ausgelotet werden, also einer Technologie, die Menschen in ihren bestehenden Aufgaben produktiver macht oder gänzlich neue Jobs ermöglicht (Frey 2019b: 13). Mit ihrem großen Flexibilisierungspotenzial kann Digitalisierung, so die These, neue Entwicklungskorridore eröffnen und Wachstums- und Standortmuster der materiellen Produktion grundlegend verändern.

Dieser Beitrag konzentriert sich im Folgenden auf die Frage, ob die Rückkehr der Produktion in die Stadt eine realistische Option ist (vgl. u. a. Läpple 2016 u. 2018; Gärtner 2019; Juraschek, Thiede, Herrmann 2018). Eine Stärkung der produktiven Basis der Städte könnte nicht nur durch Potenziale der Digitalisierung ermöglicht werden, sondern auch – wie im Folgenden noch ausgeführt wird – durch Veränderungen in der globalen Ökonomie, einen sich abzeichnenden gesellschaftlichen Wertewandel sowie die immer drängender werdende Notwendigkeit einer Dekarbonisierung der Wirtschaft.

Urbane Orte der Arbeit erfordern neue städtebauliche und architektonische Konzepte sowie eine neue Ästhetik

Von großer Bedeutung für eine mögliche Zukunft der Produktion in der Stadt ist die Flächenfrage. Dies beginnt mit einer effizienteren Nutzung von Gewerbe- und Industrieflächen durch neue flächensparende städtebauliche und architektonische Konzepte. Angesichts der hohen Flächenkonkurrenz stellt sich mit großer Dringlichkeit die Frage der *Stapelung von Funktionen*, auch für das produzierende Gewerbe. Sehr anschauliche Beispiele dazu bietet die Studie von Nina Rappaport (2015) zur „Vertical Urban Factory".[5] Gefordert ist eine flexible, möglichst nutzungsoffene städtische Gewerbearchitektur, die in flächensparender und stadtverträglicher Weise eine Integration von Produktion, Logistik, Dienstleistungen, Wohnen und sozialer Infrastruktur ermöglicht. Die neuen Orte der Arbeit sollen intelligent in den Stadtraum eingebunden und durch eine attraktive Ästhetik sichtbar und erkennbar sein. Entscheidend wird es sein, dass dies nicht auf Kosten von Grün- und Freiflächen geht, sondern Stadtgrün integraler Bestandteil dieser anspruchsvollen Formen von Nutzungsmischung ist. Neben einer Nachverdichtung durch Stapelung und einer gezielten Funktionsanreicherung kann ein kluges Lebenszyklus- und Gebietsmanagement ein sinnvoller Handlungsansatz sein, vor allem wenn es darum geht, den Bestand zu sichern und zukunftsfähig weiterzuentwickeln.

Erschöpfte Globalisierung und Wertewandel

Die Rückkehr der Produktion in die Stadt ermöglicht auch Veränderungen in der globalen Ökonomie. Wie bereits ausgeführt, zeigte sich mit der Corona-Pandemie schlagartig die enorme Störanfälligkeit einer globalisierten Ökonomie als Folge der profitgetriebenen Auslagerungs-Strategien der Produktion in sogenannte Schwellenländer.

Urban places of work – A call for new architectural and urban design concepts and for a new aesthetic

The land question has great significance with respect to a possible future for production in the city. It begins with a more efficient utilization of commercial and industrial land resulting from new space-saving urban development and architectural concepts. Considering the high level of competition for land, the question of *stacking functions* arises with greater urgency, in manufacturing as elsewhere. Nina Rappaport's study (2015) on 'vertical urban factories' offers very clear examples.[5] What is called for is a flexible, urban industrial architecture that is open to as many uses as possible and that facilitates an integration of production, logistics, services, housing, and social infrastructure in a space-saving and city-compatible way. The new places for work should be incorporated into the cityscape in an intelligent way and be visible and recognizable as a result of an attractive aesthetic. It is essential that this does not take place at the expense of green and open spaces, but rather that urban greenery be made an integral component of these sophisticated forms of a mix of uses. Aside from redensification by means of stacking and a targeted enrichment of functions, clever lifecycle and estate management may be an important approach, particularly when it is about securing and further developing existing stocks.

Exhausted globalization and a change in society's values

The return of production to the city can additionally be enabled through changes in the global economy. As already explained, the Corona pandemic has highlighted the globalized economy's enormous susceptibility to disruption because of the profit-driven outsourcing strategies of production to so-called emerging economies.

Moreover, the competitive advantages of low-wage countries and emerging economies have become increasingly fragile in recent years. Wages have also risen there, and quality issues are becoming more and more noticeable. The previous divisions of roles in a globalized world, according to which emerging economies served as an extended workbench for labour-intensive processes, is increasingly being questioned. Globalization was already losing its momentum prior to the Corona pandemic. There is now talk of a 'global trade slowdown', hence the argument that global trade has passed its historical peak.[6]

At the same time, considering the scandalous working conditions and environmentally harmful production methods of global low-cost producers, a growing demand for products produced in a fair and environmentally friendly way is emerging. More and more people want local products. They want to know *who* produces their products, *how*, and *with what materials*. People are on a search for quality and an individual aesthetic and some are also ready to contribute to a more just and sustainable world by means of their buying decisions. This has led to new niche markets, for instance in the case of textiles, shoes, furniture, food, and other consumer goods. In this context, the city with its differentiated groups of buyers and spatially concentrated purchasing power offers great potentials for new forms of a sustainable, customer-specific production. The necessary reconfiguration of a crisis-resilient globalization opens an important window of opportunity for the development of urban production.

Abb. 1:
Entwurf für eine hybride Überbauung einer Industriehalle
im Gewerbegebiet Liesing in Wien

Gestapelte Nachverdichtung, Funktionsanreicherung und
selektive Urbanisierung monofunktionaler, eingeschossiger
Gewerbebauten durch Integration von Start-ups für urbane
Produktion, Büro- und Kreativfunktionen, soziale Funktionen
(öffentliche Kantine) und urbane Landwirtschaft.
Quelle: PLAYstudio: Iván Capdevila/Vincente Iborra (ES):
Wettbewerb Europan 14

Fig. 1:
Design for a hybrid overbuilding of an industrial hall in the
Liesing industrial park in Vienna

Stacked redensification, an enrichment of functions, and a
selective urbanization of a hitherto mono-functional, one-
storey industrial buildings by integrating start-ups for urban
manufacturing, office and creative functions, social functions
(public cafeteria), and urban agriculture.
Source: PLAYstudio: Iván Capdevila/Vincente Iborra (ES):
Europan 14 competition

Zudem wurden die Konkurrenzvorteile von Billiglohn- und Schwellenländern in den letzten Jahren immer brüchiger. Die Löhne sind auch dort gestiegen und es machen sich verstärkt Qualitätsprobleme bemerkbar. Die bisherige Rollenverteilung in einer globalisierten Welt, nach der Schwellenländer vor allem als verlängerte Werkbank für arbeitsintensive Prozesse agieren, steht zunehmend in Frage. Auch bereits vor der Corona-Pandemie verlor die Globalisierung an Dynamik. Es ist inzwischen die Rede von einem „global trade slow down", also der These, dass der Welthandel seinen historischen Gipfel überschritten habe.[6]

Gleichzeitig entwickelt sich angesichts der skandalösen Arbeitsverhältnisse und der umweltbelastenden Produktionsmethoden der globalen Billigproduktion eine zunehmende Nachfrage nach fair und umweltgerecht produzierten Produkten. Immer mehr Leute wollen lokale Produkte. Sie wollen wissen, wer ihre Produkte *wie* und *mit welchen Materialien* produziert. Die Menschen sind auf der Suche nach Qualität und individueller Ästhetik und einige sind auch bereit, mit ihren Kaufentscheidungen einen Beitrag für eine gerechtere und nachhaltigere Welt zu leisten. Das führt zu neuen Nischenmärkten, beispielsweise bei Textilien, Schuhen, Möbeln, Nahrungsmitteln und anderen Konsumgütern. Hier bietet die Stadt mit ihren differenzierten Käufergruppen und der räumlich konzentrierten Kaufkraft große Potenziale für neue Formen einer nachhaltigen, kundenspezifischen Produktion. Die notwendige Neugestaltung einer krisenresistenten Globalisierung unter Berücksichtigung der ökologischen Kosten eröffnet der Entfaltung urbaner Produktion ein wichtiges Möglichkeitsfenster.

22

Neue Perspektiven durch 3D-Druck und Leichtbauroboter

Eine der spektakulärsten Möglichkeiten bieten die 3D-Drucker, also die neuen „additiven Fertigungsmethoden" auf digitaler Basis. Die Anwendungen scheinen unbegrenzt: Hörgeräte, Zahnkronen, Prothesen, Sportschuhe, Kleidung oder Automobilersatzteile; Teile gefertigt aus unterschiedlichsten Kunststoffen, Aluminium, Stahl, Titan, Glas oder Keramik. Selbst der „Druck" von Häusern oder von Nahrungsmitteln wie „Steaks" wird inzwischen getestet. Einige Autorinnen und Autoren gehen davon aus, dass die 3D-Drucker die Fertigung aus den Billiglohnländern zurückholen könnten, dass sich also eine kundenspezifische Produktion da entwickelt, wo die Verbraucher und Verbraucherinnen mit ihren individuellen Wünschen sind. Bisher ist dies nur in einigen Nischen gelungen.

Allerdings hat der 3D-Druck durch die Corona-Krise einen erheblichen Aufschwung erfahren. So wurde er vor allem als Puffer und flexibler Problemlöser bei Lieferunterbrechungen und Engpässen der globalisierten Massenproduktion eingesetzt. Während die global ausgerichtete Massenproduktion enorm störanfällig ist und sich nur sehr langsam an veränderte Markt- oder Lieferbedingungen anpassen kann, können 3D-Drucker flexibel und schnell reagieren und damit teure Produktionsausfälle verhindern helfen. Diese „Noteinsätze" während der Corona-Krise haben auch zu neuen Skalierungsoptionen geführt. So wurden inzwischen sogenannte „Druckfarmen" entwickelt, wo bis zu 500 Geräte parallel produzieren, um auf die erforderlichen Stückzahlen zu kommen. Es zeichnet sich ein starker Innovationsschub ab, dessen Zukunftsdynamiken noch nicht absehbar sind.

New perspectives because of 3D printing and lightweight robots

One of the most spectacular opportunities to promote urban production is offered by 3D printers, i. e. the new 'additive production methods' on a digital basis. The applications seem to have no limits: hearing aids, dental crowns, prostheses, sports shoes, clothing, or replacement parts for cars; parts produced from a wide range of synthetic materials, aluminium, steel, titanium, glass, or ceramic. Even the 'printing' of houses or food items such as 'steaks' is meanwhile being tested. Some authors anticipate that 3D printers might bring production back from low-wage countries, and that customer-specific production will thus develop in places where consumers with their individual desires are found. However, up to now, this has only been successful in some niches.

At the same time, 3D printing has experienced a significant upswing because of the Corona crisis. It has been used in particular as a buffer and flexible problem solver in the case of interruptions to supply and bottlenecks in globalized mass production. While globally-oriented mass production is extremely susceptible to disruptions and can only adapt to altered market or supply conditions very slowly, 3D printers can react flexibly and thus help prevent expensive production shortfalls. These 'emergency deployments' during the Corona crisis have also led to new scaling options. In the meantime, there are so-called 'printing farms' where up to 500 devices can produce in parallel to deliver the quantities required. This delivers a massive impetus for innovation whose future prospects cannot yet be foreseen.

It can, however, be anticipated that 3D printing, just like the very flexible and easily programmable lightweight robots, is at present not yet able to compete with global mass production. These new technologies can only develop their potentials if a new production logic attuned to an individualized and decentralized 'on-demand production' and a corresponding buyer's market takes shape. The industry sociologist Sabine Pfeiffer articulated this as follows: "On-demand production would undoubtedly be technically conceivable and ecologically very sensible – it can, however, only be realized in niches, since it runs counter to the principles of a capitalistic economy condemned to growth (and hence to overproduction)" (Pfeiffer 2019: 173). At this point, it becomes clear that this (in my opinion) necessary transformation is not a technical question, but a question that touches on society itself. Also, cities as places for innovations, production, and consumption, and as arenas where social controversies are vigorously conducted can play a central, transformative role. After all, the cities of today are central venues for dealing with the question of how we want to live in the future.

Evidence for a re-urbanization of industry

An interesting insight into current development tendencies with respect to a transformation of urban economies in the direction of 'on-demand production' is provided by a study of industrial start-up activities in Germany, which was conducted by the Deutsches Institut für Wirtschaftsforschung (DIW, German Institute for Economic Research) (Gornig/Werwatz 2018). The authors, who want to obtain insights into the location preferences of start-ups using digital technologies, arrive at interesting results: the intensity of new businesses being founded is nearly 40 % higher in large agglomeration areas than in

Es ist allerdings davon auszugehen, dass der 3D-Druck, ebenso wie die hoch flexiblen und leicht programmierbaren Leichtbauroboter, der globalen Massenproduktion vorerst keine ernsthafte Konkurrenz machen werden. Diese neuen Technologien können ihre Potenziale nur entfalten, wenn sich eine neue Produktionslogik im Sinne einer individualisierten und dezentralisierten „On-demand-Produktion" und entsprechende Käufermärkte herausbilden. Die Industrie- und Arbeitssoziologin Sabine Pfeiffer formuliert es wie folgt: „Eine On-demand-Produktion wäre ohne Frage technisch denkbar und ökologisch höchst sinnvoll – sie ist aber nur in Nischen umsetzbar, denn sie widerspricht den Prinzipien einer kapitalistischen, zum Wachstum (und damit zur Überproduktion) verdammten Ökonomie." (Pfeiffer 2019: 173) Hier wird deutlich, dass diese meines Erachtens notwendige Transformation keine technische, sondern letztlich eine gesellschaftliche Frage ist. Und dabei kann den Städten als Standorten von Innovationen, Produktion und Konsumtion sowie als Arenen gesellschaftlicher Auseinandersetzung eine zentrale transformative Rolle zukommen. Denn Städte sind heute bedeutende Verhandlungsorte für die Frage, wie wir in Zukunft leben wollen.

Anzeichen für eine Reurbanisierung der Industrie

Einen sehr interessanten Einblick in aktuelle Entwicklungstendenzen einer Transformation der Stadtökonomien in Richtung einer „On-demand-Produktion" bietet eine Studie des DIW zum industriellen Gründungsgeschehen in Deutschland. (Gornig/Werwatz 2018) Die Autoren, die Einsichten bekommen wollen in Standortpräferenzen neuer Unternehmen unter Berücksichtigung digitaler Rahmenbedingungen, kommen zu interessanten Ergebnissen: Die Gründungsintensität ist in den großen Agglomerationen um fast 40 Prozent höher als in den übrigen Regionen der Bundesrepublik. Und was besonders erstaunt: In den Metropolen haben Unternehmen im Lowtech-Bereich, also vor allem Betriebe der Konsumgüterindustrie, den größten Anteil an industriellen Neugründungen. Bei den industriellen Gründungen zeigen sich zwei Tendenzen: Die Gründer und Gründerinnen im Bereich der Hightech-Industrien suchen die Nähe zu Hochschulen und Forschungseinrichtungen. Die Gründer und Gründerinnen im Bereich der Lowtech-Industrien suchen die Nähe zu den Kunden. Die Forscher konstatieren, dass bei Konsumgütern noch immer die Massenproduktion dominiert. Durch den Einsatz additiver Fertigungstechnologien würden aber kleinserielle Produktionen immer preisgünstiger. „Entsprechend kann direkter und einfacher auf individuelle Kundenwünsche eingegangen werden – und da ist es von Vorteil, wenn der Kunde gleich um die Ecke ist." (Ebd.: 1010) Die Stadt könnte so mehr und mehr zum Inkubator für die Erneuerung der Industrie werden. Das Fazit der Studie: „Reurbanisierung der Industrie ist möglich, wenn die Politik die richtigen Weichen stellt." (Ebd.)

Resümee: Die Krise als Chance einer radikalen Transformation der Ökonomie und urbaner Systeme

Die Corona-Pandemie ist mit einem historisch singulären Einbruch der Wirtschaftsleistung verbunden. In dieser Krisensituation zeigt sich, dass viele Bereiche der Ökonomie nicht zukunftsfähig sind, weder ökonomisch noch ökologisch. Die Wirtschaft braucht einen starken Impuls – nicht nur für eine konjunkturelle Erholung, sondern vor allem auch für einen überfälligen Struktur-

other regions of the Federal Republic. What is particularly surprising is that, in metropolises, companies in the low-tech sector, that is, companies in the consumer goods industry, account for the biggest share of new industrial start-ups. Two tendencies can be seen when we look at new start-ups. Entrepreneurs in the field of high-tech industries seek proximity to universities and research institutions. Entrepreneurs in the field of low-tech industries seek proximity to customers. The researchers postulate that mass production will continue to dominate in the case of consumer goods. As a result of the use of additive and digital production technologies, however, small, serial productions would become more and more inexpensive. 'It will correspondingly be possible to respond to individual customer wishes more directly and simply – and it is therefore advantageous if the customer is just round the corner' (Ibid.: 1010). The city could thus increasingly become an incubator for the renewal of industry. The conclusion drawn by their study: 'A re-urbanization of industry is possible if policy-makers make the right decisions.' (Ibid.)

Conclusion: The crisis as an opportunity to radically transform the economy and urban systems

The Corona pandemic is linked with a historically unique slump in economic output. This crisis makes it clear that many areas of the economy are not sustainable, neither ecologically nor economically. The economy needs strong government stimulus – not only for an economic recovery, but in particular for an overdue structural transformation. The Sachverständigenrat (the German council of economic experts) has rightly warned that, influenced by the problems in individual economic branches, policy-makers are being tempted to take a wide range of sector-specific measures, such as a buyer's premium for vehicles, that, generally speaking, will rigidify existing structures (Sachverständigenrat 2020:17). This crisis offers a historically unique opportunity to radically transform the economy and to make it sustainable over a longer period. In addition to safeguarding employment, resilience, supply security, and sustainability should be the paramount guiding principles. Cities and towns play a key role in this. It is at the urban and regional level that crucial investments in the fields of health, education, housing, renewable energies, sustainable mobility, a circular economy, and digital infrastructure must be conceived and implemented. This also opens new perspectives for the development of a new production logic aligned with individualized and sustainably oriented urban production.

It is now up to policymakers to make the right decisions. What is needed – in addition to providing venture capital and intensifying knowledge transfer – is the provision of affordable land and commercial spaces for start-ups, intelligent governance structures for shaping the mix of uses and digitization, and a political solving of use conflicts between housing and business and urban production. What is called for today is a culture of experimentation, with open spaces of opportunities for unforeseeable futures, 'labs' as places for experiments, and breeding grounds for problem-driven innovations.

wandel. Der Sachverständigenrat warnt zurecht davor, dass sich die Politik unter dem Einfluss der Probleme in einzelnen Branchen zu einer Vielzahl an branchenspezifischen Maßnahmen, etwa einer Kaufprämie für Fahrzeuge, verleiten lässt, welche die bestehenden Strukturen verfestigen würden. (Sachverständigenrat 2020: 17) Diese Krise bietet die historisch einmalige Chance, die Wirtschaft radikal zu transformieren und zukunftsfähig zu machen. Neben der Beschäftigungssicherung sollten dabei Resilienz, Versorgungssicherheit und Nachhaltigkeit die entscheidenden Leitprinzipien sein. Eine Schlüsselrolle kommt dabei den Städten und Gemeinden zu. Auf der städtischen und regionalen Ebene müssen die entscheidenden Investitionen in den Bereichen Gesundheit, Bildung, Wohnen, erneuerbare Energien, nachhaltige Mobilität, Kreislaufwirtschaft und digitale Infrastruktur konzipiert und umgesetzt werden. Damit öffnen sich auch der Entwicklung einer neuen Produktionslogik im Sinne einer individualisierten und nachhaltig ausgerichteten urbanen Produktion neue Perspektiven.

Jetzt kommt es darauf an, dass die Politik die richtigen Weichen stellt. Es braucht – neben der Bereitstellung von Risikokapital und einer Intensivierung des Wissenstransfers – bezahlbare Gewerbeflächen und Gewerberäumen für Start-ups, intelligente Governancestrukturen zur Gestaltung der Nutzungsmischung und der Digitalisierung sowie eine politische Auflösung von Nutzungskonflikten zwischen Wohnen und Gewerbe. Gefordert ist jetzt eine Kultur der Experimente mit offenen Möglichkeitsräumen für unvorhersehbare Zukünfte und „Labs" als Experimentierorte und Keimzellen für problemgetriebene Innovationen.

24

1.   Bei der Versorgung mit lebenswichtigen Medikamenten ist Deutschland sehr stark von sogenannten Schwellenländern abhängig. Über 80 Prozent der gängigen pharmazeutischen Wirkstoffe stammen inzwischen aus China oder Indien.

2.   So hat zum Beispiel die Bundesregierung ein Förderprogramm, das sogenannte „Sprinterprogramm", angekündigt, mit dem Ziel, eine Produktionskapazität von jährlich etwa 2,5 Milliarden Schutzmasken in Deutschland aufzubauen.

3.   Unter Resilienz wird – vereinfacht formuliert – die Fähigkeit eines sozial-ökologischen Systems verstanden, Störungen zu absorbieren und sich durch strukturellen Wandel zu transformieren (vgl. Walker et al. 2004). Inzwischen gibt es auch vielfältige Versuche, dieses Konzept auf Städte zu übertragen (vgl. De Flander et al. 2014). Resiliente Städte sollten somit robuste, adaptive und innovative Strukturen entwickeln, um auf unvorhersehbare Zukünfte vorbereitet zu sein und sich in Krisensituationen neu erfinden zu können.

4.   Die folgenden Ausführungen stützen sich teilweise auf eine frühere Publikation (siehe Läpple 2019).

5.   Ein äußerst interessantes Beispiel einer vertikalen Fabrik ist die Süßwarenfabrik der Firma Manner in Wien. Mit Hilfe neuer Fertigungstechnologien und unter Nutzung urbaner Synergien ist es gelungen, nicht nur die Produktion in der Stadt zu halten, sondern Produktionskapazitäten von der grünen Wiese zurück in die Stadt zu verlagern. Siehe dazu Läpple 2019: 14f.

6.   Über Jahrzehnte wuchs der Welthandel deutlich stärker als die Weltwirtschaft (weltweites BIP). Dieser Trend hat sich seit 2012 umgekehrt. Seither wächst der Welthandel geringer als die Weltwirtschaft.

1.   Germany is extremely dependent on so-called emerging economies for its supply of vital medicines. Over 80 % of pharmaceutical ingredients currently come from China or India.

2.   The federal government has thus taken measures including announcing a funding program, the so-called 'Sprinterprogramm', with the aim of developing a production capacity of 2.5 billion protective masks per year in Germany.

3.   In this context, resilience is understood very generally, as "the capacity of a system to absorb disturbance and reorganize while undergoing change" (Walker et al. 2004). Currently, multifold approaches exist to transfer this concept onto cities (see De Flander et al. 2014). To be resilient, cities should develop robust and adaptive structures to prepare them for unpredictable futures and the ability to reinvent themselves in crisis situations.

4.   The following statements are based in part on an earlier publication (see Läpple 2019). An extremely interesting example of a vertical factory is provided by the wafer and sweets factory of the Manner company in Vienna. With the help of new production technologies and by making use of urban synergies, it has succeeded not only in keeping production in the city, but also in shifting production capacities from greenfield sites back to the city. On this, see Läpple 2019: 14f.

5.   For decades, global trade grew considerably more strongly than the global economy (worldwide GDP). This trend has reversed itself since 2012. Since that year, global trade has been growing by less than the global economy.

Literature

Crouch, Colin, 2019: Gig Economy. Prekäre Arbeit im Zeitalter von Uber, Minijobs & Co. Berlin: Suhrkamp.

Eickelpasch, Alexander; Rainer Behrend, 2017: 'Industrie in Großstädten: Klein, aber fein'. DIW-Wochenbericht, 32+33 (2017): 639–51.

Frey, Carl Benedikt, 2019a: 'In der Technologiefalle'. Süddeutsche Zeitung, 193 (22 August 2019): 11.

Frey, Carl Benedikt, 2019b: The Technology Trap. Capital, Labor, and Power in the Age of Automation. Princeton, NJ: Princeton University Press.

Frey, Carl Benedict; Osborne, Michael A., 2013: The Future of Employment: How Susceptible Are Jobs to Computerisation? Oxford Martin School, University of Oxford, Oxford, U.K.

Gärtner, Stefan, 2019: 'Strukturwandel und Produktionsarbeit im urbanen Raum'. In Arbeit: Zeitschrift für Arbeitsforschung, Arbeitsgestaltung und Arbeitspolitik, 28, 3: 285–305;

Golding, Ian; Mike Mariathasan, 2014: The Butterfly Defect: How Globalization Creates Systemic Risks, and What to Do about It. Princeton, NJ: Princeton University Press.

Gornig, Martin; Werwatz, Axel, 2018: 'Anzeichen für eine Reurbanisierung der Industrie'. In DIW-Wochenbericht, 47 (2018): 1006–11.

Habermas, Jürgen, 2020: 'So viel Wissen über Nichtwissen gab es noch nie', interview. In Kölner Stadt-Anzeiger (3 April 2020).

Juraschek, Max; Thiede, Sebastian; Herrmann, Christoph, 2018: 'Urbane Produktion. Potenziale und Herausforderungen der Produktion in Städten'. In Carsten, Hans et al (eds.): Handbuch Produktions- und Logistikmanagment in Wertschöpfungsnetzwerken. Berlin: 1113-33.

Läpple, Dieter, 2019: 'Neue Arbeitswelten: Eine Einführung'. In Informationen zur Raumentwicklung, 6 (2019): 4–19;

Läpple, Dieter, 2018: 'Perspektiven einer produktiven Stadt'. In Schäfer, Klaus (ed.), Aufbruch in die Zwischenstadt. Urbanisierung durch Migration und Nutzungsmischung. Bielefeld: transcript Verlag: 150–76.

Läpple, Dieter, 2016: 'Produktion zurück in die Stadt. Ein Plädoyer'. In StadtBauwelt, 211, 107: 22–29.

Pfeiffer, Sabine, 2019: 'Produktivkraft konkret. Vom schweren Start der Leichtbauroboter'. In Butolle, Florian; Sabine Nuss (eds.), Marx und die Roboter. Vernetzte Produktion, Künstliche Intelligenz und lebendige Arbeit, Berlin: Dietz Verlag: 156–77.

Rappaport, Nina, 2015: Vertical Urban Factory. New York: ACTAR.

Sachverständigenrat, 2020: 'So kann sich die Wirtschaft erholen'. In Süddeutsche Zeitung, 117 (22 May 2020): 17.

Tooze, Adam, 2020: 'Unsere Normalität kehrt nicht zurück'. In Blätter für deutsche und internationale Politik, 5 (2020): 47–52.

Zukin, Sharon, 1995: The Cultures of Cities. Malden/Oxford: Wiley-Blackwell.

Literatur

Crouch, Colin, 2019: Gig Economy. Prekäre Arbeit im Zeitalter von Uber, Minijobs & Co. Berlin;

De Flander, Karleen et al., 2014: Resilienz und Reallabore als Schlüsselkonzepte urbaner Transformationsforschung. In: GAIA 23/3 (2014): 284–286;

Eickelpasch, Alexander; Behrend, Rainer, 2017: Industrie in Großstädten: Klein, aber fein. DIW-Wochenbericht Nr. 32+33.2017: 639–651;

Frey, Carl Benedikt, 2019a: In der Technologiefalle. Süddeutsche Zeitung Nr. 193 (22.08.2019): 11;

Frey, Carl Benedikt, 2019b: The Technology Trap. Capital, Labor, and Power in the Age of Automation. Princeton, NJ;

Frey, Carl Benedict; Osborne, Michael A., 2013: The Future of Employment: How Susceptible Are Jobs to Computerisation? Oxford Martin School. University of Oxford, Oxford, U.K.;

Gärtner, Stefan, 2019: Strukturwandel und Produktionsarbeit im urbanen Raum. In: Arbeit: Zeitschrift für Arbeitsforschung, Arbeitsgestaltung und Arbeitspoltik 28, H. 3: 285–305;

Golding, Ian; Mariathasan, Mike, 2014: The Butterfly Defect. How Globalization creates systemic risks, and what to do about it. Princeton, NJ;

Gornig, Martin; Werwatz, Axel, 2018: Anzeichen für eine Reurbanisierung der Industrie. In: DIW-Wochenbericht Nr. 47/2018: 1006–1011;

Habermas, Jürgen, 2020: „So viel Wissen über Nichtwissen gab es noch nie", Interview. In: Kölner Stadt-Anzeiger, 03.04.2020;

Juraschek, Max; Thiede, Sebastian; Herrmann, Christoph, 2018: Urbane Produktion. Potenziale und Herausforderungen der Produktion in Städten. In: Carsten, Hans et al (Hrsg.): Handbuch Produktions- und Logistikmanagement in Wertschöpfungsnetzwerken. Berlin: 1113–1133;

Läpple, Dieter, 2019: Neue Arbeitswelten: Eine Einführung. In: Informationen zur Raumentwicklung, Heft 6/2019, 4–19;

Läpple, Dieter, 2018: Perspektiven einer produktiven Stadt. In: Schäfer, Klaus (Hrsg.); Aufbruch in die Zwischenstadt. Urbanisierung durch Migration und Nutzungsmischung. Bielefeld: 150–176;

Läpple, Dieter, 2016: Produktion zurück in die Stadt. Ein Plädoyer. In: StadtBauwelt, 211. Jg. (107): 22–29;

Pfeiffer, Sabine, 2019: Produktivkraft konkret. Vom schweren Start der Leichtbauroboter. In: Butolle, Florian; Nuss, Sabine (Hrsg.): Marx und die Roboter. Vernetzte Produktion, Künstliche Intelligenz und lebendige Arbeit, Berlin: 156–177;

Rappaport, Nina, 2015: Vertical Urban Factory. New York;

Sachverständigenrat, 2020: So kann sich die Wirtschaft erholen. In: Süddeutsche Zeitung, Nr. 117 (22.05.2020): 17;

Walker, Brian et al., 2004: Resilience, Adaptability and Transformability in Socio-ecological Systems. In: Ecology and Society 9 (2): 5.

Tooze, Adam, 2020: Unsere Normalität kehrt nicht zurück. In: Blätter für deutsche und internationale Politik, 5/2020, 47–52;

Zukin, Sharon, 1995: The Cultures of Cities. Malden/Oxford.

Die Produktive Stadt

Auf der Suche nach neuen Quartierstypen

Stefan Werrer, Architekt und Stadtplaner AKBW DASL Inhaber Labor für urbane Orte und Prozesse, Stuttgart Professor für Städtebau an der FH Aachen

Der Begriff „Produktive Stadt" greift die Transformationstendenzen in Wirtschaft und Gesellschaft auf, thematisiert neue Formen des Arbeitens mit flexibleren und urbaneren Produktionsformen, mit wechselnden Kooperations- und Kollaborationsmustern. Vor dem Hintergrund einer wachsenden Kritik an der postindustriellen Stadt stellt die Produktive Stadt nach Läpple ein Suchkonzept für die Neuorientierung und Neuerfindung der Stadt dar. Wie bei vielen früheren Themen von Europan geht es auch bei der Produktiven Stadt um die Kultivierung eines neuen Blicks auf Raumtypen und Flächenpotenziale. Darüber hinaus stellt sich aber auch die Frage nach den Schlussfolgerungen für das konkrete planerische Handeln.

Die Produktive Stadt ermöglicht das Nachdenken über eine produktive und soziale Mischung an sehr hybriden Standorten und in unterschiedlichen Quartiersformaten. Typologische Ansätze können auf unterschiedlichen Maßstabsebenen mit Strahlkraft auf ihr jeweiliges Umfeld identifiziert werden. Nachfolgend seien einzelne „produktive Stadtbausteine" beispielhaft genannt, die an vielen Orten standortbezogen entwickelt werden könnten:

- gemischte Wohnquartiere in Kombination mit urbaner Produktion
- Transformationsquartiere, die über Zwischennutzungen Raum für innovative urbane Prozesse bieten
- hybride Wissensproduktionsquartiere für Forschung und Entwicklung
- urbane Gewerbequartiere mit Aufenthaltsqualität
- urbane Katalysatoren als gemischt genutzte Stadtbausteine
- eine experimentelle Start-up- und Produktionskultur mit Coworking Spaces, FabLabs und Inkubatoren als neue Elemente einer Quartiersinfrastruktur

Quartiersentwicklungen sollten daher von Anfang an neue urbane Arbeitsformen und lokale Ökonomien einplanen. Die unter dem Schlagwort „Industrie 4.0" zusammengefassten Transformationstendenzen der Industrieproduktion wie urbane Manufakturen, vernetzte Produktion, FabLabs oder Kleinfabriken der Recyclingbranche könnten eine Rückkehr neuer städtischer Industrien in kleinteilig gemischte Quartiere ermöglichen. Es entstehen neue Formen des Arbeitens mit flexibleren und urbaneren Produktionsformen, mit wechselnden Kooperations- und Kollaborationsmustern im Sinne einer Next Economy. Auf diese Weise kann eine inklusive Stadt aus unterschiedlichen Wohnmilieus, Arbeitswelten und Lernarenen entstehen, die Möglichkeitsräume für das notwendige Entwerfen und Austesten von neuen produktiven Strukturen nach dem Prinzip „Learning by doing" bietet.

Der durch die Digitalisierung ermöglichte Wandel von Produktionsweisen, Konsummustern und Warenströmen und damit auch von Raumbedürfnissen und Ansprüchen an Wirtschaftsflächen lässt stadtverträgliche Produktion zu. Planerisches Handeln, das nicht mehr die Vermei-

Productive Cities

On a Search for New Kinds of Districts

Stefan Werrer, architect and urban planner AKBW DASL Owner Laboratory for Urban Places and Processes, Stuttgart Professor for urban development at the FH Aachen

The term 'productive city' refers to transformative tendencies in economy and society and addresses new types of work with more flexible and urban forms of production and changing patterns of cooperation and collaboration. Against this background of increasing criticism of the post-industrial city, the productive city, according to Dieter Läpple, stands for a concept of searching for a reorientation and reinvention of the city. As in the case of many previous Europan topics, "Productive Cities" also deals with cultivating a new view of spatial types and potentials for sites. However, what also arises is the question of what implications this has for concrete planning practices.

Productive cities facilitate considering a productive and social mixture operating on very hybrid sites and in different district formats. Typological approaches with a radiating impact on their respective surroundings can be identified on various scale levels. The following text names examples of individual 'productive city building blocks' that can be developed in a site-specific way in many locations:

- Mixed residential districts combined with urban production
- Transformation districts that offer interim uses space for innovative urban processes
- Hybrid knowledge production districts for research and development
- Urban commercial districts with qualities for spending time there
- Urban catalysts as mixed-use urban building blocks
- An experimental start-up and production culture with co-working spaces, fab labs, and incubators as new district infrastructure elements

The development of districts should therefore incorporate plans for new, urban forms of work from the very beginning. Transformative trends with respect to industrial production as well as urban manufactories, networked production, fab labs, or small factories for the recycling sector that are summarized under the key-word 'Industry 4.0' might facilitate a return of new urban industries in small-scale, mixed districts. They engender new forms of work with more flexible and urban forms of production, with changing patterns of cooperation and collaboration conducive to a 'next economy'. In this way, an inclusive city consisting of various living milieus, worlds of work, and learning arenas is created, offering possible scenarios for the necessary design and testing of new productive structures based on the principle of 'learning by doing'.

The transformation of production methods, consumption patterns, and flows of goods facilitated by digitization, and thus also of spatial needs and demands for economic areas makes sustainable urban production possible. Planning practices that no longer aim to avoid, but instead to moderate conflicts of use is now necessary. Cities will thus become more productive.

Werksviertel, München (Foto: Stefan Werrer)
Factory district, Munich (Photo: Stefan Werrer)

dung, sondern die Moderation von Nutzungskonflikten zum Ziel hat, ist nun notwendig. So werden Städte produktiver.

In fast allen deutschen Städten bietet die Transformation von meist größeren, bisher gewerblich geprägten Arealen Räume für innovative urbane Prozesse. Durch Nachverdichtung und Nutzungsmischung der häufig rein funktional und logistisch gedachten Produktions- und Gewerbestandorte nutzen diese Städte ihr Potenzial als attraktives Wissenschafts- und Arbeitsmilieu und werden im Wettbewerb um die „klügsten Köpfe" und Fachkräfte attraktiver. Eine Übertragung von bewährten Instrumenten des Stadtumbaus und der Innenentwicklung auf Wirtschaftsflächen könnte vielversprechend sein. So werden Wirtschaftsflächen urbaner.

Absoluten Vorrang sollte im Rahmen gesamtstädtischer bzw. regionaler Strategien die Integration der Themen Arbeit und Produktion in ressortübergreifende und regionale Kooperationen haben, flankiert von einer aktivierenden Bodenvorratspolitik (zum Beispiel von revolvierenden Grundstücksfonds) und gegebenenfalls dem Einsatz des Erbbaurechts auch auf Wirtschaftsflächen. In der konkreten Projektarbeit muss es gelingen, die relevanten Akteure und Akteurinnen und Unternehmen mit konkretem Ortsbezug zur Mitwirkung zu aktivieren sowie die bisher nur auf Nacht- bzw. Wohnbevölkerung ausgerichteten Partizipationsprozesse um Formate zu erweitern, die die Tages- bzw. Arbeitsbevölkerung einbeziehen. So ermöglichen Kommunen und Regionen Teilhabe.

In nearly all cities in Germany, the transformation of generally larger sites hitherto characterized by commerce offers spaces for innovative urban processes. By means of densification and a mixture of uses including production and commercial locations, which are often conceived purely functionally and logistically, cities of this type can utilize their potential as an attractive environment for knowledge and work and become more attractive in the competition for the 'brightest minds' and skilled workers. Transferring tried and tested instruments for urban redevelopment and internal development to business areas could be promising, as they thus become more urban.

What should have absolute priority is integrating the topics of work and production in cross-departmental and regional collaborations within the framework of citywide and/or regional strategies, in tandem with an activating land reserve policy (e.g. revolving property funds) and, if possible, also by making use of leaseholds in business areas. What must be managed in concrete project work is activating relevant stakeholders and/or businesses with a concrete relationship to the location to contribute to and expand participation processes that have hitherto only been oriented towards a night-time and/or residential population to include formats that incorporate the day-time and/or working population. This therefore enables municipalities and regions to facilitate participation.

More Than a Search Concept!

Productive cities are thus particularly suitable for cooperatively developing visions and ideas for the future of our cities. Productive uses enrich urban districts, which

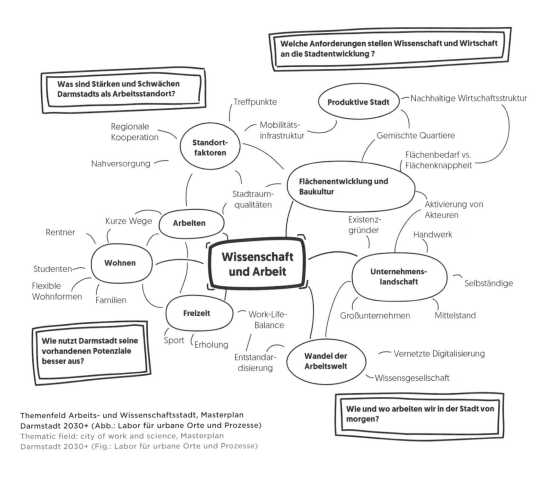

Was sind Stärken und Schwächen Darmstadts als Arbeitsstandort?

Treffpunkte

Produktive Stadt — Nachhaltige Wirtschaftsstruktur

Regionale Kooperation

Mobilitäts-infrastruktur

Gemischte Quartiere

Standort-faktoren

Flächenbedarf vs. Flächenknappheit

Nahversorgung

Flächenentwicklung und Baukultur

Stadtraum-qualitäten

Aktivierung von Akteuren

Kurze Wege

Arbeiten

Existenz-gründer

Handwerk

Rentner

Wissenschaft und Arbeit

Wohnen

Unternehmens-landschaft

Studenten

Selbständige

Flexible Wohnformen

Familien

Freizeit

Work-Life-Balance

Großunternehmen

Mittelstand

Wie nutzt Darmstadt seine vorhandenen Potenziale besser aus?

Sport Erholung

Entstandar-disierung

Wandel der Arbeitswelt

Vernetzte Digitalisierung

Wissensgesellschaft

Themenfeld Arbeits- und Wissenschaftsstadt, Masterplan
Darmstadt 2030+ (Abb.: Labor für urbane Orte und Prozesse)
Thematic field: city of work and science, Masterplan
Darmstadt 2030+ (Fig.: Labor für urbane Orte und Prozesse)

Wie und wo arbeiten wir in der Stadt von morgen?

Bürgerforum, Masterplan Darmstadt 2030+
(Abb.: Labor für urbane Orte und Prozesse)
Public forum, Masterplan Darmstadt 2030+
(Fig.: Labor für urbane Orte und Prozesse)

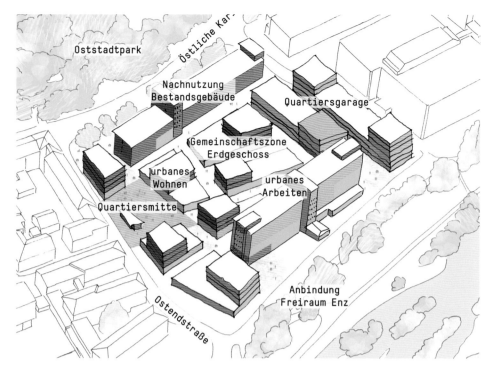

Quartierskonzept Thales-Areal,
Rahmenplan Oststadt/Nordoststadt
Pforzheim (Abb.: Labor für urbane
Orte und Prozesse)
Concept for the Thales area district,
framework plan for the Oststadt/
Nordoststadt Pforzheim (Fig.: Labor
für urbane Orte und Prozesse)

Mehr als ein Suchkonzept!

Die Produktive Stadt eignet sich somit in besonderem Maße für eine kooperative Entwicklung von Visionen und Ideen zur Zukunft unserer Städte. Produktive Nutzungen bereichern die über Jahrzehnte zusehends segregierten Stadtquartiere. Aktuelle Planungen machen deutlich, dass sich die Nutzungen der neuen Arbeitswelt in ihren räumlichen Strukturen je nach Projektpartnerschaft verändern und weiterentwickeln. Die immer größer werdenden Flächenkonkurrenzen von Wohnen und Arbeiten können nur durch eine intensive, kooperative Raumnutzung überwunden werden. Dabei bietet es sich an, Nutzungsmischung in Quartieren zu organisieren und Quartiere nutzungsorientiert zu entwickeln, sodass eine inklusive Stadt mit unterschiedlichen Wohnmilieus, Arbeitswelten und Lernarenen entstehen kann. All dies erfordert Mut zum Experiment, oder einfach gesagt: mehr Mut zur Stadt!

Der Text basiert in weiten Teilen auf der Veröffentlichung: Werrer, Stefan, „Die Produktive Stadt – Mehr als ein Suchkonzept?", 12–14. In: Bundesinstitut für Bau-, Stadt- und Raumforschung (Hrsg.): Neue Räume für die produktive Stadt, BBSR-Berichte, Bonn 2019.

Literatur:

Frank Gwildis / Stefan Werrer: *Produktive Stadt in produktiven Quartieren – Handlungsstrategie und Leitbild für eine gemischt genutzte Stadt*, in PLANERIN 03_18, 54–56

Kaye Geipel: *Stadt = Wohnen und Gewerbe. Stimmt die Formel?*, Stadtbauwelt 211 (Bauwelt 35/2016), 20–21

Dieter Läpple: *Produktion zurück in die Stadt. Ein Plädoyer*, in: Stadtbauwelt 211 (Bauwelt 35/2016), 22–29

Landeshauptstadt Stuttgart (Hrsg.): *Symposium Die Produktive Stadt. Dokumentation*, Stuttgart 2015 (www.stuttgart.de)

have been becoming more and more segregated over decades. Current planning makes it clear that functions in the new world of work are changing and developing further with respect to their spatial structures depending on project partnerships. The ever-greater competition for areas between housing and work can only be overcome by means of an intensive, cooperative use of space. This suggests a need to organize a mixture of uses in districts and developing districts in a use-oriented manner so that an inclusive city with various living environments, worlds of work, and learning arenas can come into being. All of this requires courage to experiment. Or, to put it simply: more courage for the city!

The text is based to a great extent on the publication: Werrer, Stefan, 'Die Produktive Stadt – Mehr als ein Suchkonzept?', pp. 12–14, in Bundesinstitut für Bau-, Stadt- und Raumforschung (ed.), Neue Räume für die produktive Stadt, BBSR-Berichte (Bonn, 2019).

Bibliography:

Frank Gwildis / Stefan Werrer, 'Produktive Stadt in produktiven Quartieren—Handlungsstrategie und Leitbild für eine gemischt genutzte Stadt', in PLANERIN 03, 18, pp. 54–56.

Kaye Geipel, 'Stadt = Wohnen und Gewerbe. Stimmt die Formel?', in Stadtbauwelt 211 (Bauwelt 35 (2016)), pp. 20–21.

Dieter Läpple, 'Produktion zurück in die Stadt. Ein Plädoyer', in Stadtbauwelt 211 (Bauwelt 35 (2016)), pp. 22–29.

Landeshauptstadt Stuttgart (ed.), Symposium Die Produktive Stadt. Dokumentation (Stuttgart, 2015); www.stuttgart.de (accessed in April 2020).

Ergebnisse in Deutschland und Polen
Results in Germany and Poland

Bergische Kooperation

Hilden, Ratingen, Solingen und Wülfrath-Düssel Standort / Location
~ 58.000, ~ 92.300, ~ 159.000, ~ 21.200 Bevölkerung / Inhabitants
16,7 ha, 91,9 ha, 42,5 ha, 48,42 ha Betrachtungsraum / Study Site
2,8 ha, 43 ha, 20,7 ha, 12 ha Projektgebiet / Project Site

Der Kooperationsraum „Zwischen Rhein und Wupper" will auf Grundlage des gemeinsamen Zukunftskonzeptes für das Pilotprojekt „Zukunfts-Quartiere zwischen Rhein und Wupper" regional und lokal beispielgebende Quartiersentwicklungen anstoßen, die die Möglichkeiten und Herausforderungen des technologischen und gesellschaftlichen Wandels aufnehmen. In diesem Rahmen stellen vier Städte eine gemeinsame Aufgabe für den Wettbewerb. Ziel und Aufgabe ist es, konkrete räumliche Strategien und Bilder zu entwerfen und internationale Impulse für die Quartiersentwicklung in der Region zu erhalten.

Allen Standorten gemeinsam ist die Nähe zu bestehenden oder noch auszubauenden Haltepunkten des öffentlichen Nahverkehrs, die die unterschiedlichen Maßstabsebenen miteinander verbinden. Die gemeinsame Fragestellung soll im Wettbewerb für alle Standorte auf der strategischen Ebene beantwortet werden, um konkrete Lösungsansätze für die einzelnen Standorte sowie Qualitäten und Handlungsansätze für den gesamten Kooperationsraum ableiten zu können.

1. Hilden: Unter Achtung des gründerzeitlichen Stadtgrundrisses soll ein Bebauungskonzept für ein Quartier zwischen Stadtzentrum und Bahnhof entwickelt werden, in dem neue Wohnformen und gewerbliche sowie freiberufliche Nutzungen nebeneinander entwickelt werden können.

2. Ratingen: Mit einem neuen S-Bahn-Haltepunkt will die Stadt eine großflächige Umstrukturierung einleiten. Das ausgewählte Planungsareal soll als Bindeglied sowohl für die gute Integration des Haltepunktes als auch für die Vernetzung der Stadtbereiche West und der Kernstadt fungieren. Vor allem aber soll das Gebiet prototypisch das Mit- und Nebeneinander von Arbeiten und Wohnen ausloten. Dabei geht es nicht nur um Abriss und Neubau, sondern um einen prozesshaften Wandel im Stadtteil.

3. Solingen: In Bezug auf eine Nachnutzung des ehemaligen Industriegeländes sind mehrere Szenarien möglich – wobei die Umgebungsbebauung zu berücksichtigen ist, die unter anderem durch Wohnbebauung geprägt wird. Vorstellbar seitens der Stadt ist aufgrund der zentralen Lage ein urbanes Quartier zum Wohnen und Arbeiten mit einem Nutzungsmix aus innovativem, nicht störendem Gewerbe, Wohnformen für Jung und Alt, Dienstleistungen und weiteren ergänzenden Nutzungen sowie einem attraktiven öffentlichen Raum mit hohen Aufenthaltsqualitäten und Spielmöglichkeiten für Kinder. Erwartet wird im Ergebnis ein urbanes Quartier von hoher städtebaulicher und architektonischer Qualität.

4. Wülfrath-Düssel: Es soll ein neues Siedlungsgebiet entwickelt werden, bei dem die Einzigartigkeit und die besondere, gewachsene soziale und baukulturelle Qualität des Ortes bewahrt wird. Düssel soll zu einem lebendigen Ort werden, in dem Wohnen, Arbeiten und Freizeit miteinander verbunden sind. Eine besondere Herausforderung besteht darin, die neuen Siedlungsflächen behutsam mit den bestehenden, zum Teil historischen Strukturen des Ortsteils zu verbinden.

The cooperation space "between Rhein and Wupper" wants to initiate regional and local urban quarter developments on the basis of a common future concept embodied in the project "Future Quarters between Rhein und Wupper", that include the possibilities and challenges of the technological and social changes in a constructive way. Within this framework, four cities pose a common question for the session. The objective and the task is to design specific spatial strategies and images and, additionally, to create an international momentum for the development of urban quarters in the region.

All sites are located at existing or soon-to-be-built public transport stops that should connect the different levels within the region. The common objective should be responded to on a strategic level for all four sites, not only to gain specific solutions for the specific sites but also to generate common qualities and actions for the whole cooperative space.

1. Hilden: A building concept for the area between city centre and train station must be developed that combines new forms of living with commercial, freelance, and suitable productive use whilst respecting the "Gründerzeit" city plan.

2. Ratingen: The city wants to initiate an extensive restructuring process with a potential new suburban train station. The given site should act as an integrating element for the train stop and a future link between the western city and the city centre. It should also act as a prototype for the cooperation and coexistence of working, living and productive uses. The task is not about demolition and rebuilding but about creating a process of change in the neighbourhood.

3. Solingen: There are several scenarios for the subsequent use of the former industrial area although the adjacent building with housing should be taken into account. The city envisions an urban working and residential quarter with a mixture of innovative non-disruptive commercial and productive uses, housing for the young and the elderly, and services and other complementary uses as well as attractive open spaces with playgrounds for the kids and high-quality places to stay. The expectation is of an urban quarter with high quality urban design and architecture.

4. Wülfrath-Düssel: A new district should be developed that preserves the uniqueness and specific quality of the place. It is therefore necessary to take the housing areas which serve the larger cities into account, but also to preserve the grown qualities of social structures and building culture and develop them. Düssel should become a lively place where living, working, suitable production and leisure can coexist. It will be a particular challenge is to connect and interweave the new settlement area with the existing and partly historical structures of the district.

en

Ratingen

Solingen

Wülfrath-Düssel

Bergisch Plugin

Nikolai Werner (DE) Stadtplaner / Urban Planner
Daniel Branchereau (DE) Architekt / Architect
Moritz Scharwächter (DE) Architekturstudent / Architecture student
Vassilissa Airaudo (DE) Architektin / Architect

Als ganzheitliche Antwort auf die Quartiersentwicklung der Bergischen Kooperationsräume in Ratingen, Wülfrath, Hilden und Solingen haben wir Planungsprinzipien entwickelt, die die Rahmenbedingungen und die notwendigen Weiterentwicklungspunkte definieren, die eine produktive Stadt unserer Auffassung nach im Bergischen Kooperationsraum beinhalten muss. Die Kriterien werden in Plugins gebündelt, die die produktive Lücke innerhalb der Städte schließen. Das Plugin wird bildlich in die Städte eingefügt und verbessert die spezifischen lokalen Verhältnisse des Quartiers hin zu einer produktiven Stadt. Hierfür wurden Kriterien festgelegt, die ein Umfeld schaffen, in dem sich die Nutzerinnen und Nutzer produktiv entfalten können. Die jeweiligen Plugins bieten diverse Möglichkeiten, die verschiedenen Quartiersebenen zu aktivieren. Folgende übergeordnete Plugins bilden die ökologischen, ökonomischen, soziokulturellen und funktionalen Rahmenbedingungen für eine produktive Stadt: lokaler Attraktor, Flächen entsiegeln, neue Mobilität, Gebäude aktivieren, Flächen aktivieren, flexibel nutzbare Gebäude, produktives Erdgeschoss, produktive Dachfläche, Experimentierfelder schaffen.

Bevor die Plugins auf die einzelnen Planungsgebiete angewendet werden, gilt es die Städte überregional zu vernetzen, damit die notwendige Infrastruktur zur produktiven Vernetzung gegeben ist. Dies wird durch ein Free-floating-Angebot für den Bergischen Kooperationsraum umgesetzt. Durch ein besser vernetztes Angebot an E-Mobilitätsstrecken gelangen Nutzerinnen und Nutzer zunächst zu Stationen des öffentlichen Nahverkehrs, an denen Mobility-Hubs positioniert sind. Von dort aus gelangen sie so schneller zu ihrem Ziel im Kooperationsraum. Dadurch sparen sie Zeit, die sie dann produktiver in ihrem Quartier nutzen können.

As a holistic response to the development of districts in the Bergisch cooperation sites in Ratingen, Wülfrath, Hilden, and Solingen, we developed planning principles that define the framework conditions and the necessary points for further development that a productive city in the Bergisch cooperation area, in our opinion, must encompass. These criteria are bundled together into a plugin, which closes missing productive gaps in the municipalities. The plugins are inserted visually within the municipalities and improve the local relationships of the specific district in order to make it a productive location. To achieve this, we defined criteria for creating an environment in which users are able to develop in a productive way. The various plugins offer diverse possibilities for implementation so as to activate various levels of the district. The following superordinate plugins form the ecological, economic, socio-cultural, and functional framework conditions for a productive city: local attractors, unsealing surfaces, new mobility, activating buildings, activating areas, buildings that can be used flexibly, productive ground floors, productive roof areas, creating fields for experimentation.

Before the plugins can be applied to the individual planning areas, it is necessary to link the municipalities on a supra-regional level so that the necessary infrastructure for interconnecting the individual municipalities productively is possible. This is realized by means of a free-floating offer for the Bergisch cooperation area. A better-networked range of e-mobility routes brings users to public transport stations where mobility hubs are positioned. From there, they can travel on to their destination in the cooperation area with fewer changes and shorter waiting times. This allows them to save time, which they can then utilize more productively in their district.

Kennengelernt haben wir uns während des Architekturstudiums. Nach unserem Studium wollten wir weiterhin gemeinsam an Projekten arbeiten und entschieden uns für die Teilnahme am Wettbewerb Europan 15. Schon während unserer Arbeit im Studium wollten wir nicht auf eine gute Mahlzeit verzichten: etwas Einfaches, Schnelles, Leckeres, Warmes und Abwechslungsreiches sollte gekocht werden. Dabei hat sich Pasta mit Pesto etabliert. Daraus wurde ein Ritual, bei dem wir uns Zeit genommen haben, gemeinsam Gedanken auszutauschen – der Anfang des Team Pesto.

nikolaiwerner@live.de

We got to know one another while studying architecture. After our studies, we wanted to continue working on projects together and hence participated in Europan 15 as our first joint project. Part of our workflow while studying was making sure to eat a good meal: Something simple, fast, tasty, warm, and varied was supposed to be cooked. Pasta and pesto thus quickly became established. This turned into a ritual during which we took time to exchange collective ideas and became the beginning of Team Pesto.

nikolaiwerner@live.de

Lokaler Attraktor / Local Attractor

Ein lokaler Attraktor schafft Rahmenbedingungen für ein produktives Quartier. Durch einen identitätsstiftenden Raum bzw. der Quartiercharakter gestärkt. Dies kann z.B. ein Zentrum bildendes, lokalverwurzeltes, historisches Artefakt sein.

A local attractor creates the framework conditions for a productive quarter. The character of the neighbourhood is strengthened by an identity-forming space or centre. This can, for example, be a centre-forming, locally rooted, historical artefact.

Aktivband / Activity path

Bürgerhaus / Community centre

Stahlguss / Artefact / artefact

Neue Mobilität / New Mobility

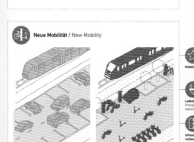

Neue Mobilität schafft die Rahmenbedingungen für ein vernetztes produktives Quartier. Durch ein vielfältiges E-Mobility- und Sharingangebot werden lokale Emissionen verringert und die Anbindung an den öffentlichen Verkehr vereinfacht. Mobility Hubs werden an wichtigen Fortbewegungsorten platziert, von dort aus können sich BewohnerInnen z.B. durch Freefloating-Angebote durch das Quartier bewegen.

New mobility creates the framework conditions for a connected productive quarter. A wide range of e-mobility and sharing services will reduce local emissions and simplify connections to public transport. Mobility hubs will be located at important transport locations, from where residents will be able to move through the neighbourhood e.g. through free-floating services.

Mobility Hub

Ladestation / Charging station

Infrastruktur verbessern / Improve infrastructure

Flächen entsiegeln / Unseal Surfaces

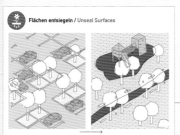

Entsiegelte Flächen schaffen einen Rückhalt für die produktive Stadt. Durch das Entsiegeln werden Flächen auf eine ökologische Weise umgestaltet, sodass sie das Mikroklima verbessern und ein resilienten Stadtraum bilden. Z.B. wird ein Stellplatz zu einer Grünfläche mit Aufenthaltsqualität umgenutzt.

Unsealed areas create support for the productive city. By unsealing, areas are redesigned in an ecological way so that they improve the microclimate and form a resilient urban space. For example, a parking space is converted into a green area with recreational quality.

Gebäude aktivieren / Activate Buildings

Ein aktiviertes Gebäude schafft Räume für produktive NutzerInnen. Das vorhandene, lokale Potenzial von Gebäuden wird leicht zugänglich gemacht. Eine Möglichkeit ist die Umnutzung von Leerstand zu vergünstigten Konditionen.

An activated building creates spaces for productive users. The existing local potential of buildings is made easily accessible. One possibility is the conversion of vacant buildings at favourable conditions.

Fläche aktivieren / Activate Areas

Eine aktivierte Fläche schafft Freiräume für produktive NutzerInnen. Einseitig genutzte Flächen müssen durch unterschiedliche Angebote vielseitig bespielbar werden. Eine zuvor landwirtschaftlich genutzte Fläche wird zum öffentlichen, produktiven Raum.

An activated area creates free space for productive users. Monotonous used areas become versatile and can be played on in a variety of ways. A previously agriculturally used area becomes a public, productive space.

Urban Farming

Quartiersplatz / Neighbourhood square

Erholung / Recreation

Sport / Sports

Flexibel nutzbare Gebäude / Buildings flexible in use

Ein flexibel, nutzbares Gebäude ermöglicht unterschiedliche, produktive Nutzungen über einen langen Zeitraum. Durch eine flexible Gebäudestruktur werden absehbare Nutzungsänderungen in der Planung berücksichtigt. Etwa ein geplantes Parkhaus wird so konstruiert, dass eine Weiternutzung zum Wohnraum möglich ist.

A building flexible in use enables different, productive uses over a long period of time. Due to a flexible building structure, foreseeable changes in use are taken into account in the planning. For example, a planned multi-storey car park is designed that it can be easily used as living space afterwards.

Gewerbe / Trade

Dienstleistung / Service

Büro / Office

Wohnen / Living

Produktives Erdgeschoss / Productive Ground Floors

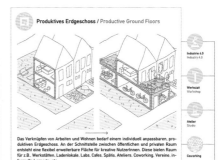

Das Verknüpfen von Arbeiten und Wohnen bedarf einem individuell anpassbaren, produktiven Erdgeschoss. An der Schnittstelle zwischen öffentlichen und privaten Raum entsteht eine flexibel erweiterbare Fläche für kreative NutzerInnen. Diese bieten Raum für z.B. Werkstätten, Ladenlokale, Labs, Cafes, Spätis, Ateliers, Coworking, Vereine, informelle Lernorte, etc.

Das Verknüpfen von Arbeiten und Wohnen bedarf einem individuell anpassbaren, produktiven Erdgeschoss. An der Schnittstelle zwischen öffentlichen und privaten Raum entsteht eine flexibel erweiterbare Fläche für kreative NutzerInnen. Diese bieten Raum für z.B. Werkstätten, Ladenlokale, Labs, Cafes, Spätis, Ateliers, Coworking, Vereine, informelle Lernorte, etc.

Industrie 4.0 / Industry 4.0

Werkstatt / Workshop

Atelier / Studio

Coworking

Produktive Dachfläche / Productive Roofs

Dachflächen werden so gestaltet, dass sie eine produktive Nutzung übernehmen. Sie haben eine nutzerunabhängige Funktion oder sind so erschlossen, dass sie vom Nutzer aktiviert werden. Vorgesehene Nutzungen dafür sind z.B. PV-Anlagen, Gründächer, Terrassen, Dachgärten, Gewächshäuser, Sportanlagen, etc.

Roof surfaces are designed that they can be used productively. They have a user-independent function or are planned in such a way that the user activates them. Intended uses include PV systems, green roofs, terraces, roof gardens, greenhouses, sports facilities, etc.

Gewächshaus / Greenhouse

Dachgarten / Roof garden

Terasse / Terrace

Photovoltaik / Photovoltaics

Experimentierfelder schaffen / Provide Experimental Fields

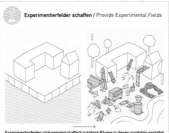

Experimentierfelder sind gemeinschaftlich nutzbare Räume in denen produktiv gestaltet wird. Impulsgebend sind hierfür angepasste Regeln, die es vereinfachen Ideen zu erproben. Dies kann z.B. bedeuten, dass Anwohner eine alternative Wohnform temporär ausprobieren.

Experimental fields are spaces that can be used collectively and in which productive design takes place. The impetus for this is provided by adapted rules that simplify the testing of ideas. This can mean, for example, that residents temporarily try out an alternative form of living.

Bergisch Plugin

Die Aufgabenstellung beinhaltet, einen ganzheitlichen Lösungsansatz zur Entwicklung der bergischen Kooperationsräume in Ratingen, Wülfrath, Hilden und Solingen zu entwickeln. Dieser soll wiederum Anstoß für weitere Städte sein, sich untereinander stärker zu vernetzten und einen einheitlichen Ballungsraum zu bilden. Als Antwort auf diese Quartiersentwicklung haben wir Planungsprinzipien entwickelt, welche die Rahmenbedingungen und die notwendigen Weiterentwicklungspunkte definieren, die eine produktive Stadt unserer Auffassung nach im bergischen Kooperationsraum beinhalten muss. Diese Prinzipien werden in übergeordneten Plugins zusammengefasst, welche die ökologischen, ökonomischen, soziokulturellen und funktionellen Rahmenbedingungen für eine produktive Stadt bilden. Um die produktive Lücke innerhalb der Städte zu schließen werden dafür notwendige Kriterien wiederum in untergeordneten Plugins gebündelt. Diese werden dann bildlich in das Planungsgebiet gesteckt und verbessern die spezifischen lokalen Verhältnisse des Quartiers im Sinne einer produktiven Stadt. Hierfür wurden insbesondere Attribute festgelegt, die im Umfeld schaffen in dem sich die Nutzer*innen produktiv entfalten können. Je nach Plugin gibt es diverse Möglichkeiten diese Kriterien zu erfüllen, um die verschiedenen Quartiersebenen zu aktivieren. Bevor die Plugins auf die einzelnen Planungsgebiete angewendet werden, gilt es, die Städte überregional zu vernetzen, damit die notwendige Infrastruktur zur produktiven Vernetzung der einzelnen Städte gegeben ist. Die Kartierung zeigt wie diese durch ein Floatingangebot für den bergischen Kooperationsraum umzusetzen ist. Durch ein besser vernetztes Angebot an E-Mobility-Strecken können Nutzer*innen zunächst mit diesen Fortbewegungsmitteln zu Stationen des öffentlichen Nahverkehres gelangen, an denen Mobility hubs positioniert sind. Dadurch gelangen sie durch weniger umsteigen und weniger Wartezeit schneller zu ihrem Ziel im Kooperationsraum und sparen Zeit welche sie produktiver in ihrem Quartier nutzen können.

The task entails developing a holistic approach to the development of the Bergisch cooperation areas in Ratingen, Wülfrath, Hilden and Solingen. This should in turn be the impetus for other cities, to network more closely with one another and to form a single agglomeration. In response to this development of neighborhoods, we have developed planning principles that define the framework conditions and the necessary development points that, in our opinion, a productive city must include in the Bergisch Cooperation Area. These principles are summarized in superordinate plugins that form the ecological, economic, socio-cultural and functional framework conditions for a productive city. In order to close the productive gap within the cities, necessary criteria are again bundled into subordinate plugins. These are then pictorially inserted in the planning area and improve the specific local conditions of the neighborhood in terms of a productive city. In particular, attributes have been defined for this purpose, which create an environment in which users can develop productively. Depending on the plugin, there are various ways to fulfill these criteria in order to activate the different levels of the neighborhood. Before the plugins are applied to the individual planning areas, it is important to network the cities nationwide, so that the necessary infrastructure for the productive networking of the individual cities is given. The mapping shows how this can be implemented through a floating offer for the Bergisch cooperation area. Through a better networked range of e-mobility routes, users can first use these means of transport to reach public transport stations where mobility hubs are positioned. As a result, they can get to their destination in the co-operation space faster and save less time and less waiting time and save time which they can use more productively in their quarters.

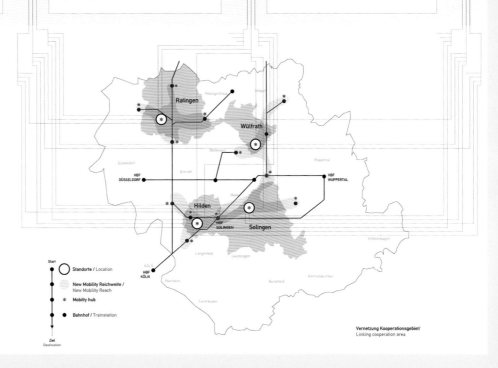

Start — Standorte / Location

New Mobility Reichweite / New Mobility Reach

* Mobility hub

Bahnhof / Trainstation

Ziel / Destination

Vernetzung Kooperationsgebiet / Linking cooperation area

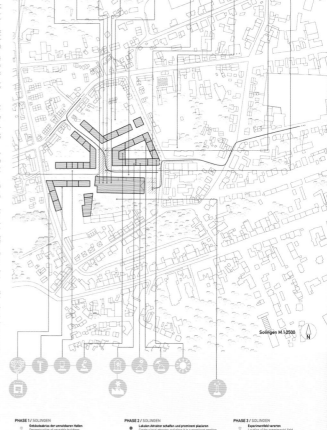

Hilden M 1:2500

Solingen M 1:2500

PHASE 1 / HILDEN

○ Zwischennutzung Postgebäude mit Garagen
  Intermediate use Post building with garages

● Gebäude Abriss
  Building Deconstruction

PHASE 2 / HILDEN

● Wohnbebauung mit produktivem Erdgeschoss ergänzen
  Add productive ground floor to residential buildings

● Produktives Erdgeschoss für Garagennutzer schaffen
  Create productive ground floor for garage users.

PHASE 3 / HILDEN

● Wohngebäude mit produktivem Erdgeschoss ergänzen
  Add productive ground floor to residential buildings

● Gebäude aktivieren
  Activate Buildings

○ Anbindung zum Bahnhof/Stadthalle stärken
  Strengthening the connection to train station/town hall

PHASE 1 / SOLINGEN

○ Gebäudeabriss der unnutzbaren Hallen
  Deconstruction of unusable buildings

● 'Grossmann' Hauptgebäude aktivieren
  Activate 'Grossmann' main building

PHASE 2 / SOLINGEN

● Lokalen Attraktor schaffen und prominent plazieren
  Create a local attractor and place it in a prominent position

● Wohngebäude mit produktivem Erdgeschoss erweitern
  Expand residential building with productive ground floor

● Baufläche als Experimentierfläche umnutzen
  Reuse building area as Experimental Field

PHASE 3 / SOLINGEN

○ Experimentierfeld verorten
  Location of the experimental field

● Wohngebäude mit produktivem Erdgeschoss erweitern
  Expand residential building with productive ground floor

○ Anbindung zur Trasse/Bushaltestelle stärken
  Strengthening the connection to the rail trail/bus stop station

Wülfrath M 1:2500

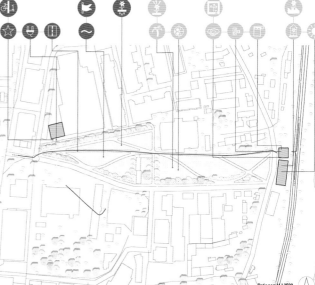

Ratingen M 1:2500

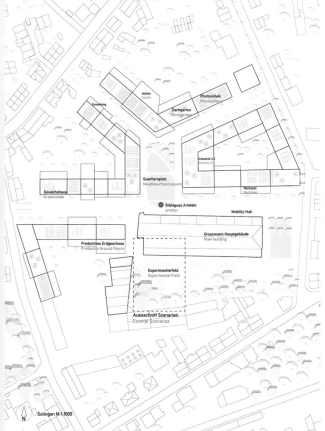

Atelier
Studio
Coworking
Photovoltaik
Photovoltaics
Dachgarten
Roof garden
Industrie 4.0
Industry 4.0
Quartiersplatz
Neighbourhood square
Gewächshaus
Greenhouse
Werkstatt
Workshop
Stahlguss Artefakt
artefact
Mobility Hub
Grossmann Hauptgebäude
Main building
Produktives Erdgeschoss
Productive Ground Floors
Experimentierfeld
Experimental Field
Aussschnitt Szenarien
Excerpt Scenarios

N Solingen M 1:1000

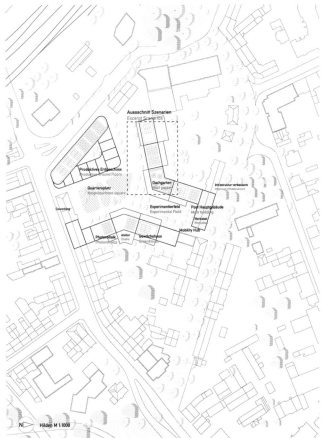

Aussschnitt Szenarien
Excerpt Scenarios
Produktives Erdgeschoss
Productive Ground Floors
Dachgarten
Roof garden
Infrastruktur verbessern
Infarous infrastructure
Quartiersplatz
Neighbourhood square
Experimentierfeld
Experimental Field
Post Hauptgebäude
Main building
Coworking
Werkstatt
Workshop
Photovoltaik
Photovoltaics
Atelier
Studio
Gewächshaus
Greenhouse
Mobility Hub

N Hilden M 1:1000

Szenario A / Solingen
Experimentierfeld wird als Wohndorf genutzt
Experimental field used as residential village

Dorf
Village

Szenario B / Solingen
Experimentierfeld wird als Filmset benutzt
Experimental field is used as film set

Filmset
Film Set

Szenario C / Solingen
Experimentierfeld wird mit unterschiedlichen Nutzungen bespielt
Experimental field is used for different purposes

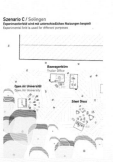

Bauwagenbüro
Trailer Office
Open Air Universität
Open Air University
Silent Disco

Szenario A / Hilden
Erdgeschosszone mit minimal produktiver Nutzung und Gärten
Ground floor zone with minimal productive use and gardens

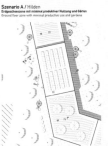

Szenario B / Hilden
Erdgeschosszone mit produktiver Nutzung und Gärten
Ground floor zone with productive use and gardens

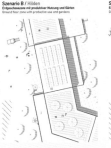

Szenario C / Hilden
Erdgeschosszone mit maximal produktiver Nutzung
Ground floor zone with maximum productive use

The Productive Region

Marc Rieser (DE) Stadtplaner / Urban Planer

Beabsichtigt wurde eine Darstellung des Verlaufs von der regionalen Strategie über die Adaption in ein städtebauliches Konzept bis hin zur exemplarischen Implementation dieses Konzepts in den Quartieren der jeweiligen Standorte.

Das erarbeitete Programm „The Productive Region" soll auf der regionalen Ebene erste Leitlinien für die zukünftige kooperative Planung bieten. Auf der städtebaulichen Ebene geht es dann um die individuelle Auseinandersetzung mit den jeweiligen Standorten und deren standortspezifischen Talenten in Verbindung mit dem anpassungsfähigen Konzept.

Dieses Konzept umfasst vier Maßnahmen-Cluster: konkrete räumliche Maßnahmen im Quartier (SPACE); Maßnahmen zur vielfältigen Belebung dieser Räume (LIFE); Maßnahmen zur ökologischen und nachhaltigen Entwicklung der Quartiere (ECOLOGY); Maßnahmen, welche den Zugang zu den geschaffenen Qualitäten ermöglichen (MOBILITY). Durch eine genaue Auseinandersetzung mit den jeweiligen Gebieten und eine darauf aufbauende Skalierung der Maßnahmen-Cluster soll so eine gleichwertige Qualität mit individuellem Charakter an allen Standorten der Region erreicht werden.

Hinzu kommen die Prozesse, welche Synergien innerhalb der Quartiere schaffen und optimieren. Das DAILY LIFE SYSTEM basiert auf der Verknüpfung der verschiedenen Schnittstellen von Nutzenden und Nutzungen in der Nachbarschaft, um so ein bedarfsgerechtes Angebot herzustellen. Der URBAN METABOLISM befasst sich mit den unterschiedlichen Ressourcen-Kreisläufen innerhalb der Quartiere und deren Optimierung.

Die Bestandteile an sich bauen aufeinander auf und funktionieren durch ihre Synergien am produktivsten. Allerdings kann und muss sich das Konzept flexibel und resilient für Veränderungen aufstellen. So ist eine Entwicklung in mehreren Phasen mit jeweils einer neuen bedarfsgerechten Skalierung der Maßnahmen-Cluster notwendig.

The intention was to depict the full course of the regional strategy, from the adaptation into an urban-planning concept to the exemplary implementation of this concept in the districts of the respective sites.

The 'The Productive Region' program that has been developed is intended to provide the first guidelines on a regional level for the cooperative future planning. On the urban planning level, what is then required is an individual examination of the respective sites and their site-specific aspects in connection with the adaptable concept.

This concept encompasses four clusters of measures: concrete spatial measures in the districts (SPACE); measures to enliven these spaces in diverse ways (LIFE); measures for developing the districts ecologically and sustainably (ECOLOGY); measures that facilitate access to the qualities created (MOBILITY). As a result of an in-depth examination of the respective areas and a scaling of the clusters of measures based on it, an equivalent quality with an individual character should thus be achieved at all the sites in the region.

Added to this are processes that create and optimize synergies within the districts. The DAILY LIFE SYSTEM is based on linking the various interfaces between users and uses in the neighbourhood so as to provide a needs-oriented offering. URBAN METABOLISM deals with the circulation of various resources within the districts as well as the optimization of this circulation.

The components themselves build on each other and function very productively as a result of their synergies. The concept can and must, however, be set up flexibly and in a way that is resilient to changes. A development in several phases with a new needs-oriented scaling of the clusters of measures for each case is thus necessary.

Marc Rieser studierte Städtebau (M.Sc.) an der TH Köln und der TONGJI University in Shanghai. Zuvor absolvierte er an der HS OWL seinen Abschluss in Landschaftsarchitektur (Ing./B.Sc.). Während des Studiums arbeitete er unter anderem für Büros wie MUST (Köln/ Amsterdam), GHP (Hamburg) und rheinflügel severin (Düsseldorf). Neben Europan konnte er sich bereits in weiteren nationalen und internationalen Wettbewerben erfolgreich platzieren.

marc.rieser@hotmail.de

Marc Rieser studied urban planning (M.Sc.) at the Technical University in Cologne and at TONGJI University in Shanghai. He previously completed a degree in landscape architecture (Ing./B.Sc.) at the OWL University of Applied Arts and Sciences. While studying, he worked at firms including MUST (Cologne/Amsterdam), GHP (Hamburg), and rheinflügel severin (Düsseldorf). Besides Europan, he has already managed achieve a ranking successfully in other national and international competitions.

marc.rieser@hotmail.de

xl 01

STRATEGY

1. THINK AS ONE REGION, NOT AS MANY CITIES

For an efficient implementation of the overall planning, it is of highest priority to understand and act as a common region. In order to ensure sustainable protection of the entire region, developments must be considered and assessed regionally. In addition to mobility, spatial development and use, these also include social issues.

2. DEVELOP NETWORKS & CIRCULATIONS, ON EVERY LEVEL

The transition from a linear economy to a circular economy spares resources in the first place, in addition, it also connects a wide variety of participants locally and regionally with one another and, in addition, encourages decentralized supply.

3. URBANITY FOR EVERY SCALE

Urbanity is often understood as having a high population density in an urban context, but it is more about the vibrant diversity of cultural and social facilities or various offers of education, work and living. For the region, this means a true-to-scale implementation of this urbanity at the urban and rural levels. In addition to the individual possibility of using space, this also includes comprehensive access to the technological standard.

4. KNOW YOUR IDENTITY

Even those who think ahead as a region should be aware of their local identity. The Bergisches Land and its towns and villages have a lot of charisma and different spatial characters, which have to be preserved, integrated and presented. In addition to spatial as well as social structures, these also have to be considered outside the planning area.

5. HOMOGENEOUS HETEROGENEITY

Regional thinking in combination with local characteristics gives rise to an equally sustainable and fair region, which is nevertheless characterized by a variety of attractive individual characteristics. This balanced diversity should be considered from the regional scale to the neighborhood with its milieus, uses and buildings. Monofunctional structures are completely to be avoided.

6. INNOVATIVE THINKING & SUPPORTING INNOVATIVE THOUGHTS

Innovative planning should be the cornerstone of a sustainable region. Again, regional issues such as mobility, sustainability or social issues are in focus. In addition, there should also be the possibility that the individual or group can engage in innovation. This usually requires space and infrastructure that should be there.

7. BRING TOGETHER WHAT BELONGS TOGETHER

Unterschiede ziehen sich an. Gleich und gleich gesellt sich gern.
As you can see, there is no firm rule as to who fits together. This should be determined individually for each city location in order to create synergies between users and / or uses. For example, the combination of Thinkers & Makers in a common spatial element can both increase productivity and minimize social differences.

8. BOOST & DEMAND

Due to the massive housing shortage in large cities, such as Cologne and Dusseldorf many manufacturing industries are displaced from the city. These must be acquired and integrated into the region.
Young and innovative companies need to be encouraged to give them a chance but also to keep them in the region. This also requires space and infrastructure. Large and financially strong companies like to jump on a good moving train, but they should also participate in the development of the region.

ratingen

The peculiarity here is that a long-term development with several phases is planned for this purpose. The planning presented here represents the kick-off for a new innovative and productive and also lively area, which on the one hand should have a positive development for the area within the planning boundaries and beyond. The new train station Ratingen - West offers new potential for the development of the area. Based on this new access to mobility, a new milieu can now be established here. The new university location is a combination of theoretical thinking and learning with practical implementation. Here, students and apprentices should work together productively with research and craftsmen. This creates a win-win situation for everyone in which a product can be experienced in one place, from the idea through to completion. The further development envisages a transformation from large-scale monostructures to small-scale multiple use. This creates space that is intended for qualitative open spaces, such as the new park as a core element and connector of the surrounding areas.

wülfrath

Structurally, the planning of the development area is based on the existing morphology of the village, but reinterprets from a sustainable perspective. Mostly one- to two-storey construction in addition to some interspersed high points, so allows a density that is not foreign to the place but still corresponds to the requirements of building on the Grünen Wiese. The adjacent landscape and its consideration is part of the development. The main focus here is the social interaction of the new inhabitants with each other and with the locals. Very small-scale production from home office to co-working can be found here. Social institutions, the club life or shared areas make the new area to be a lively for its initial situation of the place. In addition to new residents, this area should also offer alternatives for local residents who want to redefine their demands on the living space.

By connecting to a new cycle superhighway to Wülfrath and the new train station Düssel provides optimal mobility for the rural area. In addition, access to digital opportunities offers further urbanity. These include, for example, on-demand services.

hilden

Perfectly connected to the public transport, this area offers the opportunity for a new symbiosis of small-scale and perceptible productivity, with quality space for new living. The Grunderzeit urban fabric is taken up and not only the attractive outside but also a new lively inside, which offers space for the existing and new small uses, but also creates new living space. In addition, these different new and local milieus find each other in several community uses. The former fallow land in the south of the area is closed by a modern parking garage. This new gateway to the city, in addition to interior noise control, provides a hub for multimodal mobility and offers space on the roof for an attractive sports ground for the entire neighborhood. In the middle of the block there is also a new communal area and a green area created which, together with the green roof areas and shared gardens, creates a healthy microclimate. In addition, the green roof areas can be used by the local residents and, for example, provide space for community gardens in the middle of the city.

solingen

An area that has always embodied productivity and now has to reorganize as it transforms. During planning, this historical background is taken into account and illustrated by the preservation of individual structures. In doing so, however, it will be restructured in a smaller scale so that a production will be created together with a new residential district. A division into different blocks allows a variety of uses. On the one hand, there is space for all local structures, as well as any kind of production facilities. Especially a creative environment with a fable for local and sustainable development can be established here. At the same time, new flexible working models should be available for everyone on a long-term and also temporary basis.

In addition to the conversion and creation of new living, social and working space, the focus here is also on the quality of the outdoor space and, thanks to the various offers, it helps to revitalize the place. This creates a new community that meets all the needs of everyday life in the immediate vicinity and also invites the neighborhood to participate, here at Grossmann Quartier.

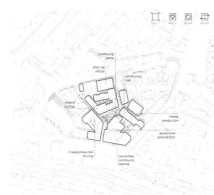
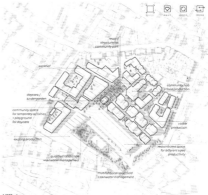

ADAPTION

SPACE

This input provides the starting point for spatial development. Through a diverse mix of space offers, creating a quality neighborhood, which can thus be claimed by different user groups. From the beginning of the planning, spatial consideration is given to inclusion. Through a phased development, certain parameters can be adjusted and optimized in the course.

LIFE

A place without life does not work. And so, in the development of the neighborhood, one should try to include as many different forms of life as possible. This includes all generations, social milieus as well as ways of life and work. Many different uses can be arranged at the same location. The spatial connection creates interfaces that lead to the further activation of the neighborhood.

ECOLOGY

Sustainable planning is a prerequisite for the development of new neighborhoods and therefore the focus is also on dealing with the topic of the circular metabolism. This includes dealing with the microclimate, water management, energy, food production, securing open spaces as well as its qualification. In addition, these factors should also be aesthetically integrated into the planning.

MOBILITY

The way of living, working and its demands on getting around are changing and mobility has to be redefined. Away from a car-oriented planning to multi-modal and sustainable mobility with multiple flexible alternatives, which allows every user barrier-free access. The planning is carried out coverage and demand-oriented for every type of neighborhood and its environment.

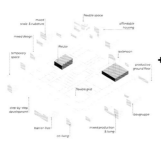
+
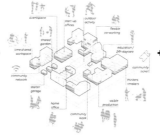
+

+
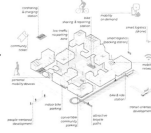

THE PRODUCTIVE REGION

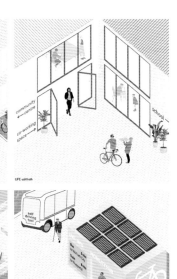

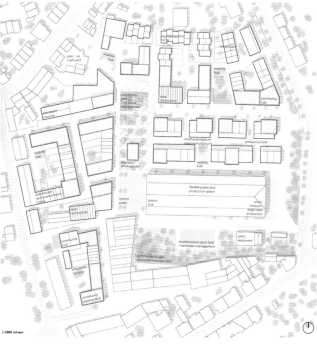

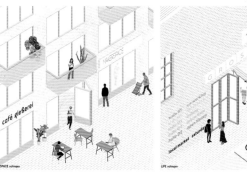

IMPLEMENTATION

DAILY LIFE SYSTEM

The Daily Life System is based on linking the different interfaces of users and residents in the neighborhood. Due to the diverse demands on these interfaces by the users, these offer a variety of possibilities. The smallest part of this system are the rooms with individual requirements such as living. These are frequented every day. The next major component is the CommunityHub. Here are claims of the surrounding neighborhood taken up, such as access to shared mobility services or co-working rooms

together with child care. The biggest part is the DistrictHub, which is a focal point for the whole district. Concerns are being concentrated here, which are frequented by many but not necessarily needed on a daily basis. This is also a meeting point for the entire district and offers space for joint activities. Parking is also to be concentrated here so that the rest of the district is free from parking areas. To make this work, the switch to shared mobility for the last few meters to the finish is also possible here.

CIRCULAR METABOLISM

Sustainable planning is the prerequisite for any development today. Thus, from the very beginning, circular flows must be considered and the influence of the measures on the area must be weighed. Resource-saving planning through the preservation of structures and reuse in combination with the addition of multi-valued structures are a start. Just as important as the use of water and its multiple use in the district is the generation of energy, as well as storage in focus. A self-sufficient

system, which can provide itself with energy and in addition also operates local food production and thus less dependent on the outside world is targeted.

Another part of this system is the social cycles that already share resources instead of owning them. Within the district, this principle can be transferred to the space requirements. By optimizing the use of such spaces, land consumption can be minimized.

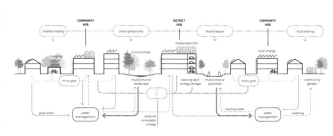

THE PRODUCTIVE REGION

Selb

Selb, Bahnhofsareal Standort / Location
~ 16.000 Bevölkerung / Inhabitants
65,7 ha Betrachtungsraum / Study Site
6,6 ha Projektgebiet / Project Site

Durch die Revitalisierung einer innerstädtischen Brachfläche und die Verbesserung der städtebaulichen Situation im direkten Bahnhofsumfeld soll ein Beitrag zur Innenentwicklung der Stadt Selb geleistet werden. Selb hat, ebenso wie die gesamte Region, einen strukturellen Mangel an gutem und individuell gestaltbarem Wohnraum, insbesondere im Mietwohnungssektor. Zudem gibt es nur sehr eingeschränkte innerstädtische Flächenpotenziale für den Geschosswohnungsbau. Daher ist eine, zumindest teilweise, Neubebauung der Fläche mit Mehrfamilienhäusern oder Stadthäusern besonders wünschenswert. Eine Nutzungsmischung mit nicht störendem Gewerbe ist an dieser Stelle unter Berücksichtigung des kleinstädtischen Charakters der Stadt ausdrücklich gewünscht. Das dann neu gestaltete Bahnhofsviertel soll verkehrlich optimal an die verschiedenen Stadtquartiere angebunden werden.

Das Areal befindet sich etwa 400 Meter nördlich des Stadtzentrums. Neben der Güterhalle steht auch das gründerzeitliche Bahnhofsgebäude heute weitgehend leer und beeinträchtigt das Stadtbild an prominenter Stelle. Das ca. 4,5 Hektar große Bahnhofsumfeld hat seine historische Bedeutung durch die drastische Abnahme des Bahnverkehrs in Selb weitgehend verloren. Weite Teile des Areals liegen brach. Vor dem Bahnhofsgebäude befinden sich der Goetheplatz und die daran anschließende Bahnhofstraße, die ebenfalls von erheblichen städtebaulichen und funktionalen Missständen geprägt sind.

Die traditionsreiche Porzellanindustrie in Selb hatte ihre zahlreichen Produktionsstandorte von Anfang an inmitten der Stadt. Auch viele der wieder prosperierenden Mittelständler produzieren, forschen und verwalten auf sehr gut eingebetteten, kernstädtischen Grundstücken und prägen das industrielle Bild der Stadt bis heute. Auslagerungen von Produktionsanlagen an den Stadtrand und die Trennung von Wohnen und Arbeiten sind dagegen in Selb Phänomene der jüngsten Vergangenheit und beschränken sich auf wenige Fallbeispiele im Westen der Stadt entlang der A 93. Die Stadt Selb möchte daher mit einer Stärkung des zentralen Bahnhofsareals und seines engeren Umfeldes als Ort von Wohnen und Arbeiten an die Tradition der innerstädtischen Produktion anknüpfen. In Selb gibt es aktuell kaum noch integrierte Gewerbeflächen für räumliche Erweiterungen oder Neuansiedlungen. Auch attraktive innerstädtische Orte für kleinteilige Dienstleister und Kreative findet man in Selb bisher kaum. Die Stadt möchte das bisher ungenutzte Potenzial seines brachliegenden Bahnhofsviertels heben. Durch die Nutzungsmischung von Wohnen, Dienstleistungen und produzierendem Gewerbe soll diesem Raum ein modernes und urbanes Flair eingehaucht werden, das jedoch gleichzeitig durch gestalterische Elemente die für die Industriegeschichte der Stadt so bedeutsame Eisenbahntradition am Standort aufgreift. Langfristig soll sich das Bahnhofsareal durch städtebauliche Impulse mit der Innenstadt und dem neuen Outlet Center zur attraktiven neuen Mitte von Selb verbinden.

Revitalizing fallow plots of land within the city and improving the urban situation around the railway station should contribute to inner development. Selb, like the region as a whole, is in need of good and individually adaptable living spaces, in particular rented flats. Additionally, there are only a few available areas within the city for the potential construction of new blocks of flats. What is therefore required is at least partial new construction with blocks of flats or townhouses. A mixture of non-disruptive businesses with a relationship to the small-scale character of the city is desired. The new railway station district should have optimal traffic links to the different parts of the city.

The area is located approximately 400 meters north of the city centre. The empty storage facility and the adjacent, largely vacant station building have had a negative influence on the city's image, existing as they do at a prominent location. The approximately 4.5-hectare-large area around the station has lost its historic significance because of the great decrease in railway traffic in Selb. There are also functional deficits. Large sections of the area are brownfields. In front of the station, Goetheplatz and the adjoining Bahnhofstraße also have urban and functional drawbacks.

From the very beginning, the traditional porcelain industry had its production facilities in the centre of the city. Many small-to-medium-sized businesses (now thriving once again) produce their output, conduct their research, and are managed on areas that are integrated into the city, and thus influence the industrial image of the city to this day. The outsourcing of production to the periphery and the separation of working and living are phenomena of the more recent past in Selb, with only a few exceptions along the A93 motorway in the west. The city wants to strengthen the tradition of production within the city with the reinvigoration of the railway station area and adjacent spaces. Potential integrated spaces for the expansion of existing commercial areas or the creation of new ones are hard to find at the moment. In addition, there are hardly any attractive locations within the city for small businesses or creative users. The city of Selb therefore wants to take advantage of the unused potential of the railway station district. This area should be given a modern and urban flair by introducing a mixture of housing, services, and producing businesses and design elements related to the city's important industrial and railway heritage. In the long term, the station area should be connected to the city centre and the new Outlet Center by urban planning trends. Together, they should form a new, attractive centre for Selb.

Scherben bringen Glück
Das Produktive Herzstück

Simon Gehrmann (DE) Architekt / Architect
Roderich Eßmann (DE) Architekturstudent / Architecture student
Margarita Vollmer (DE) Architekturstudentin / Architecture student
Robin Thomae (DE) Architekturstudent / Architecture student

In Anlehnung an die Struktur und Nutzungsvielfalt der industriellen, handwerklichen Vergangenheit der Porzellanstadt Selb entsteht auf dem Bahnhofsareal ein neues produktives Quartier. Es bietet dank dem über mehrere Generationen aufgebauten Reichtum an Erfahrung mit keramischen Erzeugnissen einen Entwicklungsraum für Innovationen in Materialforschung, Produktdesign und Industriehandwerk. Das Bahnhofsareal im Norden der Innenstadt spielte für die Entwicklung der einst renommierten Porzellanstadt eine Schlüsselrolle und ist mittlerweile ein vergessenes Herzstück Selber Stadtgeschichte. Die Zukunft der Stadt Selb steht im Zeichen des Outlet Centers und prognostiziert eine einseitige Stadtentwicklung im Sinne des Massenkonsums, welcher jedoch entscheidende Potenziale für Synergien bietet.

Die zwei grundlegenden Elemente – das Produktive Herz und die Promenade der Freundschaft – gestalten das neue Quartier zu einem einzigartigen Ort des Zusammenkommens für alle Generationen. Das Produktive Herz wird mit neuen Arbeits- und Wohnformen zum Lebensmittelpunkt von Forscherinnen und Forschern, Studentinnen und Studenten sowie Bewohnerinnen und Bewohnern der Stadt. Im Norden befinden sich Werkstätten und die Multifunktionshalle mit Außenbereichen, die zum Forschen, Entwickeln und Präsentieren genutzt werden und einen spannenden Einblick in die Produktion geben. Auf der Südseite bieten Atelierhäuser den Forscherinnen und Forscher und Studentinnen und Studenten angemessene Wohn- und Arbeitsräume mit einem Werkhof, die das Modellieren von Skulpturen und andere Projekte fördern.

Entlang der ehemaligen Bahngleise erstreckt sich die Promenade der Freundschaft, welche die Bewohnerinnen und Bewohner in ihrer Grünraumstruktur zusammenbringt und zum Austausch und Verweilen anregt. Beide Kernelemente des Entwurfs werden zum grenzübergreifenden Veranstaltungsort der Freundschaftswochen 2023 von Selb (DE) und Asch (CZ).

The project represents an extension to the future development of the city of Selb, which is currently dominated by an outlet centre and development driven by consumption. The design focuses on the formation of a specialized educational site, which is based on the past experiences and competences of the 170-year-long tradition of the porcelain industry and knowledge of materials. The railway station area in the north of the city played a key role in the economic development of Selb from a town of craftsmen to an internationally renowned production site for ceramic products. In honour of the railway station building, a public square will be created behind it as a prelude to the new productive district, and a new mobility hub will link the area with the region.

Two core elements—the Promenade of Friendship and the Productive Heart—will make the railway station area a unique gathering place for all generations. The productive heart becomes the centre of life for researchers, students, and residents, with new forms of work and housing in the form of research labs and studio houses. A multi-functional hall enables them to collaborate on product design and material science projects, and stimulates visitors who are interested in obtaining insights into the work process. The characteristic features of the residential buildings are working studios on the ground floor and an additional work yard for students to work on models, sculptures, and other projects.

The Promenade of Friendship runs through the old railway, brings residents together, and gives rise to exchange and places to spend time. The core elements of the project mentioned offer an opportunity to host events for the Bavarian-Czech friendship weeks that will take place in Selb (DE) and Asch (CZ) in 2023.

Roderich Eßmann, Robin Thomae und Margarita Vollmer sind drei Studierende an der TU Darmstadt. Sie stehen kurz vor ihrem Masterabschluss und entschlossen sich in Zusammenarbeit mit Dr. Simon Gehrmann, Architekt und wissenschaftlicher Mitarbeiter der TU Darmstadt, zur Teilnahme am Europan 15. Das Projekt „Scherben bringen Glück" basiert auf einem Studienprojekt, in dem sich die Bearbeiterinnen und Bearbeiter intensiv mit der Geschichte der Stadt Selb auseinandergesetzt haben und die Potenziale dieser in einer spielerischen Darstellungsweise aufgezeigt haben.

bolik@freiraum.tu-darmstadt.de
margarita.vollmer96@web.de
robin_th@hotmail.de
r-essmann@gmx.de
gehrmann@stadt.tu-darmstadt.de

Roderich Eßmann, Robin Thomae, and Margarita Vollmer are three students at the TU Darmstadt. They are on the verge of doing their final thesis. They decided to participate in Europan 15 in collaboration with Dr Simon Gehrmann—an architect and research assistant at the TU Darmstadt. The project 'Scherben bringen Glück' is based on a student project in which the authors examined the history of the city of Selb in detail and illustrated it potentials in a playful presentation.

bolik@freiraum.tu-darmstadt.de
margarita.vollmer96@web.de
robin_th@hotmail.de
r-essmann@gmx.de
gehrmann@stadt.tu-darmstadt.de

46

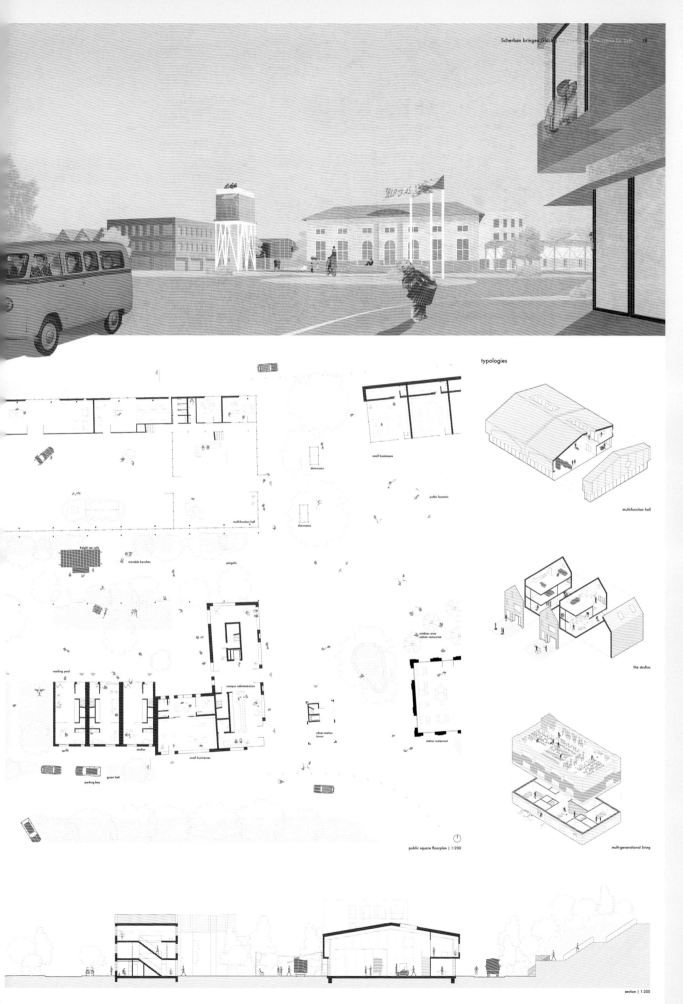

Scherben bringen Glück

typologies

small businesses

showcases

public fountain

showcases

multi-function hall

multi-function hall

freight car cafe

movable benches

pergola

outdoor area
station restaurant

the studios

working yard

campus administration

observation
tower

studios

station restaurant

small businesses

parking bay

green belt

multi-generational living

public square floorplan | 1:200

section | 1:200

Scherben bringen Glück
Das Produktive Herzstück

youth hostle
the youth hostel ist located on a slight elevation which allows to accommodate day tourist near the centre of Selb while ensuren a pleasant view over the newly formed quarter.

regional site

UAS Hof institute for material science
30 km

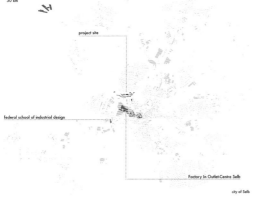

project site

federal school of industrial design

multifunction hall
the multifunction hall preludes the productive heart of Selb. It offers space for showroom and networking purposes as well as workshops and laboratories. furthermoret, it can be equipped with seating to hold public events.

promenade
he promenade is defined by a sequence of wooden posts which allows vines to grow along the way and create a kind of leafy roof. Moreover, it ensures insights into the lives and work process of researchers and product designers and thus forming the districs identity.

urban gardening
located next to the existing allotment gardens, the urban gardening area encourages young and old to communicate and garden together in the neighborhood.

Factory In Outlet-Centre Selb

city of Selb

the producitve heart of selb

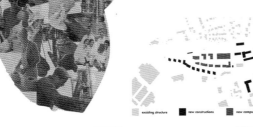

concept
The project represents an extension to the future development of the city of Selb, which is currently dominated by the outlet and a progression driven by consumption. The design focuses on the formation of an specialized educational site in Selb, which is based on past experiences and competences by porcelain industry and the citizens of Selb with the material of cera- mics. At the same time, core elements of the project offer the opportunity to host events for the Freundschaftswochen between Selb and Asch 2023.

the promenade of friendship

Tschechien (Asch)

Bayern (Selb)

building structure
In honor of the train station building that shaped the history of Selb, a public square will be implemented behind it to prelude the new productive quarter. The educational site however is located in the middle of the district and forms the „heart" or centerpiece of the district. Along the north of the centerpiece factory facilities, research labs and studio rooms are located in the form of multi-function halls. The south side of the district offers residen- tial space for students and researchers alike. These studio houses feature outstretched forecourts, which serves as an open work yard and promote the production of models, sculptures and other projects. Special use buil- dings in the form of a youth hostel and assisted living facililites are arran- ged around the centerpiece.

route links
The two main traffic axes for private transport and delivery traffic are orga- nized around the district „heart". Mobility within the campus area is solely covered by foot or bicycle. The promenade of friendship forms the primary access route with its characterisic pergola. The path preserves the existing trees and tracks of the formerly overgrown station area and creates a green recreation space with a special quality of stay. In addition, insights into the work process of researchers and creatives of the distirct are provi- ded along the main access route.

stakeholders
The development concept is realized at building level and at free spa- ce level. The promenade of friendship is to be built as part of the Bay- erisch-Tschechische Freundschaftswochen 2023. In order to promote cross-border relations between the neighboring cities of Asch and Selb, the Free State of Bavaria and the Czech Republic are investing funds to refur- bish the urban green spaces and festivities during the FW 2023. The pro- menade and the public square will thus become the scene of international relations. For the productive heart, an association of local interest groups is founded. These include the main actors of the UAS Hof with its Institute of Materials Science and the Staatliche Berufsschulzentrum für Produktdesign. In addition, the Selbwerk, the Handwerkskammer Oberfranken, as well as local companies participate in the construction of the productive center- piece. Thanks to the european funding program Interreg Europe the district can be conveyed in the field of research + innovation. With the support of the association Keramisches Herzstück e.V., a high level of knowledge about ceramic interest comes together again and Selb regains internatio- nal reputation for ceramic products and materials research.

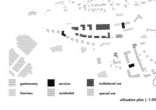

concept collage

building structure | 1:5000

existing structure   new constructions   new campus selb

communicative open spaces   new constructions   route links
existing structure

routes | 1:5000

gastronomy   services   institutional use
business   residential   special use

utilization plan | 1:5000

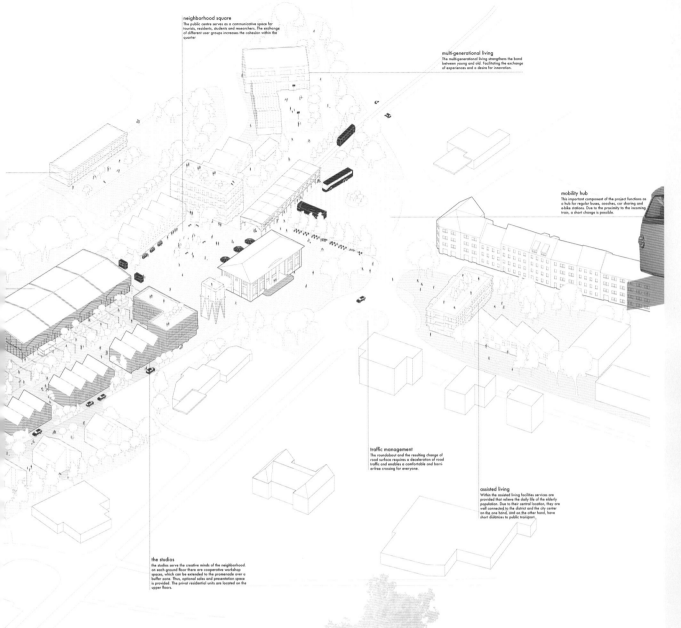

neighborhood square
The public centre serves as a communicative space for tourists, residents, students and researchers. The exchange of different user groups increases the cohesion within the quarter.

multi-generational living
The multi-generational living strengthens the bond between young and old. Facilitating the exchange of experiences and a desire for innovation.

mobility hub
This important component of the project functions as a hub for regular busses, coaches, car sharing and e-bike stations. Due to the proximity to the incoming train, a short change is possible.

traffic management
The roundabout and the resulting change of road surface requires a deceleration of road traffic and enables a comfortable and barrier-free crossing for everyone.

assisted living
Within the assisted living facilities services are provided that relieve the daily life of the elderly population. Due to their central location, they are well connected to the district and the city center on the one hand, and on the other hand, have short distances to public transport.

the studios
the studios serve the creative minds of the neighborhood. on each ground floor there are cooperative workshop spaces, which can be extended to the promenade over a buffer zone. Thus, optional sales and presentation space is provided. The privat residential units are located on the upper floors.

axonometry | 1:500

development phases

I
The realization process is characterized by three phases of development. The project starts with the formation of the districts productive heart. First, the premises of the educational institutions and the pergola of the Promenade of Friendship are implemented. The public square near the train station and the small square in the west defines the edges of the new quarter. The first phase focuses on education, local supply and office space, and resident prototypes.

II
In phase two residential units of the studios will be expanded along the south of the promenade and finalise the structure of the „productive heart". Futhermore, the realization of a youth hostel located on the north hill and an assisted-living facility in the south of Goetheplatz will heighten the diversity of use of the district and are geared towards growing numbers of tourists and future pensioners.

III
The third phase proposes an expansion of the housing units in the northwest, as this is marked as an extension area in the land-use plan to complete an overarching connection of the various districts of central Selb. The design of the new units is inspired by the family houses in the north of the district and is intended to provide more diversity and social cohesion near the campus area.

2023

development phase I

2030

development phase II

2040

development phase III

view inside the promenade

Selbstgemacht. Building the town of the future by ourselves

Alberto Montiel Lozano (ES) Architekt / Architect
Pedro de la Torre Prieto (ES) Architekt / Architect
Mitarbeit / Cooperation
David Belmonte Garcia (ES) Architekt / Architect

Die Stadt Selb ist ein perfektes Beispiel für eine postindustrielle europäische Stadt. Das einstmals am Stadtrand gelegene Industriegebiet ist nicht länger aktiv und befindet sich nun zwischen dem historischen Stadtzentrum und den Randbezirken, wodurch eine urbane Leere und eine Art Grenze entstehen. Hauptziele dieses Projektes sind die Wiedernutzung der alten Anlagen, um neuen urbanen Raum zu gewinnen, die Entwicklung neuer ökologischer Strategien, um die Verschmutzung zu beseitigen, sowie die neuerliche Anbindung der umgebenden Gebiete (Stadtzentrum, Randgebiete, Park), damit die urbanen Leerstellen mit neuen Aktivitäten und Wohnraum besiedelt werden, um neue Bewohnerinnen und Bewohner anzuziehen.

Wir schlagen den Einsatz von „Bausteinen" vor, ein autonomes Wohnraumsystem zur Wiederbesetzung der leeren Standorte des Wettbewerbsgebietes und zur Neunutzung der unbenutzten Gebäude, mit attraktiven Wohnstätten für neue Bewohnerinnen und Bewohner: Studierende, Pendlerinnen und Pendler, junge Familien und Seniorinnen und Senioren. Der Umfang jedes Bausteintyps kann je nach Ausmaß der sich verändernden Anforderungen der Stadt gewählt werden.

Um das Problem der Verschmutzung zu lösen und eine neue urbane Landschaft herauszubilden, planen wir einen produktiven Park in der Nähe des Bahnhofes. Wir schlagen die Pflanzung ergiebiger Vegetation vor, um der Verschmutzung mittels Phytosanierung Herr zu werden. Die Pflanzen sollen in der Folge zu einer Erweiterung des Rosenthal-Parks werden. Entlang des Parks werden wir Orientierungspunkte (die Inseln) über jene Orte setzen, von denen wir mit Sicherheit wissen, dass es dort Verschmutzungen gibt. Sie werden die Routen entlang des Parks und industrielle Aktivität anzeigen. Nachbarschaftsverbände können sich um diese ergiebige Vegetation des Parks kümmern und ihre eigenen Lebensmittel ziehen. Die Strategie zur erfolgreichen Revitalisierung der Stadtverbindungen umfasst drei Schritte:

1. Neunutzung der bestehenden Wege, um wertvolle isolierte Gebiete wie den Bereich des Lokschuppens wieder anzuschließen
2. Anbindung der Radwege an die Ost-West-Achse, um diese an das Zentrum anzuschließen
3. Umwandlung der Nord-Süd-Achse zwischen dem Bahnhof und dem Stadtzentrum zu einer Fußgängerzone

The city of Selb is a perfect example of a post-industrial European city. The industrial area that was once situated on the outskirts has become unproductive and now stands between the historic city centre and the suburbs, giving rise to an urban void and a barrier. Reusing the old facilities in order to generate new urban spaces, proposing new ecological strategies for the removal of contamination, reconnecting the surrounding areas (city centre, suburbs, park), and filling the urban voids with new activities and housing in order to attract new residents to Selb are the main goals of this project.

We propose using 'building blocks', constructing an autonomous housing system to reoccupy the empty sites in the competition area, and converting unoccupied buildings into attractive dwellings for a new population: students, commuters, young families, and seniors. The extent to which each kind of building block is used can be chosen based on the city's changing needs.

In order to resolve the contamination problem and to generate a new urban landscape, our plan features a productive park in the railway station area. We propose planting productive vegetation in order to remove the contamination by means of phytoremediation. As the plants grow, they will also create an extension to the Rosenthal Park. Throughout the park, we will position landmarks (islands) in places where we are sure that contamination is present. They will accompany paths through the park, and serve as testimony to the city's past industrial activity. An association of neighbours can manage the productive vegetation of the park and also obtain their own food there. The strategy for effectively revitalizing connections in the city has three clear steps:

1. Reusing existing paths to reconnect isolated valuable areas such as the engine shed area.
2. Successfully connecting cycling paths to the east-west axis in order to connect it to the city centre.
3. Pedestrianizing the north-south axis between the railway station and the city centre.

Alberto Montiel und Pedro de la Torre sind Architekten der Universität Málaga, wo sie einander auch kennenlernten. Während ihrer Zeit an der Universität nahmen sie erfolgreich an etlichen Wettbewerben für Studierende teil, sowohl auf lokaler als auch auf nationaler Ebene. Auch im Bereich der Forschung sind sie aktiv: Alberto war 2012 Teil des Solar Decathlon Teams, das den zweiten Platz belegte; Pedro war 2013 Junior-Assistent des Fachbereichs Geschichte. Um ihren Horizont zu erweitern und andere Möglichkeiten der Ausübung von Architektur kennenzulernen, gingen sie 2015 nach Deutschland, um in dort ansässigen Architekturbüros zu arbeiten. Neben der Arbeit finden sie immer noch Zeit, um gemeinsam an Architekturprojekten zu arbeiten.

montiel_1986@hotmail.com

Alberto Montiel and Pedro de la Torre are both architects who met while studying at Málaga University. During their university years, they participated in and won several competitions for students, on both local and national levels. They also keep one foot in research: Alberto was part of the Solar Decathlon Team of 2012, which won the second prize; Pedro collaborated as a junior assistant in the history department in 2013. Looking to expand their horizons and learn about other ways of approaching architecture, they went to Germany in 2015 to work in local architecture firms. While working, they still find time to create architecture together.

montiel_1986@hotmail.com

Selbstgemacht

Building the town of the future by ourselves
Europan 15 - Selb (DE)

The town

The park

The paths

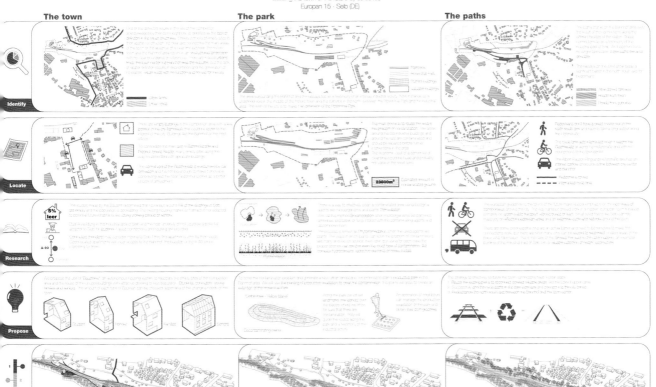

Identify

Locate

Research

Propose

Timeline   Selb 2023

Selb 2030

Selb 2040

SITE PLAN 1/2000
0   15   50   75m

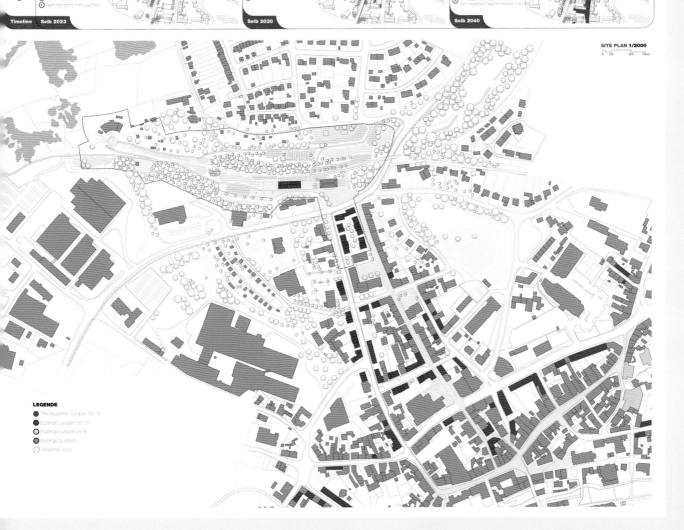

LEGENDE
- The Bausteine, Europan DE 15
- Buildings Europan DE 13
- Buildings Europan DE 9
- Buildings to reform
- Pedestrian zone

Selb**stgemacht**

Building the town of the future by ourselves

Europan 15 · Selb (DE)

Polluting agents

Phytoremediation

Phytoextraction
Absorption, accumulation and translocation of metals or organic compounds.

Phytovolatilization
Absorption and transformation of pollutants into less toxic compounds.

Phytostabilization
Contaminants accumulate in the roots, preventing them from spreading on the ground.

Phytostimulation
The presence of the plant stimulates microbial activities, favouring the degradation of contaminants.

Phytodegradation
Enzymes produced by different plants that catalyze the degradation of soil contaminants.

Contaminated Land

Phytoremediation - natural decontamination

Low vegetation

Grass
Family
Process
Pollutant

Cabbage
Family · Brassicaceae
Process · Phytoextraction
Pollutant · Heavy metals

Broccoli
Family · Brassicaceae
Process · Phytoextraction
Pollutant · Heavy metals

Cauliflower
Family · Brassicaceae
Process · Phytoextraction
Pollutant · Heavy metals

Kohlrabi
Family
Process · Phytoextraction
Pollutant · Heavy metals

Medium-height vegetation

Sunflower
Family · Asteraceae
Process · Phytoextraction
Pollutant · Heavy metals

Colza (Raps)
Family · Brassicaceae
Process · Phytoextraction
Pollutant · Heavy metals

Mustard
Family · Brassicaceae
Process · Phytoextraction
Pollutant · Heavy metals

Rye
Family · Poaceae
Process · Phytostimulation
Pollutant · Hydrocarbons

Hyacinth
Family · Asparagaceae
Process · Phytoextraction
Pollutant · Cresote

High vegetation

Mulberry
Family · Moraceae
Process · Phytostimulation
Pollutant · Hydrocarbons

Pine
Family · Pinaceae
Process
Pollutant

Poplar
Family · Salicaceae
Process · Phytodegradation
Pollutant · Heavy metals

Willow
Family · Salicaceae
Process · Phytodegradation
Pollutant · Hydrocarbons

Apple tree
Family · Rosaceae
Process · Phytostimulation
Pollutant · Hydrocarbons

AXONOMETRIC 1/1000

SELB AŠ PAVILION

BAHNHOF

TYPE OF CONTAMINATION
hydrocarbons
heavy metals
cresote

TYPE OF REGENERATION
brassicaceae
GELBE INSEL - hyacinth dahlia
rye
mustard
60 % colza 40% fescue
couch grass
70% grass 30% geophytes
sunflower
apple tree

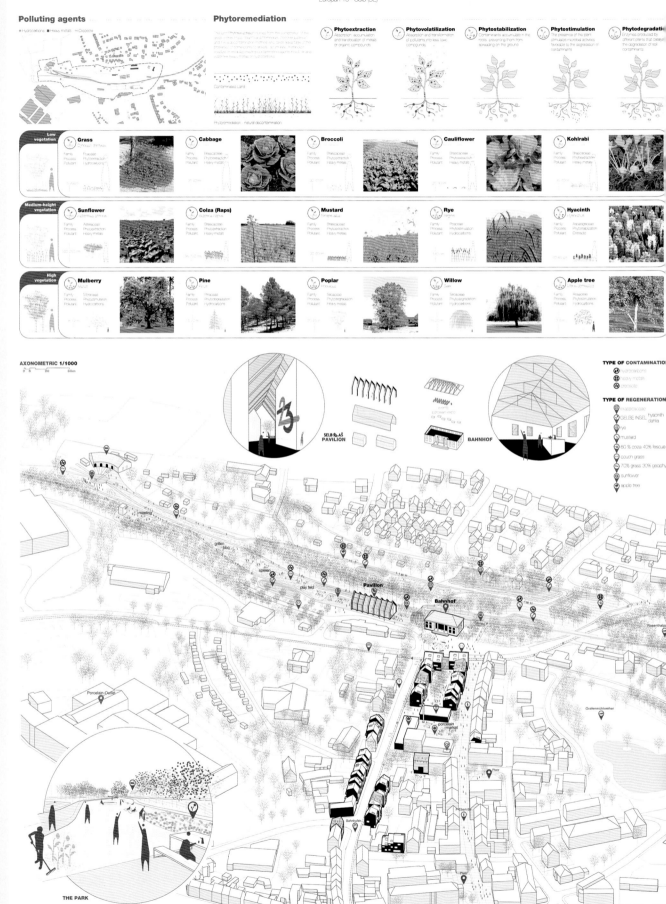

THE PARK

Pavillon

Bahnhof

Porcelain-Outlet

porcelain market

Selbstgemacht

Building the town of the future by ourselves
Europan 15 · Selb (DE)

the 'Bausteine' 1/200

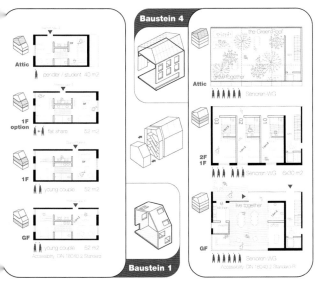

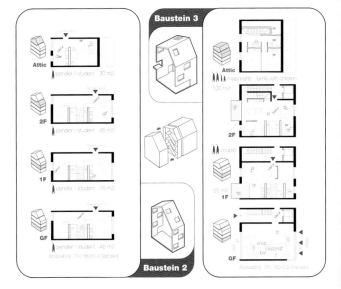

Baustein 4 · Baustein 3 · Baustein 1 · Baustein 2

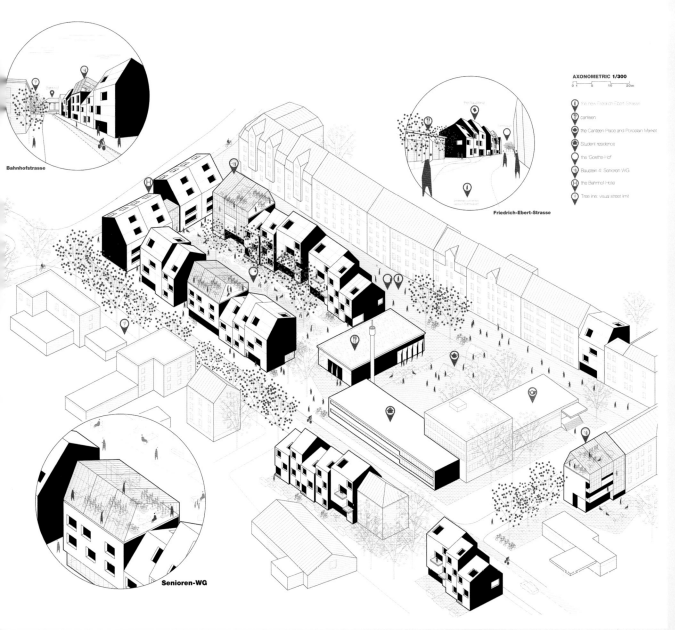

Bahnhofstrasse

Friedrich-Ebert-Strasse

AXONOMETRIC 1/300

Senioren-WG

Warschau

Bielany Standort / Location
136.485 Bevölkerung / Inhabitants
648 ha Betrachtungsraum / Study Site
115 ha Projektgebiet / Project Site

Das Stahlwerk Warschau (Huta Warszawa) lag, als es 1957 eröffnet wurde, vor den Toren der Stadt. Während der fortschreitenden Entwicklung Warschaus wurde das Werk Teil des urbanen Gewebes. Die Areale um die Stahlhütte sind maßstäblich sehr unterschiedlich und beherbergen verschiedene Nutzungen. Außer den industriellen, kommerziellen und als Lager genutzten Flächen sind Wälder und Parks, ein Friedhof, große Wohngebäude und ein Einkaufszentrum vorhanden. Obwohl die Besitzerinnen und Besitzer des Stahlwerkes öfter gewechselt haben und es Restrukturierungsmaßnahmen unterlag, verlief die Produktion kontinuierlich und das Werk ist heute ein prosperierendes Unternehmen. Die Erweiterungsflächen des Stahlwerkes bieten die Chance, die produktiven Funktionen in den urbanen Raum zu integrieren.

Das Projektgebiet liegt im nordwestlichen Teil Warschaus, im Bezirk Bielany, an einem großen intermodalen Kreuzungspunkt in Młociny, der aus einer U-Bahn-Endhaltestelle, einem Bus- und Straßenbahnloop und einer mehrgeschossigen Park-and-ride-Einrichtung besteht. Ökologische Belange, welche die Entwicklung des Areals hemmen, sind die Bodenkontamination und, im speziellen, die Lärmemissionen des Stahlwerkes.

In der Vergangenheit betrieb das Werk, obwohl es eine weitestgehend unabhängige Anlage war, kleinere Firmen und Institutionen mit Bezug zur Schwerindustrie, was einen großen Flächenbedarf zur Folge hatte und eine ausgedehnte interne Infrastruktur erforderte. Aktuelle Industriemodelle (inklusive der für Stahlwerke) weichen davon ab, die Grundlage wird durch ein Netzwerk von Partnern und Versorgern in der Stadt und der Region gebildet. Das hinterließ Spuren in der räumlichen Gestalt des Areals und führte zu Brachflächen und einer Fragmentierung hinsichtlich Eigentümerstruktur und Nutzungen. Die Aufgabe der Planer wird sein, räumliche Voraussetzungen für ein „multifunktionales Ökosystem" zu schaffen, ausgehend von der industriellen Produktion, sowie bestehende und potenzielle Synergien und Ressourcen, wie beispielsweise die Brachflächen, zu nutzen. Das bietet die Möglichkeit, das abgeschottete Areal in ein offenes, multifunktionales und gut erschlossenes Quartier zu transformieren, das in die urbane und, noch wichtiger, die soziale Struktur integriert ist. Gemeinsam mit den benachbarten Müllaufbereitungsanlagen könnte das Stahlwerk als Bindeglied einer wachsenden lokalen Kreislaufwirtschaft fungieren, in dem Schrott zu einem neuen Rohstoff recycelt wird.

Die Lage des Stahlwerkes hat, zusammen mit der Schaffung des Nationalparks Kampinos, das ausufernde Wachstum der Stadt nach Nordwesten verhindert oder begrenzt, im Gegensatz zu anderen Gegenden der Stadt. Die Umgestaltung des Werksgeländes sollte letztlich zum Schutz der umgebenden Naturräume beitragen.

The Warsaw steelworks (Huta Warszawa), which opened in 1957, was located on the outskirts of the city at the time. Due to the ongoing spatial development of Warsaw, the steelworks area has become part of the urban fabric. The areas surrounding the steelworks serve various functions and are diverse in terms of scale. In addition to industrial, storage, and commercial areas, there are also forests and parks, a cemetery, large housing estates, and a shopping centre. Although the owners of the plant have changed several times and the facility has been subjected to restructuring proceedings, it has maintained production continuity and is currently a prospering company. The reserves of land around the plant offer an opportunity to incorporate its production function into the urban space.

The project area is situated in the Bielany district in the north-western part of Warsaw, near a large interchange junction in Młociny, which consists of a metro terminus, a bus and tram loop, and a multi-storey park & ride facility. Environmental concerns that may limit development in the area include soil contamination and, in particular, the noise caused by steel production.

In the past, the Warsaw steelworks operated smaller enterprises and institutions related to heavy industry located nearby, even though it was largely a self-sufficient plant that required a vast area and an extensive internal infrastructure. Contemporary industrial models (including those that apply to steelworks) are different, since they rely on an extensive and flexible network of business partners and third-party suppliers operating in the city and the region. This has left visible traces on the area's spatial structure in the form of reduced production areas, the emergence of brownfields, and the fragmentation of the area with respect to ownership and function. The challenge that urban planners face involves creating spatial conditions for maintaining and extending a multifunctional 'ecosystem' based on industrial production, existing and potential synergies, and human and material resources, including the recovered brownfields. This could provide an opportunity to transform this enclosed area into a multi-functional, open, and accessible district that is integrated within the urban fabric and, more importantly, within the social surroundings. Along with the municipal waste treatment plants operating nearby, the steelworks could be perceived as a link in the emerging local circular economy; a plant that uses steel scrap as its principal material is in fact a large enterprise that recycles secondary raw materials.

The location of the steelworks has limited the growth of Warsaw towards the north, and, combined with the creation of the nearby Kampinos National Park, has made the scale of urban sprawl smaller than on other sides of the agglomeration. The transformation of the plant area should contribute to the protection of the natural sites in its vicinity.

54

Feedback Placemaking

Ada Jaśkowiec (PL) Landschaftsarchitektin / Landscape Architect
Michał Strupiński (PL) Landschaftsplaner / Landscape Planner

Das Industrieareal des Stahlwerkes ist von strategischer Bedeutung für die Entwicklung von Warschau in seiner Gesamtheit, weshalb wir den Gestaltungsspielraum auf vier Bereiche ausgedehnt haben: Stadt, Stadtteil, strategische Belange und Projekt. Resiliente Gestaltung besteht im ständigen Wechsel zwischen den Maßstäben und beteiligten Personen. Wir unterscheiden drei Aspekte der Resilienz: ökonomisch, ökologisch und sozial. In der produktiven Stadt muss jede Entscheidung im Hinblick darauf getroffen werden, wie sie zukünftige Entwicklungen antreibt. Somit geht es um die Vermittlung zwischen der Stadt, lokalen Stakeholdern und zukünftigen Bewohnerinnen und Bewohnern.

Die städtische Struktur des Betrachtungsraumes wird durch vier Komponenten bestimmt: öffentliche Räume, Flächen, Zonen und Punkte, welche als das Gebiet prägende Instrumente dienen. Bedeutende öffentliche Räume bilden eine Achse, die alle urbanen und Grünräume miteinander verbindet. Zonen sind unterschiedlich programmierte Gebiete, die senkrecht zur Hauptachse angeordnet sind. Flächen rahmen öffentliche Räume und bestimmen die Beziehungen und Übergänge zwischen den Zonen und den öffentlichen Räumen. Die Punkte beziehen sich schließlich auf charakteristische Strukturen, die Elemente der räumlichen Orientierung und potenzielle Landmarken darstellen.

56

Das Projekt umfasst Gebiete, die sowohl für eine permanente als für eine temporäre Entwicklung geeignet sind, und die für eine potenzielle zukünftige Erweiterung des Stahlwerkes erhalten werden. Dies erfordert einen innovativen städtebaulichen Ansatz, der den temporären Charakter und das nicht absehbare, zukünftige Wachstum des Geländes berücksichtigt. Wir schlagen vor, den temporären Standort als urbanes Experiment (behutsamer Städtebau) zu entwickeln, um die Möglichkeiten des Grundstückes auszuloten. Dies erzeugt eine Struktur, die auf geschickte Art und Weise die Produktion innerhalb der Stadt verortet und gleichzeitig einen resilienten, einladenden und offenen städtischen Raum erschafft. Nach der Testphase kann er entweder rückentwickelt oder in das Betriebsgelände des Stahlwerkes eingegliedert werden. Zu diesem Zeitpunkt verfügen wir allerdings bereits über einen umfassenden Datenbestand und ein funktionierendes Quartier.

Since the industrial area of the steelworks has a strategic significance for the development of Warsaw as a whole, we expanded the scope of the design to incorporate four scales: city, district, strategic aims, and project. Resilient design requires shifting between the scales and protagonists involved. We distinguished three aspects of resilience: economic, ecological, and social. In a productive city, every decision must be made with consideration of how it will propel further developments. It is thus a question of mediating between the city, local stakeholders, and future tenants.

The urban structure of the strategic site is defined by four components – public spaces, faces, zones and points – which act as territorialising agents. The main public spaces form an axis that links all the urban and green spaces. Zones are diversely programmed areas perpendicular to the main axis. Surfaces frame public spaces and establish the relations and transitions between zones and public spaces. Finally, points refer to characteristic structures that serve as elements that anchor spatial orientation and as potential landmark locations.

The project encompasses areas intended for both permanent and temporary development, with the latter earmarked for the steelworks' potential future expansion. This requires an innovative urban design approach based on temporality and the unpredictability of the plot's future development. We propose developing the temporary site as an urban experiment (slow urbanism) so as to explore the possibilities of the plot. This provides a framework that cleverly accommodates production within the city and creates a resilient, welcoming, and open urban space. After the trial period, the site can be either redeveloped or reincorporated into the steelworks' premises. However, by the time that happens, there will already be a vast database and a well-established neighbourhood.

Wir haben zusammen in Warschau (PL) und Delft (NL) studiert und im Laufe der vergangenen Jahre an etlichen Wettbewerben teilgenommen, sowohl im Bereich Städtebau als auch Architektur. 2016 gewannen wir mit dem Städteplan einer experimentellen Wohnanlage mit Mischnutzung den Wettbewerb Builder 4Young Architects. Nach unserem Studienabschluss in Architektur haben wir uns beruflich in Richtung Städteplanung orientiert. Unser Interesse für den Europan 15-Standort Warschau rührt von unserer Vertrautheit mit dem Gebiet und den umfassenden Dimensionen des Projektes her die eine nicht kanonische Erarbeitung erfordern, die wir in der Lage sind zur Verfügung zu stellen.

ada.jaskowiec@gmail.com

We studied together in Warsaw (PL) and Delft (NL) and have participated in several competitions, both urban and architectural, over the last few years. In 2016, we won the competition Builder 4Young Architects with an urban plan for an experimental, mixed-use housing estate. After obtaining our degree as architects, we began our professional path within the field of urban planning.

The Warsaw site in Europan 15 interested us because of our familiarity with the area and the large scale of the project, which required a noncanonical elaboration that we felt we were in the position to provide.

ada.jaskowiec@gmail.com

WARSAW - FEEDBACK PLACEMAKING
METHODOLOGY - MULTISCALAR APPROACH

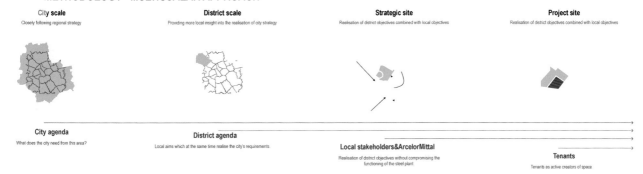

City scale	District scale	Strategic site	Project site
Closely following regional strategy	Providing more local insight into the realisation of city strategy	Realisation of district objectives combined with local objectives	Realisation of district objectives combined with local objectives

City agenda
What does the city need from this area?

District agenda
Local aims which at the same time realise the city's requirements.

Local stakeholders&ArcelorMittal
Realisation of district objectives without compromising the functioning of the steel plant.

Tenants
Tenants as active creators of space.

Cycles & scheme of relations between parties involved

CITY SCALE

Socially resilient Warsaw
Ability to attract new residents regardless of the circumstances
- Polycentric city structure: strong centre, multifunctional district centres and local community centres
- Compact urban tissue: strong preference for densification within existing urban boundaries
- Creation of local identity on multiple levels, i.e. in regard to the city, district and closest communities

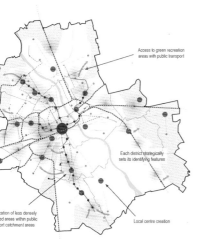

Access to green recreation areas with public transport

Each district strategically sets its identifying features

Densification of less densely populated areas within public transport catchment areas

Local centre creation

- ● Main centre
- ● District centres
- ○ Local community centres
- Densification areas
- Green recreation areas
- Accessibility of green with public transport

Economically resilient Warsaw
Ability to adapt to diverse economic situation
- Close collaboration between businesses, industry and education
- Diversity of business profiles and sizes: start-ups, family companies, through medium size businesses, international corporations to industries
- Openness to innovation: to keep updated and be able to adjust business profiles to new circumstances

Spatial pairing of industrial zones with scientific institutions

Introduction of small production and craftsmanship into local centres

Legislation conducive to start ups and local entrepreneurship

Creation of efficient multi-modal transfer points

Injection of diverse business profiles into existing office areas

- Existing office demand
- Proposed office locations
- Existing academic institutions
- Existing industry
- Proposed location of academic institutions
- Proposed location of start-ups
- Proposed location of crafts and small industry
- Proposed location of multimodal transfer point

Environmentally resilient Warsaw
Capability to adapt to changing weather and climate conditions
- Air quality: protection of aeration corridors, greenification within urban areas
- Urban heat island effect: greenification within urban areas
- Water retention: water retention reservoirs, biologically active surface, flooding protection

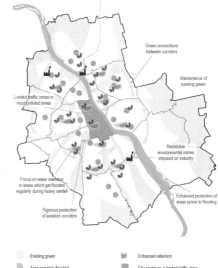

Green connections between corridors

Maintenance of existing green

Limited traffic zones in most polluted areas

Restrictive environmental norms imposed on industry

Focus on water retention in areas which get flooded regularly during heavy rainfall

Enhanced protection of areas prone to flooding

Rigorous protection of aeration corridors

- Existing green
- Area regularly flooded
- Area potentially flooded during emergency state
- Greenification within dense urban areas
- Enhanced retention
- City centre as a limited traffic zone
- Limited traffic zones in strategic spots in the city
- Clean industry

DISTRICT SCALE

District scale resolves conflicts that arise as a result of the three city-scale scenarios. It translates city-scale ambitions into spatial decisions and it makes sure that they are are fulfilled without compromising local priorities.

The city scale proposes rough spatial guidelines and directions, which form coherent scenarios on a properly abstract and systematic scale. District scale elaboration, however, already chooses particular areas for the placement of desired functions. It also establishes more precise regulations, such as the percentage of biologically active areas, density of housing or placement and expected capacity of particular infrastructure.

Densification up to the desired amount of housing units per hectare (u/ha)

Main axis serves as a major public and slow transport connection

Enhanced first/last mile communication to and from metro stations

Improved quality of existing green (e.g. recreational paths, new planting, new facilities)

Continuity of green areas

New businesses and industries develop in connection to Huta Warszawa

New district centres develop around Mlociny and Slodowiec transportation hubs

Society
- Car free connections
- Densification
- District centres
- Local community centres
- Multifunctional areas

Environment
- Upgrade of rexisting greenery
- Greenification within dense urban areas
- Enhanced retention areas
- Protected valuable ecosystem

Economy
- Small family businesses
- Office areas
- Science and education
- Startups
- Clean industry
- Local craftsmanship

Infrastructure
- New road connections
- Enhanced profile of existing roads
- Multi-modal transfer hubs

WARSAW - FEEDBACK PLACEMAKING
STRATEGIC SITE

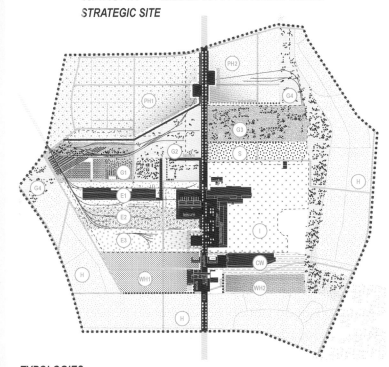

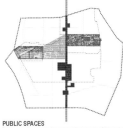

PUBLIC SPACES
Building upon the original urban concept, the extension of Kasprowicza street is created as a main axis of the new development. Such solution creates spatial connection to areas which are potentially located within the metro station catchment area, yet in reality are very disconnected. The axis acts as an organising agent to all the public spaces, urban as well as green.

SPECIAL PLACES
Characteristic elements, which help to maintain the raw and industrial character of the site. They serve as anchoring elements of public spaces. They act as potential landmark locations (such as the former rolling mill) and territorialising elements (railway tracks give directions and leading through green spaces).

ZONING STRIPES
The area is divided into zones which form stripes perpendicular to the main axis. Thanks to such spatial distribution, walking through the area allows to experience and see every type of zone, which exists within the strategic site. It contributes to the visibility of diversity and emphasises the eclectic composition of functions.

FACES
Every zone connected to the axis has a public face through which it establishes its relation to the public realm and surrounding zones. Specific function (different from the overal zone's function) is injected at the border and gradually fades out towards the middle of the zone.

— Leisure, food, commerce
···· Education, technology
--- Public functions
— Work
— Production

TYPOLOGIES
Project site

E | EXPERIMENTAL ZONE
Temporary experimental zone oriented towards flexibility and openness, providing potential future-proof solutions. It is a testing ground for the needs of the area, defined as slow urbanism. Few rules apply:
- maximum use of existing infrastructure
- renovations with the maximum flexibility as an assumption
v
E1 Area managed by Huta Warszawa
Huta Warszawa renovates two iconic buildings (rolling house and finishing house) for the use of future tenants. The company is also responsible for program and choice of tenants.
E2 Area managed by the tenants
Extension area for the E1 an E3. Current and future tenants are responsible for its management in regard to program, buildings and public spaces.
E3 Area managed by the city
Due to its proximity to the metro station, the area has a potential for a vibrant and attractive location for events, exhibitions and public oriented functions. This is where the city's objectives are realised.

PH | PRODUCTIVE HOUSING
Experimental housing typologies (co-housing, passive houses, house/warehouse ip.) linked with various productive premises, such as local workshops, small-scale companies or family businesses as well as easing larger scale industries. Productive activities may include also collective gardening, food production, wood processing.

PH1 Production:housing ratio 50:50

PH2 Production:housing ratio 20:80

G | GREEN
Green wedge, which pierces through the middle of the area, serves both as a buffer zone and a connector between more a chaotic productive zone and calmer, more residential part. It adjusts itself to the adjoining zones and gives space for the zones to extend further into public space. The border is blurred, as activities of the surrounding zones blend into the area.

G1 Productive green
It demonstrates a merger between industrial greenery and interesting and attractive public space, yet different from the park. It focuses on providing material for wood processing industry, biomass production (energy willow).

G2 Park
The main central green space of the area. It assumes extensive management of greenery to create an attractive park - leisure space for guests and inhabitants.

G3 Recreational green
Organised zone open for outdoor activities. It contains particular functions, such as, sport fields, tennis courts, outdoor gym or school playgrounds.

G4 High quality buffer green
Existing green areas in order to gain attractiveness, need maintenance and protection. Project assumes creation of recreational paths and leisure areas. It is prohibited to raise any structures within this zones as they are crucial for the ecosystem of Warsaw.

Strategic site

I | INDUSTRY
Zone, in which the industrial production continues, taking into account all the requirements, which make sure that the new developments never impede the production. However, since it becomes the part of the bigger system, it is no more completely separated from the surrounding areas. It creates links to neighbouring zones (science zone) and develops a public face supporing the main public axis. The public face serves as a zone for Huta Warszawa to present its work, become more visible in the city and regain its position. It's the area for the exchange of ideas and public exhibition of collaboration between Huta Warszawa and other entrepreneurs.

CW | COMMERCE & WORK
Commercial and office zone developed around the newly built shopping mall. By creation of public space in front of the shopping mall, the complex gets connected to the main axis and provides significant numbers of visitors to the area.

S | SCIENCE
Location of scientific and research institutes as well as education facilities in direct vicinity of Huta Warszawa allows for close cross-disciplinary cooperation. It brings mutual benefits. Huta receives scientific backup, which allows them to implement new technologies and solutions once needed. Educational institutions receive financing which, enables them to develop new solutions and explore innovative ideas. This constant exchange builds up resilience of both parties involved.

H | HOUSING
The project assumes densification of the least dense parts of the existing dwellings areas up to the desired amount of housing units per hectare (uha), which varies from area to area. Most dense areas are the ones best communicated with public transport!

WH | WORK & HOUSING
Areas located closest to the metro station have the benefit of the best accessibility in the area. Hence, they are required to provide multifunctional areas including highest density dwellings (min. 80 units / ha), work spaces for the district and the city, as well as supporting commercial, cultural and educational facilities. As a result, it requires new typologies which combine dwellings, office spaces and facilities within one building or a plot.

TRANSITIONS

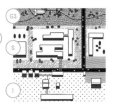

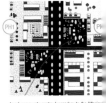

School, placed in the zone PH2, extends its sport fields into recreational green and links them to a bigger system of plenair sport facilities.

Tall office buildings protect from road noise. Smooth transition towards housing is provided by hybrid typologies, combining housing and work spaces.

Productive dwellings of Placówka face the recreational greenery, which gradually turns into productive green. Both green areas are publicly accessible.

New district centre is built around the Młociny mobility hub and requires opening of the premises of Huta Warszawa for public access.

Spatial pairing of Huta Warszawa and scientific institutions allows for direct exchange of knowledge and creates innovation-friendly environment.

Local community centre (secondary to the Młociny mobility hub) provides public spaces for adjacent residential and productive areas.

PLACEMAKING

Main axis as seen towards Młociny station
The main public axis provides attractive space for both residents and guests. It provides both temporary and permanent functions. Due to maintenance of the steel mill's premises and infrastructure, the raw industrial vibe of the area is maintained. As a result, Huta Warszawa returns to the collective awareness and caters new local identity, which allows the inhabitants to be proud of their city.

Between recreational and productive green
Greenery serves as a buffer between noisy, chaotic productive zones and more calmer housing areas. Each green area gets assigned a function, thanks to which it can be fully used by people, industry and businesses. Space is formed with territorialising elements, such as railway tracks, which suggest directions, or patterns or density of planting, which draw borders between different zones.

Innovative zone as seen towards the finishing house
The most vibrant and dynamic zone of the area. Propelled by its temporal character, it acts like a trial-error experiment, whose aim is to explore the possibilities of the plot in order to be able to choose for permanent functions which will work well. The city redevelop itself, which might be risky in other areas, but here it comes at low cost. It's an experimental test ground for technology, science, urbanism or food production.

WARSAW - FEEDBACK PLACEMAKING
PROJECT SITE - TIMELINE OF DEVELOPMENTS

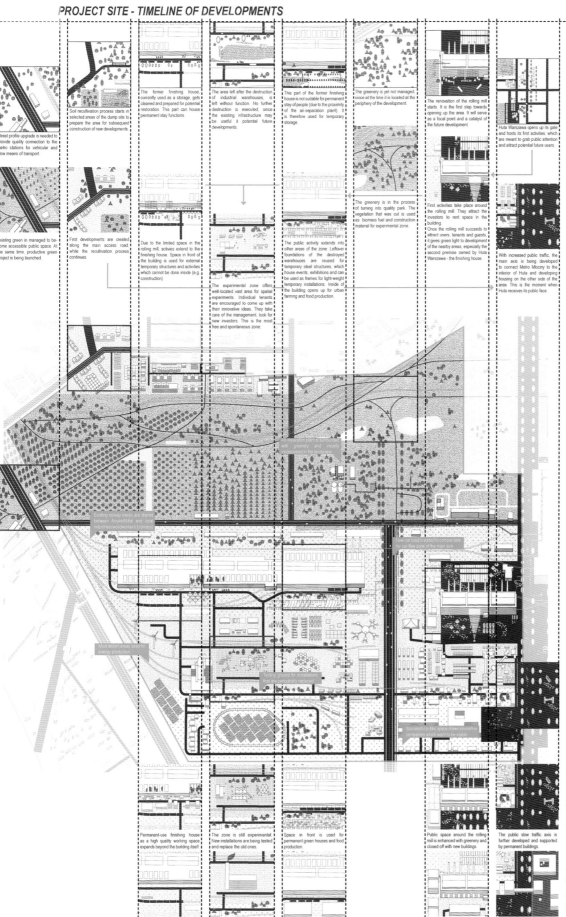

Street profile upgrade is needed to provide quality connection to the metro stations for vehicular and slow means of transport.

Soil recultivation process starts in selected areas of the dump site to prepare the area for subsequent construction of new developments.

The former finishing house, currently used as a storage, gets cleaned and prepared for potential restoration. This part can house permanent stay functions.

The area left after the destruction of industrial warehouses, is left without function. No further destruction is executed, since the existing infrastructure may be useful in potential future developments.

This part of the former finishing house is not suitable for permanent stay of people (due to the proximity of the air-separation plant). It is therefore used for temporary storage.

The greenery is yet not managed, since at the time it is located at the periphery of the development.

The renovation of the rolling mill starts. It is the first step towards opening up the area. It will serve as a focal point and a catalyst of the future development.

Existing green in managed to become accessible public space. At the same time, productive green project is being launched.

First developments are created along the main access road, while the recultivation process continues.

Due to the limited space in the rolling mill, activies extend to the finishing house. Space in front of the building is used for external temporary structures and activities which cannot be done inside (e.g. construction).

The experimental zone offers well-located vast area for spatial experiments. Individual tenants are encouraged to come up with their innovative ideas. They take care of the management, look for new investors. This is the most free and spontaneous zone.

The greenery is in the process of turning into quality park. The vegetation that was cut is used as biomass fuel and construction material for experimental zone.

The public activity extends into other areas of the zone. Leftover foundations of the destroyed warehouses are reused for temporary steel structures, which house events, exhibitions and can be used as frames for light-weight temporary installations. Inside of the building opens up for urban farming and food production.

The greenery is in the process of turning into quality park. The vegetation that was cut is used as biomass fuel and construction material for experimental zone.

First activities take place around the rolling mill. They attract the investors to rent space in the building.
Once the rolling mill succeeds to attract users, tenants and guests, it gives green light to development of the nearby areas, especially the second premise owned by Huta Warszawa - the finishing house.

Huta Warszawa opens up its gate and hosts its first activities, which are meant to grab public attention and attract potential future users.

With increased public traffic, the main axis is being developed to connect Metro Młociny to the interior of Huta and developing housing on the other side of the area. This is the moment when Huta receives its public face.

Permanent-use finishing house as a high quality working space expands beyond the building itself.

The zone is still experimental. New installations are being tested and replace the old ones.

Space in front is used for permanent green houses and food production.

Public space around the rolling mill is enhanced with greenery and closed off with new buildings.

The public slow traffic axis is further developed and supported by permanent buildings.

Finishing house is brought back to its former use or gains a new function in an expanding industry.

Empty spaces are being used for development of clean, modern industry.

Finishing house is brought back to its former use or gains a new function in an expanding industry.

The rolling mill serves as a new administrative building, industrial buildings fill up the square.

The public slow traffic axis is kept, however, with a narrower profile.

2020 - LAUNCH

The development starts. First renovation works are being implemented around the rolling mill buildings and in the green areas (as they are the most time consuming). The main focus of the first phase if to attract public attention, create the awareness of ongoing change and design a frame which can be then filled with activities.

2020-2035 - PROCESS

The most important aspect of the whole process is the timeline of the developments. In such organic process, it is important to decide what precedes and what follows, because each event triggers another and only the success of the former one can give green light to the next step. It is important that this process happens hierarchically and is constantly monitored and adjusted. The described events are suggestions of possible development of matters. However, they are meant to create as flexible frame as possible, to be able to adjust decision on the go without changing the whole strategy.

2035 - EVALUATION

Permanent developments

Developments which have been going on outside the zone B, are mostly developed at this point. The green strip is established and serves as a quality space for the residents of Placówka and neighbouring areas. Placówka is densified with new housing and production facilities and serves as a meaningful community centre. Quick and efficient access with public transport is provided to the residential areas in the strategic zone and around. Slow traffic axis through the area is finished and functions as a main connection.

Temporary developments

Within 15 years, a decision has to be made about the future of the Zone B, owned by ArcelorMittal. Due to the temporary character of the developments, the area can be easily brought back to the state in which ArcelorMittal can use it for its own purposes.

Due to the fact that the surrounding areas have already developed and function as a new system, the expansion of the industry does not compromise the newly build neighbourhood. The public spaces, green spaces, distric centre and local community centre are already established.

AFTER 2030 - OPTION 1
Experimental phase of the Zone B gives ground for permanent developments

Based on the knowledge and experience collected in the experimental phase, new permanent program is created for the redevelopment of the Zone B. This enables for more precise reassessment of areas needed for i.e. offices, housing, industry, facilities. Experiment turns into reality.

AFTER 2030 - OPTION 2
Huta Warszawa extends its activities into Zone B

The favourable economic situation allows Huta Warszawa to extend its activity. As a result, Zone B is reappropriated by industrial programme. Due to temporary character of the experimental zone, the area is roughly intact and ready to redevelop.

NEW neighborHUT

Edyta Nieciecka (PL) Architekturstudentin / Architecture student
Stanislaw Tomaszewski (PL) Stadtplaner / Urban Planner

Unser Projekt soll aufzeigen, dass urbane und industrielle Gebiete in Symbiose existieren und einander ergänzen können. Um die räumliche Struktur dieses Stadtteils zu strukturieren und seine Ausbreitung zu begrenzen, sollte die Stahlindustrie zu einem integralen Bestandteil eines produktiven Stadtviertels werden. Die aktuellen Produktionsbedingungen im Werk begrenzen die Verschmutzung der Umwelt so weit wie möglich. Das Hauptproblem bei der Gestaltung ist somit der verursachte Lärm bei der Herstellung. Um dieses Problem zu lösen, wurde der Gebäudegrundriss so ausgelegt, dass die frei stehenden Volumina und Gebäudeeinheiten den Schall abschirmen.

Die Idee, das Gebiet des Stahlwerkes in die Stadt zu integrieren, setzt die Nutzung bestehender grüner Korridore voraus. Dazwischen sollten zudem Entwicklungsgebiete lokalisiert werden. Die Vegetation unterstreicht die Bedeutung der Grenze, die nicht als Hindernis verstanden wird, sondern als funktionaler Übergang zwischen urbanisierten und unerschlossenen Bereichen.

Da wir an die Vorstellung des Übergangs von einer linearen zu einer Kreislaufwirtschaft glauben, präsentieren wir in unserem Projekt eine neuartige Recycling-Industrie innerhalb der Stadt. Durch die Nutzung des Verbindungspotenzials schaffen wir eine intermodale Schnittstelle, die den Straßen- und Schienenverkehr unterstützen wird, den Schwerpunkt jedoch auf den umweltfreundlicheren Schienenverkehr legt. Als Ergänzung der intermodalen Schnittstelle bildet das Lagerhaus für die Aufarbeitung und den Umbau von Containern ein Containerdorf. Dieser Bereich soll in erster Linie bieten: Dienstleistungen, Entspannungsorte, Büroeinheiten und Kulturveranstaltungen. Da wir die Idee von Produktivität umsetzen wollen, planen wir Gewächshäuser, die Lebensmittel für die Bedarfe der Stadt bereitstellen werden. Doch in erster Linie stellen sie kürzere Versorgungswege zwischen Konsumentinnen und Konsumenten und Produzentinnen und Produzenten sicher. Wichtigster Anziehungspunkt dieses Gebietes ist ein Freizeitpark, der auf den industriellen Charakter des Gebietes Bezug nimmt und durch Lehrpfade bereichert wird, welche auf die Geschichte und Funktionsweise des Stahlwerkes eingehen.

Our project aims to show that urban and industrial areas can exist in symbiosis and complement each other. In order to systematize the spatial structure of this part of the city and prevent its sprawl, the steelworks should become an integral part of a productive city district. The current steelmaking process limits pollution as much as possible. The main design problem is therefore the noise caused by production. In order to deal with this, the building layout is shaped in such a way that the freestanding volumes and building units in the design have a noise-insulating function.

The idea of integrating the areas of the steelworks into the city proposes making use of naturally existing green corridors and situating areas for development between them. The greenery also emphasizes the importance of a boundary, understood as a functional transition between urbanized and undeveloped areas, but not as a barrier.

Reflecting our belief in the idea of a transition from a linear to a circular economy, we present a project offering a new recycling industry within the city itself. Taking advantage of communication potential, we create an intermodal port to support road and rail transport, with a focus on rail as the more ecological option. In cooperation with the intermodal port, a warehouse for revitalizing and converting containers creates a container village. This space will primarily offer services, places to relax, office units, and cultural events. Since we want to continue the concept of productivity, we have designed greenhouses to provide food for the needs of the city. First and foremost, however, they ensure shorter food supply chains between consumers and producers. The main attraction of this space is an amusement park. It will make reference to the industrial character of the area and be enriched by educational routes that make reference to the history and functioning of the steelworks.

Wir haben einander an der Technischen Universität Warschau im Rahmen der Fachrichtung „Architektur und Stadtplanung – Die Stadt als Ort der Entwicklung" kennengelernt. Wir waren bei der Vorbereitung unserer Abschlussarbeit über die Huta Warszawa Stahlwerk, als der Wettbewerb ausgeschrieben wurde, beschlossen wir, zusammenzuarbeiten. Im Zuge dieser Kooperation lernten wir einander besser kennen und waren, trotz dieser kurzen Zeit der Zusammenarbeit, erfolgreich. Aktuell sind wir beide beruflich im Bereich Architektur und Stadtplanung tätig.

eda.nieciecka@gmail.com

We met while doing our Master's degree at the Warsaw University of Technology on the topic of 'architecture and urban planning—the city as a place of development'. We both began preparing a thesis in connection with the area of the Huta Warszawa steelworks. When we heard about the competition, we decided to participate. While taking part in it, we got to know each other better and, despite this brief relationship, achieved success. Both of us are currently working professionally in architecture and urban planning.

eda.nieciecka@gmail.com

WARSAW NEW NEIGHBORHUT

VISUALISATION OF THE NEW AREA FROM
FAIRGROUND ROLLERCOSTER

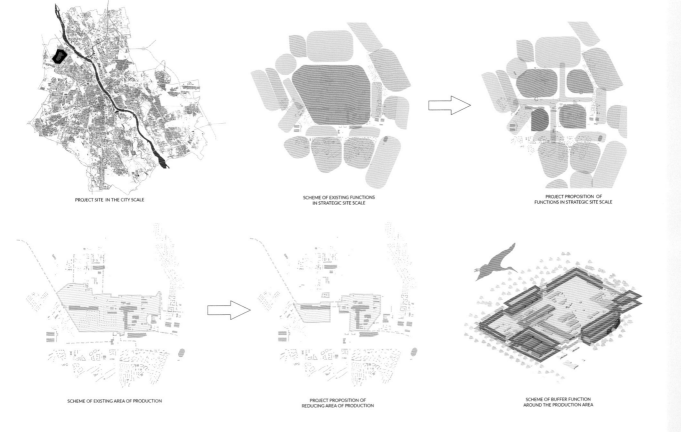

PROJECT SITE IN THE CITY SCALE

SCHEME OF EXISTING FUNCTIONS
IN STRATEGIC SITE SCALE

PROJECT PROPOSITION OF
FUNCTIONS IN STRATEGIC SITE SCALE

SCHEME OF EXISTING AREA OF PRODUCTION

PROJECT PROPOSITION OF
REDUCING AREA OF PRODUCTION

SCHEME OF BUFFER FUNCTION
AROUND THE PRODUCTION AREA

WARSAW

NEW NEIGHBORHUT

GREEN AREAS AND CONNECTIONS
IN URBAN SCALE
SCALE 1:100.000

MAIN COMMUNICATION AND
CONNECTIONS IN URBAN SCALE
SCALE 1:100.000

PUBLIC TRANSPORT AND PLANNED
STATIONS IN URBAN SCALE
SCALE 1:100.000

FUNCTIONS OF URBAN AREAS
SCALE 1:100.000

VISUALISATION OF RESIDENTIAL AREAS

VISUALISATION OF ALLOTMENT GARDENS

VISUALISATION OF MARKET PLACE

GREEN AREAS AND CONNECTIONS
IN STRATEGIC SITE SCALE
SCALE 1:100.000

PROJECT: MAIN COMMUNICATION AND
PLANNED STATIONS IN STRATEGIC SITE SCALE
SCALE 1:100.000

PROJECT: MAIN PEDESTRIANS' CONNECTION IN
STRATEGIC SITE SCALE
SCALE 1:100.000

WARSAW   NEW NEIGHBORHUT

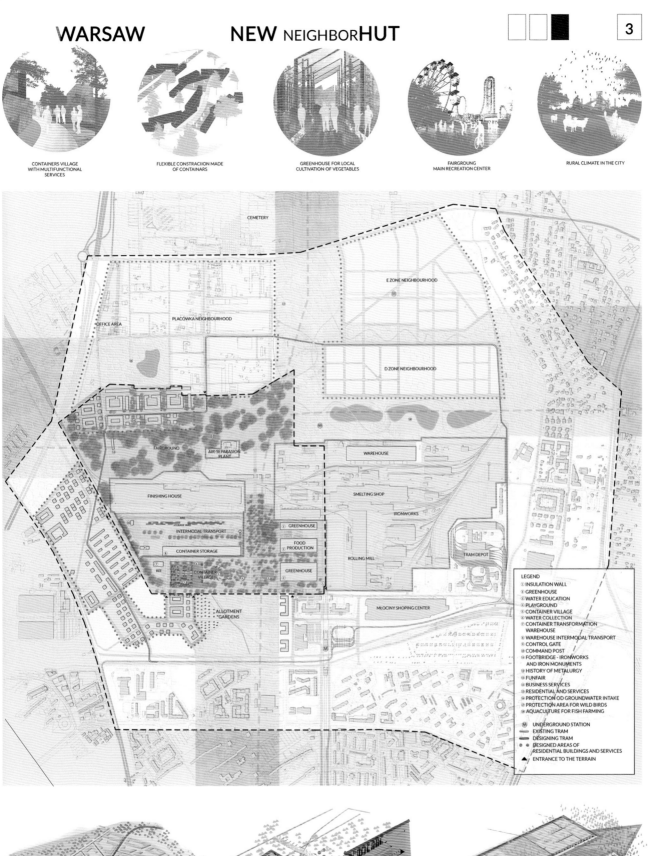

CONTAINERS VILLAGE
WITH MULTIFUNCTIONAL
SERVICES

FLEXIBLE CONSTRACIION MADE
OF CONTAINARS

GREENHOUSE FOR LOCAL
CULTIVATION OF VEGETABLES

FAIRGROUNG
MAIN RECREATION CENTER

RURAL CLIMATE IN THE CITY

CEMETERY

E ZONE NEIGHBOURHOOD

OFFICE AREA

PLACÓWKA NEIGHBOURHOOD

D ZONE NEIGHBOURHOOD

FAIRGROUND

AIR-SEPARASION
PLANT

WAREHOUSE

FINISHING HOUSE

SMELTING SHOP

GREENHOUSE

IRONWORKS

INTERMODAL TRANSPORT

FOOD
PRODUCTION

CONTAINER STORAGE

ROLLING MILL

TRAM DEPOT

CONTAINER
VILLAGE

GREENHOUSE

MŁOCINY SHOPING CENTER

ALLOTMENT
GARDENS

LEGEND
① INSULATION WALL
③ GREENHOUSE
④ WATER EDUCATION
⑤ PLAYGROUND
⑤ CONTAINER VILLAGE
⑥ WATER COLLECTION
⑦ CONTAINER TRANSFORMATION
   WAREHOUSE
⑧ WAREHOUSE INTERMODAL TRANSPORT
⑨ CONTROL GATE
⑩ COMMAND POST
⑪ FOOTBRIDGE - IRONWORKS
   AND IRON MONUMENTS
⑫ HISTORY OF METALURGY
⑬ FUNFAIR
⑭ BUSINESS SERVICES
⑮ RESIDENTIAL AND SERVICES
⑯ PROTECTION OD GROUNDWATER INTAKE
⑰ PROTECTION AREA FOR WILD BIRDS
⑱ AQUACULTURE FOR FISH FARMING

Ⓜ UNDERGROUND STATION
▬ EXISTING TRAM
▬ DESIGNING TRAM
• • DESIGNED AREAS OF
   RESIDENTIAL BUILDINGS AND SERVICES
▲ ENTRANCE TO THE TERRAIN

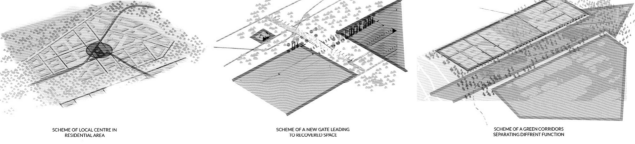

SCHEME OF LOCAL CENTRE IN
RESIDENTIAL AREA

SCHEME OF A NEW GATE LEADING
TO RECOVERED SPACE

SCHEME OF A GREEN CORRIDORS
SEPARATING DIFFRENT FUNCTION

Volcano

Michał Purski (PL) Architekt / Architect

Mitarbeit / Cooperation:
Inez Wawszczyk (PL) Architekturstudentin / Architecture student

Das Gebiet des Stahlwerkes liegt in einer ungeeigneten Umgebung, die gute Anbindung macht diesen Bereich dennoch zu einem attraktiven Stadtteil von Warschau. Der Ort stellt also einen Wert dar, der das Potenzial für die Entwicklung bildet, nicht zuletzt wegen der Nähe zum Nationalpark Kampinos oder der Anbindung an die Autobahn.

Die erste Achse ist die natürliche Verlängerung der Kasprowicza Straße, die alle wesentlichen Attribute aufweist, beispielsweise U-Bahn- und Busstationen sowie ein Einkaufszentrum. Diese Achse verfügt über ein großes kommerzielles Potenzial, welches sich über das gesamte Viertel verbreiten ließe.

Eine weitere Achse beginnt in der Na-Skarpie-Allee nahe der Weichsel und des Palais Brühl und führt in das Naturschutzgebiet Łosiowe Błota. Der Charakter dieses Weges ist weniger formal, sondern eher zwanglos und kulturell.

Die dritte Achse ist eine grüne Verbindung. Der Nationalpark Kampinos, das Naturreservat Łosiowe Błota und bereits bestehende ökologische Korridore sind zurzeit nicht miteinander verbunden. Eine Bepflanzung in beiden Richtungen – sowohl auf der Nord-Süd- als auch auf der Ost-West-Achse – sorgt für Kontinuität.

Die Idee beruht darauf, alle vorhandenen Qualitäten zu maximieren und die Nutzung dieser wertvollen Parzellen zu stärken. Das Grundprinzip ist also die Realisierung eines sogenannten geschlossenen Kreislaufes, dessen Zweck es ist, sich zu einer autarken Einheit zu entwickeln, von der Selbstversorgung mit Energie bis hin zu Unterhaltung und Freizeit. Ein weiterer Grundpfeiler ist die Bündelung möglichst vieler Funktionen, um die größtmögliche Effizienz jeder Parzelle zu gewährleisten und dadurch den Standort attraktiver zu machen. Drei verschiedene Ebenen verbinden und teilen gleichzeitig. Die Gießerei ist die unterste, dann folgt die Produktion auf der mittleren Ebene und ganz oben kommunale Straße und Wohnraum. Die Anordnung der Funktionen trägt dazu bei, unstrukturierte öffentliche und private Räume zu vermeiden und bündelt die Vorzüge beider Elemente.

The area of the steelworks is located in an inconvenient neighbourhood, but its good connections still make it an attractive district of Warsaw. The location is the value that provides the potential for development, especially due to the closeness to the Kampinos National Park and motorway connections.

The first axis is the natural extension of Kasprowicza Street, which contains all major attributes such as metro and bus stops and a shopping centre. This axis has strong commercial potential that could be extended throughout the district. The other axis has its roots on Na Skarpie Avenue near the Vistula River and the Brühl Palace, heading towards the Łosiowe Błota Nature Reserve. The character of this axis is less formal and more casual as well as cultural.

The third axis is the green axis. While Campinos National Park, the Łosiowe Błota Nature Reserve, and already existing ecological corridors are currently not connected, greenery planted in both directions – on the north-south and east-west axes – provides continuity.

The idea is based on maximizing all the advantages already present and enhancing the use of these precious parcels of land. The core value is thus an implementation of a so-called closed circuit, the aim of which is to give rise to an independent unit, whether in terms of energy self-sufficiency or entertainment and leisure.

Another core pillar is combining as many functions as possible in order to increase the efficiency of each plot of land and the appeal of the site as a whole. Three distinct levels divide and unite at the same time. The steelworks is the lowest level, production the middle level, and the municipal boulevard and housing the top level. A distribution of functions helps avoid chaos in public and private spaces and compounds the merits of both.

Atelier-purski ist ein Architekturbüro in Kielce, Polen, das 2014 von Michał Purski gegründet wurde. Es handelt sich dabei sowohl um ein Architekturbüro als auch um eine private Schule, die junge Menschen ausbildet, die sich an Architekturfakultäten bewerben.

Michał Purski ist ein 26 Jahre alter Architekt, der 2018 seinen Abschluss an der Technischen Universität Warschau machte. 2014 gründete er Atelier-purski.

Inez Wawszczyk ist 22 Jahre alt und Studentin am Fachbereich Architektur der Technischen Universität Schlesien.

michal.purski@gmail.com

Atelier-purski is an architectural studio from Kielce, Poland that was established by Michał Purski in 2014. It is an architecture studio and private school that educates young people applying to faculties of architecture.

Michał Purski is a twenty-six-year-old architect who graduated from the Faculty of Architecture at the Warsaw University of Technology in 2018.

Inez Wawszczyk is a twenty-two-year-old student in the Faculty of Architecture at the Silesian University of Technology.

michal.purski@gmail.com

VOLCANO

The area of Foundry seems to be an inconvenient neighbourhood. Thereby good communication is the value, providing the immense potential of future development.
There are three core values in the idea.
Fist, the grid, that includes three major axis. First, the municipal, as an extension of Kasprowicz street into Campinos National Park. Second, the private, connection between Bruhl Palace and Łosiowe Błota Nature Reserve. Third, the green, uniting ecological corridors.
Second, the closed circuit, the purpose of which is to become an independent unit, ranging from energy self-sufficiency ending up entertainment and leisure.
Third, the layers, which are mixing as many functions possible into one, to provide escalation of efficiency of every parcel and to raise the appeal of the site.

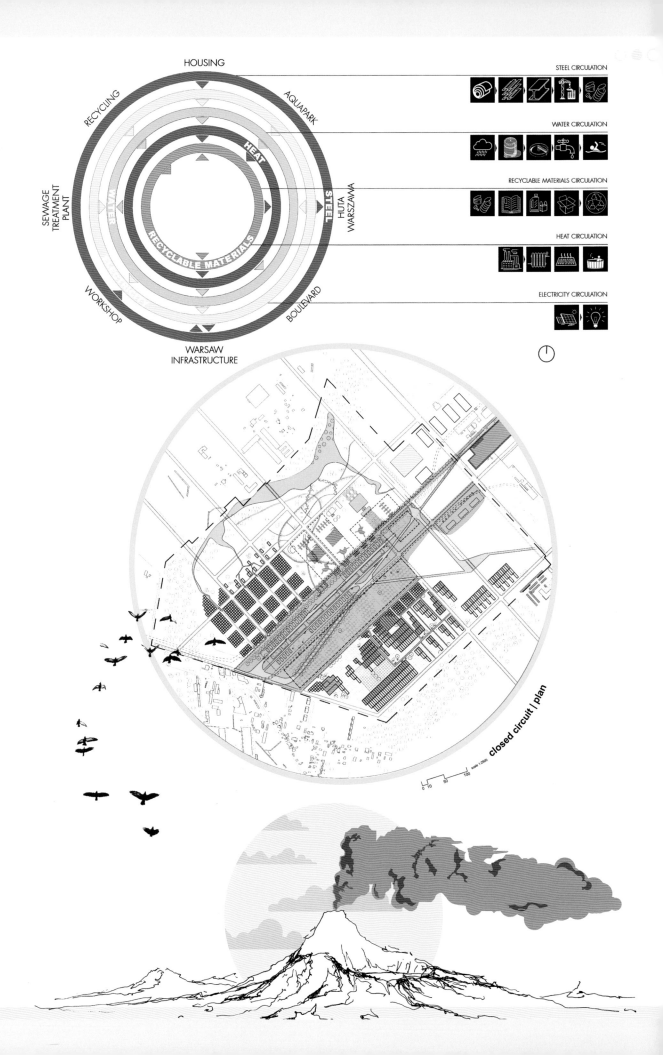

HOUSING

RECYCLING

AQUAPARK

SEWAGE
TREATMENT
PLANT

HEAT

WATER

STEEL

HUTA
WARSZAWA

RECYCLABLE MATERIALS

WORKSHOP

BOULEVARD

WARSAW
INFRASTRUCTURE

STEEL CIRCULATION

WATER CIRCULATION

RECYCLABLE MATERIALS CIRCULATION

HEAT CIRCULATION

ELECTRICITY CIRCULATION

closed circuit | plan

scale 1:2000

0 10   50   100

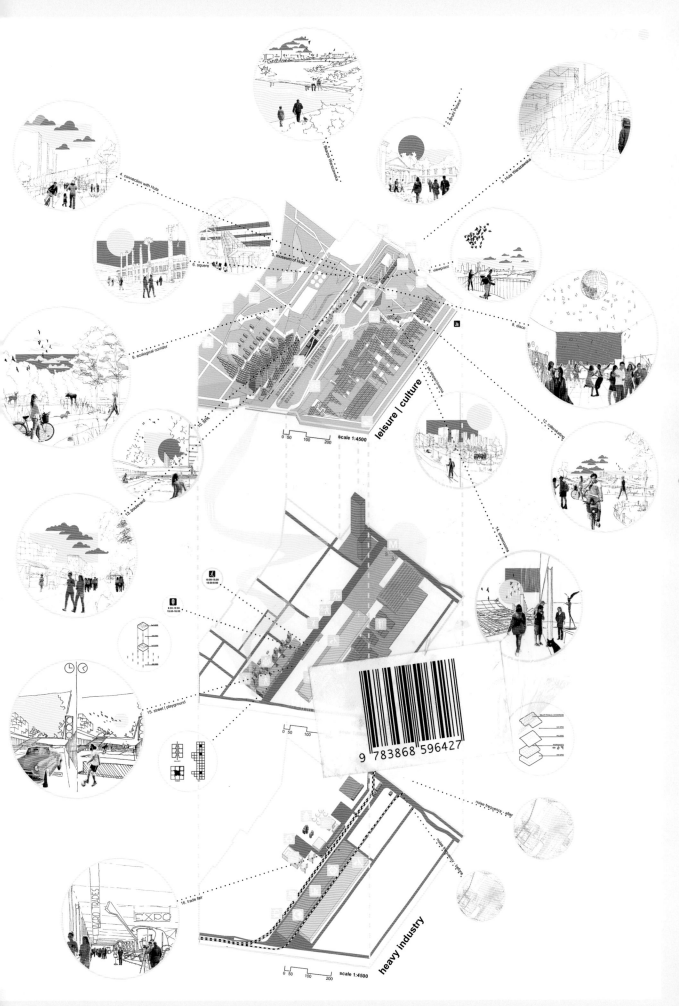

leisure | culture

heavy industry

Weil wir suchen ... (und finden)

Peter Stubbe FRICS, Vorstandsvorsitzender
GEWOBAG AG, Bremen

Europan ist eine Initiative. Europan sucht innovative und experimentelle Ansätze für Standorte, an denen konventionelle, alltägliche Lösungen keinen Erfolg haben. Europan ist für junge Architektinnen und Architekten, die in einem internationalen Kontext Fuß fassen möchten. Europan steht also für Veranstaltungen, die sich tentativ, aufgeregt, ephemer, kurzum: vital um etwas bemühen, das die Beteiligten im Vorweg nicht kennen.

Das schließt nicht aus, dass der Rahmen, der in den Europan-Wettbewerben gesetzt ist, nicht Hinweise gäbe: „Die Stadt bewohnbar machen", „Zuhause in der Stadt", „Mobilität und Nähe", „Zwischenorte", „Suburban Challenge", „Adaptable City", „Productive City" waren Titel für Europan-Wettbewerbe der vergangenen Jahrzehnte. Sie formulieren eine Entwicklung, die die Städte genommen haben oder nehmen sollten. Sie sind gleichermaßen ergebnisoffen wie programmatisch.

Dem von Europan regelmäßig wiederholten „Suchen" steht auch nicht entgegen, dass das Ergebnis manifest ist: Es werden Preise vergeben. Es werden Häuser gebaut. Es geschieht immer wieder in europäischen Städten. Es zeigt, dass Europa schon lange nicht mehr „nur" eine Idee ist, sondern Grund und Boden hat. Es gibt entsprechend eine Organisationsstruktur, die von Staaten getragen und den Vertreterinnen und Vertretern korporativer Akteurinnen und Akteure repräsentiert wird.

Um uns zum „Suchen" zu ermuntern, gibt es wie in der Physik zwei Pole, zwischen denen Europan seine Spannung aufbaut und entwickelt: die Foren als Orte der thematischen Öffnung und der gemeinsamen Befragung und die Jurys als Orte der Fokussierung, der Verständigung auf Antworten. Schon atmosphärisch hat mich beides eingenommen:

Die Foren durchziehen eher elegische Wortbeiträge, die mit großem Ernst wiederholen, wie bemerkenswert und besonders es doch sei, wenn uns ausgerechnet an diesem abgelegenen, der Welt bislang unbekannten, aber nun einmal in Rede stehenden Ort die für Stadtentwicklung typischen, mehrschichtigen Themenstellungen begegnen. Mit dem Perspektivwechsel, im Einzelfall das Grundsätzliche zu suchen, suchen die Foren eine Verbundenheit, eine Anschlussfähigkeit der verschiedenen Sichten an denselben Ort. Das Stilmittel der Foren, Wiederholung und Nuancierung aneinanderzureihen, ist dazu eine vielfach bewährte Übung.

In der Jury arbeiten wir dann unsere Unterschiede heraus, verschwören uns zur Uneinigkeit, vergewissern uns unserer je eigenen, individuell gebildeten, eingestanden selektiven Wahrnehmung, indem wir auf Details hinweisen, die für das Ganze stehen und Bedeutung haben. Denn wir brauchen diese gemeinsame Attitüde der Akribie, die vordergründig polarisieren mag, weil sie unserer gemeinsamen Sorge Ausdruck verleiht, dass wir uns am Ende bitte doch einigen wollen. Damit das auch tatsächlich passiert, damit eine auf Uneinigkeit eingeschworene

Because We Seek ... (and Find)

Peter Stubbe, CEO
GEWOBAG AG, Bremen

Europan is an initiative that seeks innovative and experimental approaches to sites where conventional, everyday solutions do not succeed. Europan is for young architects who would like to gain a foothold in an international context. Europan therefore promotes activities that strive in a tentative, inspired, ephemeral, and, in short, vital way for something that the participants do not know in advance.

This does not mean that the framework in which the Europan competitions are positioned does not provide guidance: 'Living in the City', 'At Home in the City', 'New Housing Landscape', 'In Between Locations', 'Sub-Urban Challenge', 'The Adaptable City', and 'Productive Cities' were titles of Europan competitions of the past decades. They formulate a development that the cities and municipalities have or were in the position to take up. They are both open with respect to the outcomes and programmatic at the same time.

The 'seeking' regularly repeated by Europan in no way precludes the concrete manifestation of the outcome. Prizes are awarded. Buildings are built. This has happened several times over in European cities and municipalities. This demonstrates that, for a long time now, Europe has been more than just an idea; instead, it is something with a solid foundation. Correspondingly, there is an organizational structure that is supported by countries and represented by proxies of corporate stakeholders.

To encourage us to 'seek', there are, as in physics, two poles between which Europan structures and develops its tension: the forums as places for thematic opening, for collective inquiry – and the juries as places for focusing and coming to a shared understanding of responses. I have previously given some thought to the atmosphere of both:

The forums are pervaded by rather elegiac verbal contributions, which repeat with great earnestness how remarkable and special it is when we encounter the multi-layered topics that are typical in urban development at these distant locations, which were hitherto unfamiliar to the world, but are suddenly now under discussion. With the change in perspective brought by seeking what is fundamental in each individual case, the forums search for a connectedness, for an ability to integrate different perspectives on the same location. The stylistic means of the forums: forming a sequence of repetition and nuancing is thus a practice that has frequently been proven.

In the jury, we then map out our differences, agree to disagree, assure ourselves of our personal, individually formed, and admittedly selective perception by pointing to details that stand for the whole and have meaning. After all, we need this collective attitude of meticulousness, which might polarize superficially but only because it expresses our shared concern; we nevertheless want to come to an agreement in the end. In order for this to actually occur, a culture of debate that has agreed to disagree ultimately arrives at a selection of prize-winners;

69

Debattenkultur in eine Auswahl von Preisträgerinnen und Preisträgern mündet, braucht es gleichermaßen akribische Wettbewerbsregeln und die Lust und Phantasie der Jurymitglieder, zwischen Mikro und Makro an beliebigen Stellen zu wechseln. Wenn sie sich verausgabt haben, freuen sie sich, dass für die schriftlichen Würdigungen schon alles zusammengetragen ist.

Beides: die unterschiedlichen Kulturen von Forum und Jury, sind hilfreich, weil in Europan-Wettbewerben Aufgaben und Entwürfe auffallend unterschiedlich und oft genug sperrig sind, sodass sich alle Beteiligten aus der Sicherheit, es vorher gewusst zu haben, lösen können müssen.

Dass mit der Produktiven Stadt scheinbar eine „neue" Nutzungsart in den Mittelpunkt gestellt wurde, mag auch hilfreich gewesen sein. Tatsächlich ist „das Wohnen", traditioneller Schwerpunkt von Europan, der Produktiven Stadt nicht wirklich fern oder fremd. In der Produktiven Stadt verstecken sich die „Gewerbeimmobilien" nicht hermetisch hinter dem Werkstor in einem Sektor, der ihnen mit der Charta von Athen zugewiesen wurde. Sie müssen es nicht mehr, weil die Produktive Stadt einen Typus post-industrieller Arbeit begrifflich voraussetzt und auch nur diesen einen Typus von Arbeit zu- und einlässt, der ohne Lärm und Dreck auskommt – und damit wohnverträglich ist.

„Productive City" meint zwar Orte der Arbeit. Aber eben einer Arbeit, die ihre Form, ihre Themen und ihren Platz in der Stadt erst sucht. Arbeit als Suche? Erinnern wir uns: Das war schon bei den Jägern und Sammlern so – und hat sich vielleicht gerade wieder einmal nicht erledigt, weil die Digitalgesellschaft so demonstrativ gern nach „Lösungen" sucht.

70

but it also requires detailed competition rules and the desire of jury members to alternate between the micro and the macro in diverse areas. When the jury members have worn themselves out, they are happy that everything necessary for the assessments has already been compiled in written form.

Both of the different cultures of the forum and jury, are helpful because, in Europan competitions, tasks and designs are strikingly diverse and often enough unwieldy, which means that all those involved must be able to detach themselves from the certainty of having known something beforehand.

The fact that a seemingly 'new' form of use has become the central focus with the productive city might also have been helpful. In reality, 'housing' is a traditional focus of Europan, and the productive city is not really distant or alien. In productive cities, 'commercial real estate' is not concealed hermetically behind the factory gate in the sector assigned to it by the Charter of Athens. It must no longer remain hidden, because the productive city supposes a type of post-industrial work conceptually, and also allows for and tolerates only this one type of work: which manages without noise and dirt – and is thus resident-friendly.

Even though 'productive cities' denote places for work, it is a sort of work that first seeks its form, its topics, and its place in the city. Work as seeking? Let us recall: That was already the case for hunters and gatherers – and has perhaps not died out specifically because the digital society so gladly seeks 'solutions'.

Regionale Quartiers- entwicklung

Uta Schneider
Architektin und Stadtplanerin SRL DASL
Geschäftsführerin der Bergischen Struktur- und
Wirtschaftsförderungsgesellschaft mbH

„Eine Stunde mehr Zeit" – so das Motto des Zukunfts- konzeptes für den Kooperationsraum „Zwischen Rhein und Wupper", der sich im StadtUmland.NRW-Wettbe- werb zusammengefunden hat. Ziel ist es, für die Men- schen in der Region einen Mehrwert an Lebensqualität zu generieren, durch engere Lebenszusammenhänge, kürzere Wege, alternative Mobilitätsangebote. Um hierfür beispielhafte Lösungen zu erlangen, haben sich die Städte Hilden, Ratingen, Solingen und Wülfrath stellvertretend für den Kooperationsraum am Europan 15-Wettbewerb beteiligt. Die Aufgabenstellung war eine Herausforde- rung – für die beteiligten Städte ebenso wie für die Teil- nehmerinnen und Teilnehmer. Einerseits ging es um ganz konkrete Fragestellungen für vier sehr verschiedene Standorte im Bestand und in der Neuentwicklung, die andererseits für viele vergleichbare Gebiete in allen Städten des Kooperationsraumes stehen. Gesucht wurden also regionale, übertragbare Ansätze, die beispielhaft auf die Stadtquartiere in den vier Städten herunterge- brochen werden und dafür individuelle städtebauliche Lösungsvorschläge entwickeln sollten.

Die Bandbreite der sieben eingereichten Beiträge machte die Komplexität der gestellten Aufgabe deutlich. Die regionale Jury bewertete vor allem die in allen Arbeiten enthaltenen systematischen Ansätze positiv, die mit unterschiedlicher Qualität und Körnigkeit Kriterien und mögliche Lösungsansätze für übergeordnete (regionale) Herausforderungen darstellen. Weniger befriedigend war vielfach die Umsetzung auf die konkrete städte- bauliche Ebene der verschiedenen Standorte, was sicher auch dem Umfang der Gesamtaufgabe geschuldet war. Gleichwohl war die regionale Jury sich einig, dass die Wettbewerbsbeiträge die Diskussion um die Entwicklung von „ZukunftsQuartieren" im Kooperationsraum anregen und im Einzelfall auch an den konkreten Standorten in Hilden, Ratingen, Solingen und Wülfrath weiterentwick- elt werden könnten.

Von den drei regional ausgewählten Wettbewerbsbei- trägen hat die nationale Jury zwei Arbeiten mit Preisen ausgezeichnet. Beide Arbeiten zeigen beispielgebend Instrument und Prozess für eine zukunftsgerichtete Quartiersentwicklung im Bestand wie auch auf freier Fläche, die sowohl regionalen Rahmenbedingungen als auch aktuellen technologischen und gesellschaftlichen Entwicklungen, die wesentlichen Einfluss auf Stadt- und Regionalentwicklung haben, Rechnung tragen. Sie machen aber auch deutlich, dass die entwickelten Werkzeuge jeweils individuell auf den Standort, die stadträumliche Situation und die Akteurskonstellation angepasst werden muss.

Für eine Umsetzung in die kommunale und regionale Praxis wird jetzt nach geeigneten Wegen gesucht.

Regional Neighbourhood development

Uta Schneider
Architect and Urban Planner SRL DASL,
Managing director of the Bergische Struktur- und
Wirtschaftsförderungsgesellschaft mbH

'One hour more time' – this is the motto of the future concept for the cooperation space 'Between the Rhine and the Wupper', which came together in the StadtUm- land.NRW (City Surrounding Region North Rhine-West- phalia) competition. The aim is to generate added value in terms of quality of life for people in the region by means of more closely interwoven life contexts, shorter distances, and alternative mobility options. To come up with exemplary solutions for this, the municipalities of Hilden, Ratingen, Solingen, and Wülfrath participated in the EUROPAN 15 competition representatively for the cooperation space. The task was a challenge – for the cities involved as well as for the participants. It involved concrete questions for four different sites that, on the one hand, already exist or are being newly developed and, on the other, also represent many comparable areas in all the cities and towns in the cooperation space. What were thus sought were transferrable, regional approaches that can be interpreted for urban districts in the four cities and are hence supposed to develop proposals for individual urban development solutions.

The spectrum of the seven contributions that were sub- mitted makes the complexity of the task that was set clear. The regional jury was particularly positive in its assessment of the systematic approaches found in all the works, which present criteria and possible approaches to solutions for superordinate (regional) challenges with various qualities and granularities. In many cases, the implementation on the concrete urban development level of the different sites was less satisfactory, a factor that surely also has to do with the scope of the task as a whole. The jury was nevertheless in agreement that the competi- tion contributions stimulate the discussion of the devel- opment of 'ZukunftsQuartieren' (Future Districts) in the cooperation space and, in individual cases, might also be further developed at the concrete sites in Hilden, Ratin- gen, Solingen, and Wülfrath.

Based on the three competition contributions selected regionally, the national jury awarded prizes to two works. Both of these present exemplary instruments and pro- cesses for a future-oriented development of factors that already exist in the district as well as of open areas that take into account both regional framework conditions and also current technological and social developments that considerably influence urban and regional develop- ment. However, they also make it clear that each of the tools developed has to be adapted individually to the site, the urban development situation, and the constella- tion of stakeholders.

Suitable approaches to implementing the ideas in mu- nicipal and regional practice are being sought.

Bergische Kooperation

Dr.-Ing. Irene Wiese-von Ofen, Architektin und Stadt-
planerin, Inhaberin Beratungsbüro BBASS
Beigeordnete für Planung, Bau und Boden der Stadt
Essen a. D., Essen

Die Bergische Kooperation ist hervorgegangen aus dem
Bergischen Städtedreieck, dem Zusammenschluss der
drei Städte Wuppertal, Solingen und Remscheid. Vor zwei
Jahren haben sich 20 Gebietskörperschaften im Großraum zwischen Ruhrgebiet und Rheinschiene mit insgesamt ca. 2 Millionen Einwohnern zu einer Zusammenarbeit
in den Feldern Wohnen, Mobilität und Freizeit zusam-
mengeschlossen, um die allein auf kommunaler Ebene
nicht mehr lösbaren Aufgaben gemeinsam zu gestalten.
Gegründet wurde dafür unter anderem die Bergische
Struktur und Wirtschaftsförderungsgesellschaft, die
Trägerin der Auslobung des von ihr und Europan Deutschland ausgelobten Wettbewerbs war, an dem sich aus der
Bergischen Kooperation die Städte Hilden, Ratingen,
Solingen und Wülfrath beteiligt haben. Es ging und geht
weiterhin um den „Urbanen Wandel: Heimat zwischen
Rhein und Wupper".

Gleichzeitig ist das internationale Leitthema des Europan
15-Verfahrens „die Produktive Stadt 2", da sich der Wettbewerb bereits im vorangegangenen Verfahren E 14
mit der Verknüpfung von Wohnen und produktiven Nutzungen und der Umstrukturierung gewerblich genutzter
Flächen in Gebiete mit größerer Nutzungsbreite ausei-
nandersetzte.

Dass erneut dieses Leitthema gewählt wurde, zeigt die
Komplexität der Thematik der Transformation, verbunden mit der Herausforderung, in den umzustrukturieren-
den Quartieren auch der Gestaltungsaufgabe „Heimat"
zu schaffen gerecht zu werden. Heimat umfasst in den
Städten und ländlichen Gemeinden Europas immer
das Wohnen, Arbeiten und Produzieren, das Konsumie-
ren wie auch den gestalteten Freiraum und weitgehend
die Kulturlandschaft.

Die Aufgabenstellungen für den Wettbewerb waren
insoweit für Hilden das gründerzeitlich geprägte Bahnhofsviertel, für Ratingen ein Gewerbegebiet und teilweise Wohngebiet zwischen West- und Kernstadt, für
Solingen eine Gewerbebrache und für Wülfrath ein neuer
Siedlungsbereich auf der grünen Wiese (nicht zuletzt
wegen der Wohnnachfrage des nahen Düsseldorfs).

Diese vielfältigen, unterschiedlichen Standortsituationen
zu entwickeln, unter der gleichen Anforderung an gemischte Quartiere, wie sie die Auslobung in ihrer ganzen
Komplexität formuliert hat, war die Aufgabe des Wettbewerbes, die das lokale Beurteilungsgremium in seiner
Auswahl zu bewältigen hatte. Es ging dabei um geeig-
nete, den gemeinsamen Zielen des Wettbewerbes wie
der lokalen Situation gleichermaßen Rechnung tragende
Lösungen.

Die Vorauswahl aus den sieben eingereichten Arbeiten
zur Weitergabe an das Deutsch-Polnische Gesamt-Preis-
gericht, das über die Vergabe der endgültigen Preise
entscheidet, wurde von der lokalen Jury mit folgender
Zusammensetzung getroffen:

Bergische Kooperation

Dr.-Ing. Irene Wiese-von Ofen, architect & urban
planner, owner of the consulting office BBASS, town
councillor for planning, construction and soil of the city
of Essen, Essen

The Bergische Kooperation emerged from the Bergisch
Tri-City Area, an alliance between the three cities of
Wuppertal, Solingen, and Remscheid. Two years ago,
twenty regional authorities in the area between the Ruhr
region and the Rhine River, with its total of circa two
million inhabitants, joined forces to collaborate in the
fields of housing, mobility, and leisure time so as to jointly
design tasks that can no longer be dealt with solely on a
communal level. The Bergische Struktur und Wirtschaftsförderungsgesellschaft, which, along with EUROPAN
Deutschland e.V., was responsible for the call for submissions to the competition – in which, from the Bergische
Kooperation, the municipalities of Hilden, Ratingen,
Solingen, and Wülfrath participated – was established
for this purpose along with various other associations.
It was and continues to be about 'Urban Transformation:
Home Between the Rhine and the Wupper'.

At the same time, the guiding topic of the Europan 15
competition on an international level is 'Productive
Cities 2' (edition E 14 of the competition having already
examined the interlinking of housing and productive uses
and the restructuring of commercially used areas in
regions with a broader spectrum of uses).

Selecting this guiding topic for a second time shows the
complexity of the theme of transformation, combined
with the challenge of also addressing the design task of
'home' in the districts to be restructured in an equitable
way. In the cities and rural communities of Europe, 'home'
always encompasses housing, work, production, consumption, and, to a great extent, also the designed open
space and cultural landscape.

The task for the competition was thus, for Hilden, the
railway district shaped by the Wilhelmine era; for Ratingen, a commercial area and partially residential area
between the western part of the city and the urban core;
for Solingen, an industrial wasteland; and, for Wülfrath,
a new housing area on a green meadow (due, among
other reasons, to the demand for housing near Düsseldorf).

Developing these multifaceted, diverse site situations
based on the same demand for mixed districts, as the call
for submissions formulated with all its complexity, was
the task for the competition, which the local jury also
had to address in making its selection. It was thus a
question of finding suitable solutions that take the common aims of the competition and the local situation into
account to an equal extent.

The local jury made a pre-selection from the seven works
submitted and then handed it over to the German-Polish
jury, which decided on how the prizes would ultimately
be awarded, with the following composition:

Prof Kunibert Wachten (chairperson), Christof Gemeiner,
Jochen Kral, Dr Claudia Panke, Prof Rolf Westerheide,
Uta Schneider, Peter Stuhlträger, Dr-Ing. Irene Wiese-

Prof. Kunibert Wachten (Vorsitz), Christof Gemeiner, Jochen Kral, Dr. Claudia Panke, Prof. Rolf Westerheide, Uta Schneider, Peter Stuhlträger, Dr.-Ing. Irene Wiese-von Ofen, Tim Kurzbach (der Solinger OB wurde zum Teil durch Hartmut Hoferichter vertreten).

Die Arbeiten bezogen sich auf:
1. Stadt Hilden, 56.000 EW, 26 km², 2149 EW/km², Aufgabe: Umgestaltung eines Quartiers
2. Stadt Ratingen, 91.000 EW, 88 km², 984 EW/km², Aufgabe: Wohnen und Arbeiten vereinen
3. Stadt Solingen, 158.700 EW, 89 km², 1780 EW/km², Aufgabe: Neunutzung einer Brache
4. Stadt Wülfrath, 21.000 EW, 32 km², 652 EW/km², Aufgabe: ein neuer Siedlungsbereich

Ausgewählt wurden drei Arbeiten als engere Wahl zur Entscheidung durch das Preisgericht:

Bergisches Plugin: Die Arbeit entwickelt neun Planungsprinzipien, die theoretische Schlüssigkeit mit praktischen Prozessen für Bestand wie Neubau verbinden. Die regionale Entwicklung wird thematisch in erster Linie über Mobilitätskonzept-Überlegungen einbezogen. Eine Übertragbarkeit der entwickelten Prinzipien auf die jeweiligen Standorte in der Region wird auf überzeugende Weise durch die Vorschläge verdeutlicht. Dadurch könnte auch dem An- spruch, eine regionale Identität zu ermöglichen, Rechnung getragen werden, wenn man diese Vorstellungen nutzt und sie zu räumlichen Konfigurationen dreidimensional übersetzt.

Co-Productive Cities: Living Lab Bergische Kooperation: Durch eine systematische Herangehensweise mit sechs ausgewählten Prinzipien einer regionalen Strategie soll eine Quartiersentwicklung erreicht werden: MIV-frei, grün, multifunktional, wenig versiegelt, mit positiver Energiebilanz, experimentellem Umgang mit Baustoffen und dem Erhalt sowie Ausbau identitätsstiftender Elemente des Bestandes. Diese Grundprinzipien sind in einem mehrstufigen Planungsprozess lokaler und regionaler Akteurinnen und Akteure zielgruppengerecht anzuwenden.

The Productive Region: Die Arbeit entwickelt eine Art Werkzeugkasten für eine jeweilige lokale Adaption spezifisch räumlicher und funktionaler Potenziale. Dazu gehören standortspezifische Dichten, Nutzungsüberlagerungen verschiedener Anspruchsniveaus, eine nachhaltige Grünstruktur, neue Produktionsweisen sowie Mobilitätsveränderungen. Der besondere Beitrag der Arbeit liegt darin, eine zukunftsweisende Programmatik mit lokalen Begabungen als Impuls für eine regionale Entwicklung übertragbar kooperativ zu gestalten.

Die mit örtlichen Vertreterinnen und Vertretern der vier beteiligten Gemeinden und von außen kommenden Fachleuten besetzte Jury diskutierte in spannenden Auseinandersetzungen um eine örtliche Perspektive verglichen mit den mehr abstrakten nationalen und internationalen Sichtweisen und Erfahrungen und einigte sich einstimmig auf diese drei vielversprechenden Arbeiten, auf deren konkrete Umsetzung die örtlichen Vertreterinnen und Vertreter vereinbarungsgemäß ein besonderes Gewicht legten.

von-Ofen, Tim Kurzbach (the Lord Mayor of Solingen was represented in part by Hartmut Hoferichter).

The works pertained to:
1. The city of Hilden, 56,000 inhabitants, 26 km², 2149 inh./km²; task: redesigning a district
2. The city of Ratingen, 91,000 inhabitants, 88 km², 984 inh./km²; task: uniting housing and work
3. The city of Solingen, 158,700 inhabitants, 89 km², 1780 inh./km²; task: new use for a wasteland
4. The town of Wülfrath, 21,000 inhabitants, 32 km², 652 inh./km²; task: a new housing area

Three works were shortlisted for the consideration of the German-Polish jury:

Bergisch Plugin: The work develops nine planning principles that combine theoretical soundness with practical processes for the existing stock of buildings as well as new construction. Regional development is incorporated thematically first and foremost by means of considerations regarding mobility concepts. The ability to transfer the principles developed to the respective sites in the region is clarified in a persuasive way by the proposals. If these ideas are utilized and translated three-dimensionally into spatial configurations, the aspiration to facilitate a regional identity can thus also be taken into account.

Co-Productive Cities: Living Lab Bergische Kooperation: Developing a district is achieved by means of a systematic approach with six selected principles for a regional strategy: absence of motorized private transport, green, multifunctional, a minimum of sealed land, with a positive energy footprint, an experimental handling of building materials, and the preservation and further development of identity-forming elements of what already exists. These basic principles are to be applied by local and regional stakeholders in the context of a multiphase planning process in a target group-suitable way.

The Productive Region: The work develops a sort of set of tools for a specifically local adaptation of specific spatial and functional potentials. They include site-specific densities, the overlapping use of various target levels, a sustainable green structure, new methods of production, and changes in mobility. The particular contribution made by this entry lies in the way that it conceives a future-oriented program in collaboration with local talents as an impulse for a regional development that can be transferred cooperatively.

In fascinating discussions, the jury, which consisted of local representatives of the four municipalities involved along with outside experts, compared a local perspective with the more abstract national and international perspective and experience, and unanimously agreed on these three promising works, upon whose concrete implementation, as agreed, the local representatives put particular emphasis.

Deutsche Preisträgerinnen und Preisträger im Ausland

German Award-Winners Abroad

Hyvinkää (FI)

Hyvinkää Standort / Location
~47.000 Bevölkerung / Inhabitants
95 ha Betrachtungsraum / Study Site
27 ha Projektgebiet / Project Site

76

Hyvinkää ist Teil des Großraumes Helsinki. Das Zentrum von Helsinki ist sechzig Kilometer entfernt und kann mit dem Auto oder Zug in weniger als einer Stunde erreicht werden. Hyvinkää wurde in Folge des Baus der Eisenbahnlinie in den 1850er Jahren gegründet. Die Grundwasservorkommen auf dem Salpausselkä-Kamm bildeten die Grundlage für die damals wachsende Wollindustrie. Dank der Luftqualität und der Kiefernwälder wurde der Ort später auch durch Sanatorien und Wintertourismus populär. Seitdem hat sich Hyvinkää zu einer lebendigen Stadt entwickelt, auch wenn es noch immer von den früheren Spannungen zwischen Industrie, Hochkultur und Natur geprägt ist. Die Entwicklung des Stadtzentrums westlich der Haupteisenbahnlinie ist ein Schlüsselprojekt der Entwicklungsstrategie von Hyvinkää.

Das Zentrum der Stadt Hyvinkää liegt heute auf beiden Seiten der finnischen Haupteisenbahnlinie. Auf der östlichen Seite befindet sich ein neuer Einkaufsbezirk mit Wohnungen und Verwaltungs-, Freizeit- und Kulturdienstleistungen, die in alte Industriegebäude eingebettet sind. Im Westen befindet sich ein ehemaliger Bahnhof, der zu einem Stadtteil mit Wohnraum und öffentlichen Dienstleistungen entwickelt werden soll. Ziel ist es daher, für das Projektgebiet ein städtebauliches Konzept mit verschiedenen Funktionen, einschließlich produktiver Nutzungen, zu finden.

Die Dichte des Gebietes ist relativ gering, es gibt mehrere bewaldete Parzellen, die noch nicht bebaut sind. Viele der Gebäude sind veraltet und erfordern eine architektonische und funktionale Aufwertung. Wenig qualifizierte Brücken über Eisenbahnlinien, stark befahrene Verkehrsadern, überdimensionierte Kreuzungen und große, offene Parkplätze stellen verkehrliche Herausforderungen dar. Auf der östlichen Seite befinden sich ein großer Schulcampus und ein Stadtblock, die mit der westlichen Seite verbunden werden müssen. Einige der Gebäude im Projektgebiet haben historischen Wert und stehen unter Denkmalschutz. Der Bahnhof und seine Umgebung wurden als Architekturdenkmäler anerkannt und erhielten den RKY-Status (kulturell bedeutsame gebaute Umgebung).

Das Thema der Produktiven Stadt wird duch folgende Fragen aufgegriffen: 1) Wie kann der westliche Teil des Geländes mit dem übrigen Stadtzentrum und seinen Funktionen verbunden werden und so zu einem Ganzen werden? 2) Wie kann eine Identität für den westlichen Teil des Stadtzentrums geschaffen werden? 3) Wie können Verkehrsflächen – Straßen, Parkplätze, Brücken, Radwege usw. – transformiert werden? 4) Wie kann „Park-and-Ride" in das Verkehrsnetz und das Stadtzentrum integriert werden? 5) Wie können neue Gebäude in die bestehende Struktur integriert werden? 6) Wie können veraltete Bausteine aktualisiert werden? 7) Wie kann die Kleinproduktion in das städtische Gefüge integriert werden? 8) Wie kann das Gebiet schrittweise entwickelt werden, ohne seine Lebensfähigkeit zu verlieren?

Hyvinkää is part of the Greater Helsinki area. The city centre of Helsinki is only sixty kilometres away and can be reached by car or train in less than one hour. Hyvinkää was established when the railway line was first built in the 1850s. Its location on the Salpausselkä ridge with its pure groundwater reserves was the basis for a flourishing wool industry. Sanatoriums and winter tourism became popular thanks to the quality of the fresh air and pine forests. Since then, Hyvinkää has developed into a lively city, although it is still affected by the past tension between industry, high culture, and nature. Developing the city centre is one key project in Hyvinkää's urban development strategy. The goal is to create a city plan for the area to the west of the main railway line, and to create a vibrant, well-functioning, pleasant, and safe city centre.

Today the centre of the city of Hyvinkää is located on the two sides of Finland's main railway line. On the eastern side, there is a new shopping district, with housing and administrative, recreational, and cultural services embedded in old industrial buildings. To the west of the project area, there is a former railway yard that is being developed into an urban district with housing and public services. The objective is thus to find an urban concept with various functions, including productive uses, for the project area.

The density of the area is relatively low compared with the rest of the city centre, and there are several wooded lots that have not yet been built up. Many of the buildings are outdated and require an architectural and functional upgrade. There are also traffic challenges in the area: bridges over railway lines, busy traffic arteries, oversized intersections, and large, open parking areas. On the eastern side are a large school campus and a city block that need to be linked with the western side. Some of the buildings in the project area have historical value and are landmarked. The railway station and its surroundings have been recognized as architectural monuments and received RKY status (culturally significant built environment).

The task is to create an urban concept for the project area. Productive themes will be addressed by asking: 1) How can the western part of the site be connected with the rest of the city centre and its functions, and thus make it into a whole? 2) How can an identity for the western part of the city centre be created? 3) How can traffic areas – roads, parking, bridges, bike lanes etc. – be addressed? 4) How can park & ride be integrated within the traffic network and the city centre? 5) How can new buildings be integrated within the existing structure? 6) How can outdated building blocks be updated? 7) How can small-scale production be integrated within the urban fabric? 8) How can the area be developed in stages without losing its viability?

The Green Ring

Radostina Radulova-Stahmer (DE/AT) Architektin / Architect
Deniza Horländer (DE) Architektin / Architect
Viktorija Yeretska (AT) Architekturstudentin / Architecture student

Um die räumliche Trennung durch die Eisenbahn zu überwinden, schlagen wir vor, die fragmentierten Flächen des Stadtkerns von Hyvinkää durch Grünraumverbindungen ringförmig zusammenzuführen. Prägende Elemente sind dabei die drei verschiedenen Brückenverbindungen über die Bahngleise, die Wald-Brücke, die Platz-Brücke und die aktive Brücke für Fußgängerinnen und Fußgänger und Radfahrerinnen und Radfahrer. Die größte Herausforderung ist es, die zentralen Orte der Stadt gut erreichbar zu machen und gleichzeitig flexibel zu sein und den regen Autoverkehr vom Zentrum fernzuhalten. Eine der Stärken von Hyvinkää ist die Kompaktheit der Stadtstruktur. Die Hauptarbeitgeber in der Stadt befinden sich in der Nähe der Autobahnen in der Peripherie, sodass es nicht notwendig ist, durch das Stadtzentrum zu fahren.

Übergeordnetes Leitziel des Projektes ist einerseits die Einrichtung einer großräumigen Fahrradautobahn entlang des grünen Korridors in Nord-Süd-Richtung mit einer Schleife auf dem Projektgelände, welche die großen Arbeitgeber und die Wohngebiete anbindet. Ein besonderer Schwerpunkt liegt dabei auf den Radinfrastrukturen. Das Radwegenetz wird ausgebaut und mit grünen Verbindungen überlagert, um ein hochwertiges Fahrraderlebnis zu schaffen. Andererseits werden öffentliche Sammelgaragen in der Peripherie des Stadtzentrums vorgeschlagen, um den motorisierten Individualverkehr abzufangen und die Auto-Infrastruktur zu reduzieren. Dafür wird ein dichtes Radverkehrsnetz geschaffen und es werden alternative Mobilitätsmöglichkeiten wie E-Vans, E-Ruftaxis und E-Car-Sharing angeboten.

Das Herzstück der produktiven Nutzungen ist das neue Gewächshaus, das sich auf dem isolierten Bahnhofsgelände befindet. Es dient als Kultur- und Gemeinschaftszentrum und bietet Nutzungen wie Fahrradreparatur, Mobilitätszentrale, Gastronomie, Kultursauna und einen regionalen Markt.

In order to deal with the spatial separation caused by the railway, we propose uniting the fragmented areas of the city centre of Hyvinkää in the form of a ring by means of connections between green spaces. One of the formative elements for this is provided by the three different bridge links over the railway tracks, the Forest Bridge, the Square Bridge, and the active bridge for pedestrians and cyclists. The big challenge is making it easy to reach central locations in the city whilst being flexible at the same time, as well as keeping heavy automobile traffic away from the centre. One of Hyvinkää's strengths is the compactness of its urban structure. The main employers in the city are found near the motorways on the periphery, which means that it is not necessary to drive through the city centre.

One superordinate key objective of the project is to introduce a large-scale bike throughway along the green corridor in the north-south direction, with a loop on the project site that links major employers and residential areas. A particular emphasis is thus put on cycling infrastructure. The network of cycling paths will be developed and overlaid with green connections to create a high-quality cycling experience. Another is the proposal to position collective public garages on the periphery of the city centre in order to absorb motorized private transport and reduce the infrastructure for cars. To do so, a dense network of cycling paths will be created, and alternative mobility options such as e-vans, e-taxis, and e-car-sharing will be provided.

The central element of the productive uses is the new greenhouse situated on the isolated railway station grounds. It serves as a cultural and community centre and offers uses such as bicycle repair, a mobility centre, gastronomy, a sauna, and a regional market.

STUDIOD3R – Büro für Architektur, Stadtgestaltung und Forschung wird seit 2010 von den Schwestern Deniza Horländer (Dipl.-Ing. Architektin DE) und Radostina Radulova-Stahmer (Dipl.-Ing. KIT Architect NL) geführt. Das Projektspektrum reicht von kleinteiligen Raumexperimenten über Objektentwürfe und Renovierungen bis hin zu städtebaulichen Projekten. Sie arbeiten in unterschiedlichen Maßstäben und entwickeln räumliche Lösungen durch das Oszillieren zwischen systemischem Denken und ortsspezifischer Sensibilität. Mit ihrer architektonischen Tätigkeit tragen sie voller Begeisterung, Mut und Hingabe zur Gestaltung von Themenfeldern wie Urbane Produktion, städtische Kreislaufwirtschaft, urbane Biodiversität, smarte Räume, post-motorisierte Gesellschaft und neo-Straßenräume bei.

info@studiod3r.com

STUDIOD3R—Büro für Architektur, Stadtgestaltung und Forschung has been run by the sisters Deniza Horländer (Dipl.-Ing. architect, DE) and Radostina Radulova-Stahmer (Dipl.-Ing. KIT architect, NL) since 2010. The spectrum of projects ranges from small-scale spatial experiments to object designs, and from renovation to urban planning projects. They work on various scales and develop spatial solutions by oscillating between systemic thinking and site-specific sensitivity. With their architectural work, they contribute great enthusiasm, courage, and talent for designing thematic fields such as urban production, a closed-loop urban economy, urban biodiversity, smart spaces, post-motorized society, and innovative street spaces.

info@studiod3r.com

Hyvinkää FI   The Green Ring – Closing Cycles, Linking Spaces

To link the separated areas of the railways we suggest to frame the fragments of Hyvinkää's city core with a green ring, expanding the existing green areas. Defining elements are three bridges crossing the rails: the Forest bridge, the light bridge and the square bridge. Bicycle lanes and pedestrian zones in the green ring become a part of public space in our vision. They close gaps between functions situated on the both sides of the railway. Mobility is reorganized in order to reduce and keep motorized traffic away from the centre. The third spaces in-between is defined by the new greenhouse building at the train station that integrates small scale building stock in its village-like structure and introduces productive functions to the area. The greenhouse functions as a catalysator and magnet for the transformation and further adaptation of the site.

Hyvinkää is embedded into the beautiful natural landscape primarily consisting of pine forests providing high air quality, still there is a need to strengthen the green network within the city itself.

In order to create a functioning connection between the adjacent western and eastern pieces of the city center we suggest an expansion and connection of the already existing green areas around the train station in order to close this green loop. While framing the core of the city it leads the way along it's main attractions (e.g. Church, Woolen Mill) thus creating distinctive brand for Hyvinkää. The green ring is also lined by high buildings with up to five stories to ensure an easy orientation within the quarter.

As the railway station area, on both sides of the railway line, is the heart of the city's food scene we suggest to introduce a new productive force to the site that becomes the center of this ring - the greenhouse is placed directly at the train station.

An important and very defining element are the several bridge connections across the train rails: they are now influenced by the ever growing significance of bicycle lanes and public space instead of motorways - as the majority of the urban areas are easily reachable by bike. The

western and eastern parts of the city are connected by two main large bridges with distinctive characters: the plaza brige and the park bridge. The space, no longer used for car traffic, gain a new purpose and function as lanes for non motorized individual traffic. In this area a new public zone is activated, reachable directly from the train station and meant to be used by residents as well as tourists and newcomers. The third very light pedestrian bridge is placed on the north of the station replaces the outdated one.

One of the main resources that Hyvinkää has to offer is vacant space. The creative and productive force of Hyvinkää is unfolded by the public activities of it's inhabitants and guests. In our design we suggest a reactivation and conversion of exsiting vacant buildings - such as the former Rentto Factory building, oversized infrastructure and huge rooftops of the shopping malls opposite to the train station as productive spots.

Large scale functional distribution

Implementation of large scale bike highway along green corridor making a loop on the project site in the green ring

Public parking garages keep the cars outside of the centre. Car infrastructure ist scaled down and a dense cyclin network network is created

Distances to different facilities and functions

Morphologies of green space ring and public square sequence

Event bridge with local market and summer street festival

Forest bridge creating a continous biodiversity corridor throuth the city and linking the centre fragments

Reduction of waste quantities at events and catering establishments.

Ensure long-term supply and disposal, increase recycling and recovery.

Space use and emissions of the motorized traffic are reduced.

Inner development with high environmental quality connect: Green space and open space, biodiversity, local climate, networking, public transport, bicycle and pedestrian routes.

Multifunctional design and ecological management of urban green and open spaces.

Urban buildings and facilities are constructed, renovated and managed in an environmentally friendly manner.

Resource-friendly and environmentally friendly production and consumption.

Open spaces for fauna and flora and a high level of biodiversity are maintained internally despite the development of settlements.

Increasing the proportion of recycled materials in building construction and civil engineering.

greenhouses & roof gardens

greenhouses & roof gardens

greenhouses & roof gardens

new car park

Plaza bridge

Strategic plan 1:2.000 - The green ring connects all railway fragments

Hyvinkää FI The Green Ring — Closing Cycles, Linking Spaces

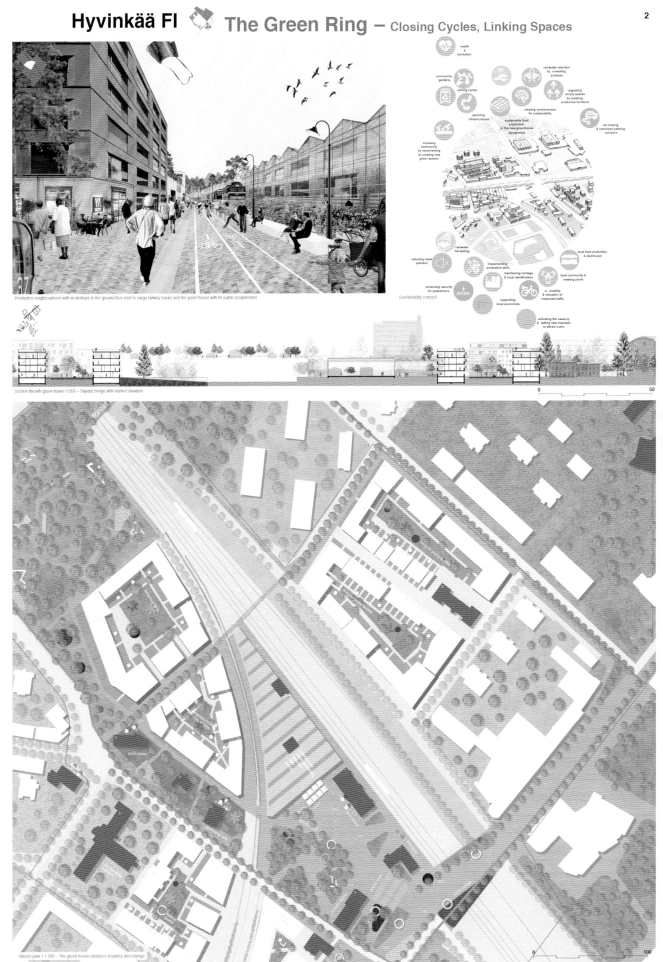

Productive neighbourhood with workshops in the ground floor next to cargo railway tracks and the green house with its public programmes

Sustainability concept

Section through green house 1:500 – Square bridge with market situation

Master plan 1:1.000 – The green house catalyses frequency and change

Offices
Health
Catering
Service
Profession
Production
Social
Residential
Sports
Art/Culture

ogrammatic distribution

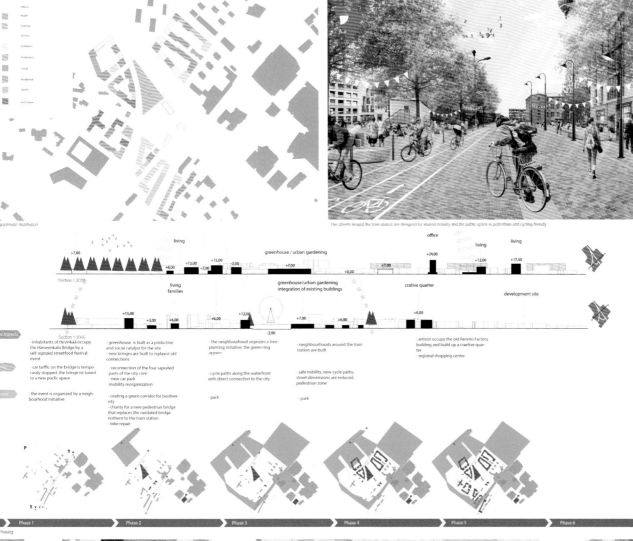

The streets around the train station are designed for shared mobility and the public space is pedestrian and cycling friendly

living
office
living
living

+7,00
greenhouse / urban gardening
+24,00
+15,00
+12,00   -2,00   +7,00   +12,00   +17,50
+6,00   +7,00   +7,00   +0,00   +7,00

Section 1:2000
living
families
greenhouse/urban gardening
integration of existing buildings
crative quarter
development site

+15,00
+3,00   +6,00   +6,00   +12,00   +7,00   +6,00   +6,00
-2,00

Section 1:2000

ocial Aspects
- inhabitants of Hyvinkää occupy the Hämeenkatu Bridge by a self-oginzed streetfood festival event
- car tarffic on the bridge is tempo-raraly stopped, the bringe ist tuned to a new puclic space
- the event is organized by a neigh-bourhood initiative

- greenhouse is built as a priductive and social catalyst for the site
- new bringes are built to replavce old connections
- reconnection of the four saprated parts of the city core
- new car park mobility reorganization
- ceating a green corridor for biodiver-sity
- charity for a new pedestrian bridge that replaces the outdated bridge nothern to the train station
- bike repair

- the neighbourhood orginizes a tree-planting initiative, the green ring appers
- cycle paths along the waterfront with direct connection to the city
- park

- neighbourhoods around the train station are built
- safe mobility, new cycle paths, street dimensions are reduced, pedestrian zone
- park

- artiest occupy the old Rennto Factory building and build up a craetive quar-ter
- regional shopping center

P

Phase 1   Phase 2   Phase 3   Phase 4   Phase 5   Phase 6

Phasing

Ground floor plan green house 1:500

0   50

Tuusula (FI)

Tuusula, Hyrylä Standort / Location
~ 38.600 Bevölkerung / Inhabitants
41 ha Betrachtungsraum / Study Site
15 ha Projektgebiet / Project Site

Die Gemeinde Tuusula ist als Teil des Großraumes Helsinki nur eine halbe Stunde von der Hauptstadt und 15 Minuten vom Flughafen Helsinki-Vantaa entfernt. Tuusula bietet eine Kombination aus aktiven städtischen Zentren und landschaftlichen Qualitäten. Die drei Zentren – Hyrylä, Kellokoski und Jokela – besitzen jeweils eine eigene Identität. Die Entwicklungsstrategie für Tuusula besteht in Wachstum durch Verdichtung.

Der Projektstandort, das Anttila-Landwirtschaftszentrum, befindet sich in einer wunderschönen Landschaft am See Tuusulanjärvi, der einen integralen Bestandteil der Identität und des kulturellen Erbes von Tuusula darstellt, in der Nähe des Zentrums von Hyrylä.

Anttila diente als Forschungs- und Ausbildungseinrichtung für Landwirtschaft, ist heute jedoch zum größten Teil verlassen. Große Scheunen und Forschungsgebäude sowie Wohnbauten stehen für eine neue Nutzung zur Verfügung. Einige der alten Wirtschaftsgebäude eignen sich zur Lebensmittelproduktion, sie ließen sich jedoch ebenso in etwas Neues umwandeln, sogar in Wohngebäude. Ziel ist es, neue Ideen und Konzepte für das Gebiet zu finden. Wie können lokale Lebensmittelproduktion, Dienstleistungen und Wohnbau in Anttila auf neue Art und Weise koexistieren? Wie kann Anttila zu einem produktiven, post-agrarischen Dorf werden?

Das Wettbewerbsziel ist die Schaffung einer Vision für das Anttila-Areal. Die Teilnehmenden sind aufgerufen, eine neue Nutzung für die alten Gebäude vorzuschlagen und auch den Wohnbau mit einzuschließen. Themen zur Entwicklung werden in folgenden Fragestellungen behandelt:

Für welche Art der Produktion könnten die alten, denkmalgeschützten Gebäude geeignet sein? Könnte Anttila als Plattform zur Entwicklung ökologisch nachhaltiger Produktionsmethoden für Lebensmittel dienen? Wie wird sich die Lebensmittelherstellung in Zukunft entwickeln? Welche Art von Einrichtungen ist dazu nötig? Wie könnten Herstellung und Wohnbau in Anttila auf neue Art und Weise koexistieren? Was könnte Anttila für Hyrylä, die Menschen, die im Großraum Helsinki wohnen oder Touristinnen und Touristen aus der ganzen Welt bieten? Wie kann sich Anttila als beliebte Destination in Tuusula neu erfinden? Welche Art von temporären Nutzungsmöglichkeiten könnte Anttila bieten? Wie wird die Neuentwicklung von Anttila im kulturellen Erbe von Tuusula Widerhall finden? Welche Rolle wird der Tuusulanjärvi in der Zukunft von Anttila spielen?

The town of Tuusula is part of the Greater Helsinki area, located only half an hour from Helsinki and fifteen minutes from the Helsinki-Vantaa airport. Tuusula is a combination of active municipal centres and peaceful countryside. The three centres – Hyrylä, Kellokoski, and Jokela – each have their own identity. Tuusula's urban strategy is one of growth by means of densification.

The project site, the Anttila farming centre, is situated in the beautiful rural landscape around Lake Tuusulanjärvi, (an inherent part of Tuusula's identity and cultural heritage) near the centre of Hyrylä.

Anttila once served as a research and education centre for farming, but has now become mostly vacant. Large barns and research buildings as well as housing are available for new uses. Some of the old farm buildings are suitable for food production, or could be converted into something new, perhaps even housing. The goal is to find new ideas and concepts for the area. How might local food production, services, and housing coexist in Anttila in a new way? How might Anttila become a productive, post-agrarian village?

The task of the competition is to create a vision for the Anttila area. Participants in the competition are asked to propose new uses for the old buildings and to incorporate housing on the site. Productive themes will be addressed by asking:

What kind of production might be suitable for the old, protected buildings? Might Anttila function as a platform for developing ecological food production methods? How will food production evolve in the future, and what kinds of facilities will it require? How might production and housing coexist in Anttila in a new way? What could Anttila offer for Hyrylä, for people who live in the Greater Helsinki area, or for international tourists? How can Anttila reinvent itself as a popular destination in Tuusula? What kinds of temporary uses could Anttila have? How will the new development of Anttila resonate with the cultural heritage of Tuusula? What kind of a role will Lake Tuusula play in the future of Anttila?

60°North

Natalia Vera Vigaray (ES) Architektin / Architect
Patxi Martin Dominguez (ES) Architekt / Architect
Josep Garriga Tarrés (ES) Architekt / Architect
Emmanuel Laux (DE) Architekt / Architect
Agnes Jacquin (FR) Landschaftsarchitektin / Landscape Architect
Alexandra Jansen (PL) Ökonomin / Economist

Die auf dem Projektgelände entwickelte Kartoffelsorte „Timo" hat eine kurze Vegetationsperiode und ist daher besonders für das finnische Klima geeignet. Ähnlich wie bei der Kartoffelsorte sind die Eingriffe für den Ort maßgeschneidert.

60°North schlägt einen ganzheitlichen und offenen Entwicklungsansatz für Anttila vor. Das Projekt arbeitet mit dem Bestehenden, es bemüht sich, die Besonderheiten des Ortes zu verstehen und anzuerkennen: Ökologie, Menschen, Erbe, Wissen und Materialien sind ein ebenso wichtiger Teil wie gebaute und natürliche Ressourcen.

Das Projekt verbindet die verschiedenen produktiven Aktivitäten genauso wie die an der Wertschöpfungskette von Lebensmitteln beteiligten Akteurinnen und Akteuren: von Landwirtinnen und Landwirten über Forscherinnen und Forscher bis zu Endverbraucherinnen und Endverbraucher. Offene Räume schaffen produktive Plattformen für den Austausch auf lokaler und globaler Ebene und verknüpfen Anttila und seine zukünftigen Bewohnerinnen und Bewohner mit der Metropolregion.

Zur Aktivierung des Ortes schlägt das Projekt fünf Hauptinterventionen vor: In den historischen Gebäuden des alten Bauernhofes wird ein Forschungszentrum für Landwirtschaft und Nahrungsmittelproduktion errichtet, welches zusammen mit einer offenen Genossenschaft in den angrenzenden Produktionsgebäuden das produktive Herz des Ortes bildet. Inspiriert von den „Miljö-Formationen" der finnischen Bauernhöfe gruppieren sich dazu mehrere Cluster aus Wohngebäuden um einen zentralen, offenen Hof herum, welcher Auffindbarkeit und Durchwegung auf dem Gelände sicherstellt und die Funktion des Außenraumes als gemeinschaftlich genutzter und bewirtschafteter Raum unterstreicht. Zusätzlich wird der Zugang zum See geöffnet und mit öffentlichen Funktionen aktiviert.

The 'Timo' potato variety, which was developed on the project site, has a short growing season and is thus particularly well suited to the Finnish climate. Like the potato variety, the interventions on site are tailor-made.

60°North proposes a holistic and open development approach for Antilla. The project works with what already exists: it strives to understand and recognize the special characteristics of the location: ecology, people, heritage, knowledge, and materials are aspects that are just as important as the built and natural resources.

The project interlinks various productive activities as well as the stakeholders involved in the chain of added value for foodstuffs: from farmers to researchers, producers to end consumers. Open spaces provide productive platforms for exchange on a local and global level and link Antilla and its future residents with the metropolitan region.

To activate the site, the project proposes five main interventions: A research centre for agriculture and food production, which forms the productive heart of the site along with an open cooperative association in the adjacent production buildings, will be erected in the farmyard's old historical buildings. Inspired by the 'Miljö formations' of Finnish farms, several clusters of residential buildings are grouped around an open, central courtyard, which ensures visibility and movement on the site and underscores the function of outdoor space as a communally used and cultivated space. Moreover, access to the lake is opened up and activated with public functions.

Das 60°North-Team wurde nach einem Europan-Forum in Brüssel gegründet und arbeitet seit 2019 europaweit als digitales Büro. Das interdisziplinäre Team besteht aus der französischen Landschaftsarchitektin Agnes Jacquin, der polnischen Ökonomin Alexandra Jansen, dem deutschen Architekten Emmanuel Laux sowie die spanischen Architektinnen und Architekten Natalia Vera Vigaray, Patxi Martin Dominguez und Josep Garriga Tarrés, die gemeinsam das Büro Office Shophouse betreiben.

hi@office-shophouse.com
www.office-shophouse.com

The 60°North team was established after a Europan Forum in Brussels and has worked as a digital firm since 2019.
The interdisciplinary team is made up of the French landscape architect Agnes Jacquin, the Polish economist Alexandra Jansen, the German architect Emmanuel Laux, and the Spanish architects Natalia Vera Vigaray, Patxi Martin Dominguez, and Josep Garriga Tarrés, who jointly manage the firm Office Shophouse.

hi@office-shophouse.com
www.office-shophouse.com

60°North
TIMO POTATOES

Tuusula (FI)
Europan15

A door to natural resources

The Anttila site constitutes a strategic place of meeting, an interface
between rural and urban life, a place for agricultural production and
experimentation.

60 North - How to grow food in Anttila for future generations.

Multiple challenges such as CO2 impact of transport, population growth, threats
to biodiversity, scarce resources, climate change, succession of farmers, food
sovereignty, and lack of awareness of consumers will affect the worldwide food
production and consumption. Taking into account its specific location (60°N), and
in line with its heritage of research centre in agronomics, the new Anttila will be
a laboratory to imagine and experiment local solutions to overcome upcoming
global challenges in food production.

Creating links between people, multiplying sinergies.

Anttila is an interface that brings the consumer closer to the farmer so to answer
the questions: "Who grew my food and how?" and "Who eats my food?". On-site
productive activities become opportunities to engage strangers in a meaningful
interaction. Together, they learn about food production and about each other.
Visits of the research and production facilities and food tastings are organised for
tourists, local pupils and professionals.

Anttila, the peri-urban area as interface between different worlds.

The proposal turns Anttila's hybrid character at a crossroads between urban and
rural into an opportunity. It draws a new vision for peri-urban areas: that of an
interface between two worlds. It creates meaning and societal cohesion while
rebalancing powers between urban and rural, currently in favour of the urban
(cities eat products and territories). It envisages a better-optimised urban densification and new, mutualised infrastructures for farmers.

Tailor-made and iterative urbanisation process.

The proposal outlines possible scenarios that take into account Anttila's specific
features, and make the fullest use possible of the site's assets: its natural resources, location, cultural and historical heritage, and skills. The scenarios will
unfold in stages. Their roll out will be a participatory and iterative process made
of engagement with local stakeholders and testing phases.
The project is governed by sustainability principles and fully respects the environment and local ecosystems.

2019	2020	2023	2025	2025 and forth	General proposal scheme
Current status	**Stage 1**	**Stage 2**	**Stage 3**	**Stage 4**	A mixed community open and engaged to its closest
Open call for a change through Europan E15 competition.	Summer sauna construction festival to activate the site and engage with local and external stakeholders.	Implementation of research and productive activities. Renovation of the old barn. Activation and definition of the urbanisation scheme with inhabitants.	Site planning and set up of the common area. Pasture maintenance and transhumance around Tuusula lake. Housing pilot projects and first construction jobs.	Final stages of housing construction. Pasture mainte- nance systematization through transhumance along a larger territory.	context. A replicable model in the peri urban territory of Helsinki.

Section 1:2000

Site Plan 1:2000

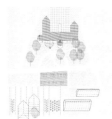

A research center mediates the future

The barn will host the cow facilities of the Agriculture
Research Center for future farming and sustainable food
production, a restaurant and a farm shop.

A productive cooperative in old walls

Crops, wool, wood and fish produced locally are stored and
processed in the existing buildings. Needed equipment is
put at the disposal of farmers, students and inhabitants.

An edible landscape for common ground

The central field is a residents' place of meeting. Gardening
lots are available to grow orchards and the existing house is
turned into a common space.

A hedonistic shoreline with minimal footprint

A sauna, swimming facilities, a summer kiosk with terrace
and stage, a small marina for the cooperative boats and
ferry stop while the ARC research on aquaculture solutions.

Fostering a sense of community with the Miljo

The arrangement of the housing units is inspired by the
"Miljö" of Finnish farms. A central yard serves as a shared
space. This layout allows visibility and flux through the plots.

60°North
TIMO POTATOES

Tuusula (FI)
Europan 15

Farm architecture

To maintain and strengthen its unique spatial quality and exposure
to nature, the proposal follows a gentle intervention, acknowledging
and reusing the characteristic built structures and incorporating elements of vernacular architecture.

Live, work & host - The tupa

In order to introduce diversity in the combination of housing and working, the project proposes housing types with an additional space, a modern interpretation of the tupa. A main room traditionally found in Finnish farmhouses, the tupa is the heated core of the house and hosts a range of activities: from work to relaxation and social gathering. Its uses vary from house to house. The possibility of an informal or external use of the tupa helps to build up cross-connections between the housing clusters.

Research & exchange - The research centre

The rehabilitated old barn provides the infrastructure for the research centre. Laboratories, workshop spaces, conference and training rooms and a library are at the disposal of researchers who work on innovative, integrated freshwater aquaculture solutions. Start-ups in the food realm start their operations in rentable spaces and benefit from the link to other actors in the sector. Knowledge is shared in courses taught to future farmers. A restaurant and a farm shop add to the attractiveness of Anttila for locals and visitors alike.

Produce & meet - The cooperative

The cooperative includes mutualised infrastructures for farmers of the cooperative to transform, package and ship their products. A multifunctional workshop, a milking parlor and dairy production unit, a warehouse and a distribution unit are set up. Goods are sold in the market hall to locals and visitors. The building includes a recycling and compost station. The infrastructure is also accessible to players of the research and innovation centre, allowing them to experiment and create synergies between researchers and practitioners.

Play & Perform - Common ground for diversity

The site is a key recreational spot of the Tuusula lake. The landscape constitutes a beautiful backdrop to a variety of available leisure activities: from the sauna and the wellness centre on the pier, to the scattered sport facilities such as the swimming pool, rowing boats, bike paths meandering on the site, and summer events such as open theatre and cinema, concerts or construction festivals. The Anttila research centre includes a restaurant and café and a marketplace, attracting additional visitors to the site.

Housing cluster - All housing types are considered to be wooden buildings and in their appearance contemporary interpretations of a Finnish farmhouse type. Housing units are clustered around the Miljö as a shared space.

The old barn, Anttila research centre - The project proposes to make use of existing built structures, renovate them and add spaces. Hereby the level of investment and thus the level of transformation can organically grow with the formation of the institution.

The marketplace - The space in between existing barn buildings is covered with a glass roof and creates a new common space of gathering and meeting. Different activities could be hosted in this space during the cold seasons.

The common sauna - The shore is set up to allow a range of recreational activities. A pier on the water allows residents and passers-by to enjoy the view and rest, inside or outside the sauna and swimming pool facilities.

Section of a housing cluster 1:500

Section of the Anttila research centre 1:500

Section of the lake facilities 1:500

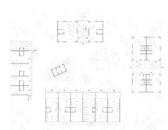

Ground floor plan of a housing cluster 1:500

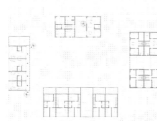

Upper floor plan of a housing cluster 1:500

Type A
A two-storey block of flats with a varying number of 1- and 1.5 room apartments. A common hallway serves as a climatic buffer zone and connects the units to the common space, which offers addition al season extending the dwellings.

Type B
Two-storey houses with open ground floor. A double height space serves as a buffer zone and gives residents the possibility to program this space. The upper floors offer a range of different division possibilities.

Type C
A semi-detached house type with a shared association and meeting space. The sizes of the houses vary depending on the requirements of the developer. The central area serves as a multi-functional space for events.

Type D
This type offers the possibility to combine individual houses around a shared space. Spaces for families or friends, multi-generational houses or temporary stay. The central area links the units and adds a generous space to the type.

Property developer
To ensure diversity of units and residents, a palette of mixture should be installed. Upper price segment can, on its own, co-finance common spaces.
Types: A - B - C
Ownership for residents: private and rental
Price range: €€€

Cooperative
A group of private individuals that finance a plot. This model assures more individual units at lower prices due to the independent development.
Types: B - C
Ownership for residents: cooperative
Price range: €€

Private financing
Developed and financed by private individuals. Hybrid models of financing to ensure the realisation of combined housing types.
Types: C - D
Ownership for residents: private
Price range: €€

Public Housing
Units developed and financed by public commission. Ownership remains public and ensures affordable prices.
Types: A - B
Ownership for residents: rental
Price range: €

01 Visitor's center	05 Workshops / labs	07 Market hall	10 Milking parlor	13 Recycling&compost station		
02 Conference rooms	06 Library	08 Crop production	11 Dairy production	14 Workshop		
03 Restaurant	06 Public square	09 Sheep barn	12 Bar / Kiosk	15 Warehouse & distribution		

Ground and first floor plan of the barn 1:500

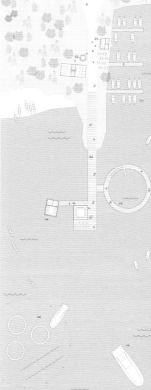

01 Bar / kiosk	03 Waterfront rental	05 Swimming pool	07 Jacuzzi
02 Changing rooms	04 Pier	06 Sauna	08 Aquaculture (BTA)

Ground floor plan of the lake facilities 1:500

60°North
TIMO POTATOES

Tuusula (FI)
Europan15

A model for productive peri-urban

Anttila is assertively integrated into a variety of networks and scales
to reinforce its position, attractiveness and identity. Seasonality
gives rhythm to activities and flows of people, animals and products.

Beyond administrative limits: the scale of the Tuusula Lake.

The proposal activates the existing lake-bound identity by promoting the lake's agricultural patrimony and heritage. With the Anttila cooperative as a model, a network of farmers could be formed. Planting hedges and wildflowers at lake scale encourages biodiversity. Cooperation at lake level puts in place a compost sharing mechanism to foster closed-loop agriculture. The yearly transhumance of Anttila sheep around the lake not only maintains the shores but becomes an expected yearly event.

Energy cycle.

Buildings and greenhouses are heated using the thermal potential of the lake. The geothermal solution consists in tapping the lake's surface waters in summer and storing them under the ground until the next winter thanks to aquifer thermal energy storage (ATES). In winter the calories are used for heating. The system can be reversed by tapping cold winter surface water and using it in summer to cool down the buildings. It presents the advantage of being carbon-neutral and respectful of the environment and biodiversity.

Edible territory and common goods: The right to pick.

The jokamiehenoikeus is a Finnish principle guaranteeing to everyone the right to roam freely and enjoy the countryside independently of whom it belongs to. In Anttila, visitors and locals experience an edible landscape: they meander around the fruit trees planted along routes that converge towards a common space. The fruit tree becomes a meeting place. Initiated in Anttila, this principle can be extrapolated to other sites around the lake.

The scale of the Greater Helsinki metropolitan area.

The research centre in agronomics will put Anttila and Tuusula Lake on the national map. The site is integrated into a transport and mobility network at metropolitan level through train and bus connections.
We further propose a vision for the metropolitan landscape based on an ecological continuity composed of patches of forests and fields. These patches connect Tuusula to Helsinki through a system of ecological and productive corridors and slow mobility path for cyclists and the sheep's transhumance.

Metropolitan productive landscapes
The metropolitan area includes multiple fertile milieus, often ignored by the urbanization processes. The project starts from these productive landscapes to compose the urban development and recreate productive continuities.

Traffic
The project maintains the existing streets and paths. Selective additions create a coherent bike and pedestrian network and connect Anttila to the region. Car access to the site is limited. Parking lots are grouped in the center and on the edges of the site.

Water management
The project proposes the use of valley gutters as floodplains. Their position is defined by the topography and the localization of sandy soil to allow infiltration. The 25 cm deep ditches are covered with wet meadows to foster biodiversity.

Tuusula lake Plan 1:20000

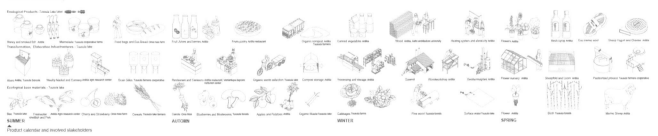

Product calendar and involved stakeholders

Autumn - Right of picking
The inhabitants and schoolchildren participate in the harvesting of apples and rustic vegetables and in the annual planting of new fruit trees. The edible territory fruits feed school canteens and the Anttila restaurant.

Summer - Gardening the Territory
In the fields the harvest is launched. On the lake the inhabitants of Tuusula and the region celebrate the summer season enjoying the new infrastructure of the lake. Thanks to the IMTA aquaculture a wide variety of fishes populate the lake.

Winter - Productive Interiors
The landscape is covered with snow leaving crops dormant. Timber cutting and forestry activities take over. In greenhouses, seedlings are grown under cover to prepare for the next growing season.

Spring - Pedestrian Transhumance
To celebrate the arrival of spring the flock starts a great pedestrian transhumance around the lake. The passing of the sheep raises awareness of passers-by and locals on urban and ecological processes and sparks discussions about food production.

Romainville (FR)

Romainville, Ormes und Chemin Vert Standort / Location
~26.000 Bevölkerung / Inhabitants
15 ha Betrachtungsraum / Study Site
2,7 ha Projektgebiet / Project Site

Im südlichen Teil der Stadt, in der Nähe der Autobahn A 3 und der Überreste einer nicht mehr in Gebrauch befindlichen Straßeninfrastruktur, bietet der Standort, ein verlassenes urbanes Gebiet, das auf die Ankunft der Straßenbahn (T1) wartet, eine fantastische Gelegenheit für die Entwicklung eines neuen „Stadtteils", der an das Stadtzentrum angeschlossen werden soll und neue Formen städtischer Aktivität (Gewerberäumlichkeiten, Stadtlogistik etc.), begleitet von einem Wohnbauprogramm, kombiniert, das die Entwicklung neuer Nutzungen und öffentlicher Einrichtungen fördert. Durch den Einsatz der neuen Straßenbahn begünstigt muss dieses aktuell isolierte Territorium in der Lage sein, Synergien zu entwickeln, die es an andere Zentren im östlichen Ballungsraum anbinden (Montreuil, Noisy-le-Sec, Fontenay-sous-Bois), und für größere territoriale Gleichheit zu sorgen. Die Stadt verfolgt eine Politik der Freiwilligkeit, die Ko-Konstruktion, Artenvielfalt und Natur in der Stadt fördert.

Der Projektstandort, der an die Stadt Montreuil grenzt und damit an der Einfahrt zu Romainville liegt, ist ein Ort der urbanen Vernachlässigung und der Straßeninfrastruktur für Schwerverkehr, die mit dem Bau der Straßenbahnlinie T1, die Bobigny mit Val de Fontenay verbinden soll, verschwinden wird.

Obwohl die Fernstraße A 3 einen massiven Riss in die Landschaft schlägt und eine Quelle des Ärgernisses ist (Umweltverschmutzung, Lärmpegel), stellt sie dennoch einen großen Vorteil für den Standort dar und verfügt über urbanes logistisches Potenzial.

Entlang der T1 sollen neue Bauprogramme jene Vielfalt fördern, die am Standort bereits vorhanden ist, und Wohnbautypologien für eine Vielzahl an Bedürfnissen und Erwartungen hervorbringen, die mit neuen Einwohnerinnen und Einwohnern einhergehen. Der Standort stellt eine echte Chance dar, zwei Sektoren der Stadt miteinander zu verbinden und territoriale Kontinuität zu entwickeln, während er gleichzeitig Stadtplanung um die Straßenbahnstation „Libre pensée" schafft. Die A 3 erlaubt die Gestaltung neuer Aktivitäten (Stadtlogistik, Kreislaufwirtschaft), die neuen lokalen Verbindungen zugutekommen.

Located in the southern part of the municipality, near the A3 motorway and close to remnants of an obsolete road infrastructure, the site, an abandoned urban area awaiting the arrival of the tramline (T1), provides a tremendous opportunity to develop a new 'piece of the town' that is connected to the town centre and combines new forms of urban activity (business premises, urban logistics, etc.) in connection with a housing program, and thus promotes the emergence of new uses and public facilities. Favoured by the arrival of the new tramline, this currently isolated area must be able to develop synergies that link it to other centres in the eastern metropolitan area (Montreuil, Noisy-le-Sec, Fontenay-sous-Bois) and generate greater territorial equity. The municipality has a voluntary policy that favours co-construction, biodiversity, and nature in the city.

Bordering the city of Montreuil and therefore at the entrance to Romainville, the project site is an area of urban neglect and abandoned heavy road infrastructures that will disappear with the construction of the T1 tramline linking Bobigny and Val de Fontenay.

While the A3 motorway creates a strong rupture in the landscape and is a source of nuisance (e.g. pollution, noise), it also presents a major advantage for the site and elicits urban logistics potentials.

Along the T1 tramline, new building programs should encourage more of the diversity already present on the site and produce housing typologies for the variety of needs and expectations that will come with new inhabitants. The site presents a real opportunity to connect two areas of the municipality and to develop territorial continuity, while also giving rise to urban planning around the 'Libre pensée' tram stop. The A3 motorway facilitates the programming of new activities (urban logistics, a circular economy) that serve new local connections.

Bridging Productivities

Sascha Bauer (DE) Architekt, Bewerter des Kulturerbes / Architect, heritage evaluator
Jonas Mattes (DE) Student Architektur und Landschaftsplanung / Architecture and Urban Planning Student
Jannis Haueise (DE) Student Architektur und Landschaftsplanung / Architecture and Urban Planning Student
Ender Cicek (DE) Student Architektur und Landschaftsplanung / Architecture and Urban Planning Student
Mitarbeit / Cooperation
Larissa Petrescu (DE) Studentin Architektur und Landschaftsplanung / Architecture and Urban Planning Student

Eine produktive und integrative Stadt nutzt ihre gewachsene Vielfalt, um einen Nährboden für das zu schaffen, was noch kommen kann. Der Entwurf sucht nach den räumlichen Anforderungen für Interaktion und adäquaten Wandel und bildet ein Konzept zur Verknüpfung der lokalen Identitäten. Wir reflektieren die Rolle des öffentlichen Raumes und wollen dessen Potenzial in unserer gebauten Umwelt diskutieren.

Die Autobahnüberführung ist ein starkes räumliches Element in der bestehenden Struktur. Ein vollständiger Abriss wäre eine verpasste Chance, sie in etwas Neues zu verwandeln, das der kollektiven Identität des Gebietes dienen kann. Wir schlagen vor, einen Teil der Autobahnüberführung zu erhalten und die eingesparten Kosten direkt in lokale Potenziale zu investieren. Temporäre Events entlang und unter der Überführung können ein gemeinsamer Startpunkt für die Entwicklung sein. Dies schafft eine Chance für Nachbarinnen und Nachbarn und lokale Gruppen, sich zusammenzutun und über die weitere Entwicklung auszutauschen.

Die unterschiedlichen Ebenen auf der Brücke erzeugen unterschiedlichste Raumqualitäten. Große produktive Typologien und öffentliche Sporteinrichtungen auf den verschiedenen Ebenen erlauben ein Zusammenspiel von öffentlichen Räumen und Produktivität. Die vorhandene Struktur und gewachsene Vielfalt des Stadtviertels „Ormes" zeichnen sich durch eine robuste Mischung aus Nutzungen und unterschiedlichen Typologien aus. Durch die natürliche Fortsetzung des authentischen Musters können unterschiedliche Formen der Produktivität in enger Nachbarschaft zueinander entstehen und für weitere Generationen angepasst werden. Ein neuer öffentlicher Platz an der Station „Libre Pensée" dient als Quartiersauftakt. Von hier entwickelt sich die Verknüpfung der ehemals getrennten Stadtviertel entlang der neuen Straßenbahnlinie.

A productive and integrative city uses its developed diversity to create a fertile basis for what might arrive in the future. The design looks for the spatial requirements for interaction and suitable transformation and provides a concept for linking local identities. We reflect on the role of public space and want to discuss its potential in our built environment.

The bridge over the autobahn is a strong spatial element in the existing structure. Completely demolishing it would be a missed opportunity to transform it into something new that can support the collective identity of the area. We propose retaining one part of the bridge over the autobahn and directly investing the costs saved in local potentials. Temporary events on and beneath the bridge can serve as a collective starting point for development. This creates an opportunity for neighbours and local groups to join forces and exchange ideas for further development.

The various levels on the bridge give rise to very diverse spatial qualities. Large productive typologies and public sport facilities on the different levels facilitate interplay between public spaces and productivity. A robust mixture of uses and various typologies characterizes the existing structure and developed diversity of the 'Ormes' city district. By continuing the authentic pattern in a natural way, various forms of productivity can arise in close proximity to one another and be adapted for further generations. A new public square at the 'Libre Pensée' station serves as a prelude to a new district. From that point, the link to the formerly divided city district develops along the new tramline.

Wir bei Studio Cross Scale sehen uns als Planungsmanufaktur, die zwischen zeitgenössischer Handlung und Achtung der Tradition arbeitet. Wir sind ein Team aus Planerinnen und Planern, Praktikerinnen und Praktikern und Macherinnen und Machern, das über die Komplexität aller Maßstäbe hinweg denkt. Nicht jedes Projekt ist mit den gleichen Voraussetzungen ausgestattet, jede Bauherrenschaft ist individuell. Dies ist unser Antrieb für eine architektonische Auseinandersetzung mit unterschiedlichsten Maßstäben und Disziplinen, die im konstruktiven und interdisziplinären Austausch erarbeitet werden.

info@studiocrossscale.com
www.studiocrossscale.com

At Studio Cross Scale, we regard ourselves as a planning factory that works between contemporary action and respect for tradition. We are a team of planners and makers that thinks beyond the complexity of norms. Not every project is equipped with the same prerequisites, since each contractor authority is individual. This is motivates our architectural examination of diverse scales and disciplines, which are elaborated in constructive and interdisciplinary exchange.

info@studiocrossscale.com
www.studiocrossscale.com

BRIDGING PRODUCTIVITIES

a network concept to enhance local identities

A productive and inclusive city uses its grown diversity to develop a breeding ground for what else can come. We pose the question of spatial requirements for interaction and adequate change. We reflect on the role of public space and want to discuss its potential in our built environment.

The proposal connects different layers of the area. A local key figure is the existing highway overpass as a binding element between existing and new identities. The bridge provides public spaces with various qualities and the saved money for demolition costs is directly reinvested into local potentials. A pattern extracted from the current fabric is extended across the new site evolving to larger mixed-use typologies closer to the new tramline.

keeping the overpass

The highway overpass is a strong spatial element in the current fabric, demolishing it completely would be a missed chance to transform it into something new that can serve the common identity of the area. By keeping the highway overpass, we propose to keep the part of the structure that is the hardest and most expensive to demolish. By saving the costs of demolition, public money is directly reinvested into local potentials.

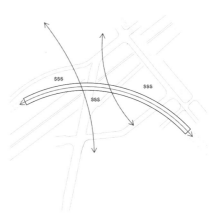

productive plus

Standing on top or below, the bridge provides public spaces with various qualities. By introducing a second level alongside the highway overpass a mix of larger scale productive programs and public sport facility can be integrated to the area. The different levels provide various scales of interaction within the area and can foster local communities and identities.

extending the productive pattern

The existing fabric and the grown diversity of the Ormes neighborhood features a robust mix of uses, different typologies and flexibility to be adapted for further generations. A natural continuation of the authentic pattern allows to give room for different ideas of productivity to exist in close proximity next to each other.

weaving identities

The buildings along the new tramline form a new urban connection between the formerly separated neighborhoods. A new public space at the "Libre Pensée" station will act as a new entering point. The typologies along the road feature a flexible structure and are thought to be developed during the process of the project.

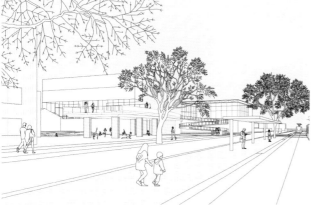

Romainville (FR)

right away
event & construction

During the demolition of the old A186 infrastructure temporary events are hold along and under the overpass, to reshape the heritage of the area from a car centered to a people centered environment.

Neighbors and local communities can come together and share their experience and thought about new developments.

2020
upgrading the overpass

During the construction of the new tram the start and end points at the overpass are built - the spiral and the pool. The construction can be funded with the money saved from keeping the overpass.

After the infrastructure is set the continuation of the typical small-scale pattern is formally under control but can take place mostly on its own.

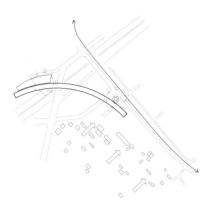

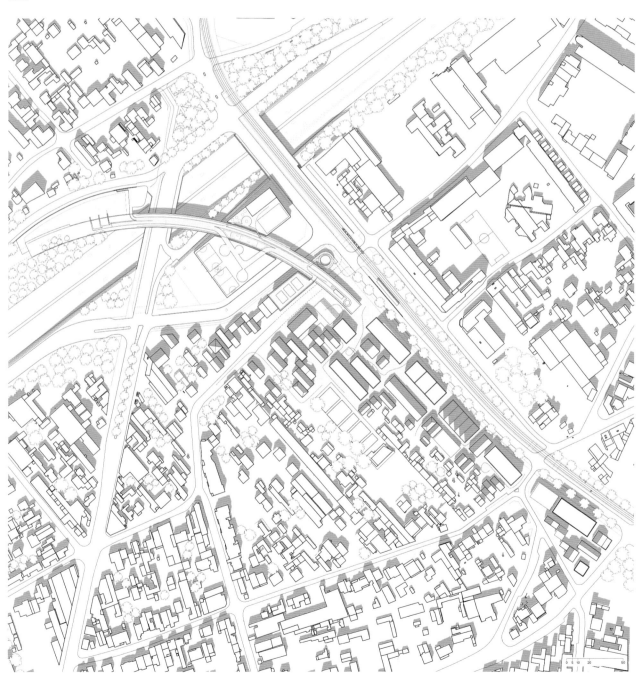

Romainville (FR)

2023
welcoming the tram

When the new tram line is opened in 2023 the overpass as a public sports-park will be mostly completed. From now on the development will focus on the connection towards the new tramline. Learnings from local community events and the overall process can be implemented to adept flexible and ever changing programs.

2023+
adjusting & finishing

The large logistic buildings alongside the bridge can be built in the last stage - by now the needs and wishes of the neighborhood can be defined and the typology's in their final form can be designed in a cooperative manner including residents and the city.

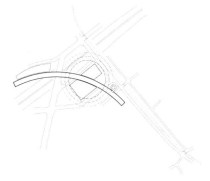

2nd level
sports court

The sports court sits on top of the logistics hub and is connected to the overpass. It features a roofed area and locker rooms and showers for the rest of the sports facilities.

the roof

The end of the overpass sits atop of a public square right next to the new tram station. The area beneath becomes a sun and rain protected urban space – the upper level offers a calmer area.

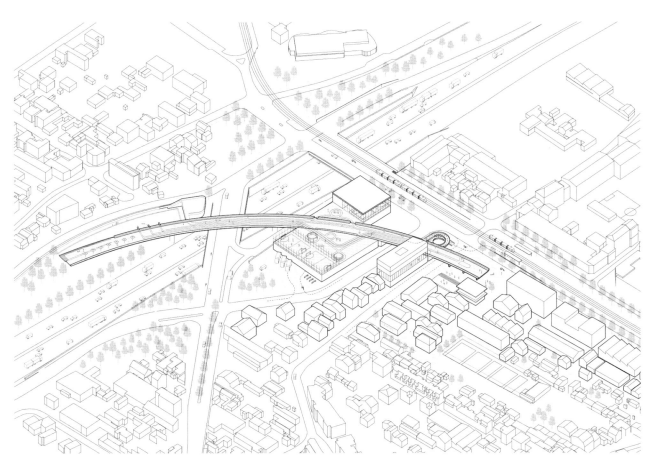

the pool

The other end of the overpass is defined by a pool sitting right next to it to set a programmatic connection to the adjacent neighborhoods. The area can be accessed over the overpass or from the corner of the street.

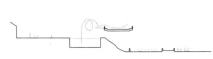

the ramp

The ramp is the main access on the bridge. Revolving once around itself it gives a stair free access to the upper level. The attached building accommodates sports facilities on the level of the overpass.

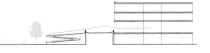

Guovdageaidnu (NO)

Márkan, Guovdageaidnu (Kautokeino) Standort / Location
2000 Bevölkerung / Inhabitants
3200 ha Betrachtungsraum / Study Site
387 ha Projektgebiet / Project Site

Guovdageaidnu ist eine kleine Stadt im Norden von Norwegen mit starker Sámi-Identität. Sie liegt am Fluss Guovdageaineatnu. Die Hauptindustrie in Guovdageaidnu ist die traditionelle Sámi-Rentierhaltung, aus der sich mittlerweile an die 1000 kleine neue Unternehmen gebildet haben. Guovdageaidnu ist auf sämtlichen Ebenen – vom Kindergarten bis zur höheren Schule – ein norwegischer Vorreiter was die Bildung angeht. Wie kann nun die Gemeinschaft Nutzen ziehen aus traditionellem Know-how und Autarkie in Verbindung mit fortschrittlicher Aus- und Weiterbildung, Informations- und Kommunikationstechnologien sowie Hightech-Lösungen?

Die Gemeinde Guovdageaidnu beteiligt sich seit kurzem an einem staatlichen Programm zur strukturellen und kommerziellen Umstrukturierung der Kommune. 2017 setzte die Gemeinde einen Plan für das Stadtzentrum Márkan um. Dieser erwies sich jedoch als wenig geeignetes Instrument für den Zweck der industriellen und kommerziellen Restrukturierung. Das liegt zum Teil daran, dass der Plan keine attraktiven Grundstücke für neue Unternehmensinitiativen vorsah. Die Gemeinde räumt ein, dass eine Notwendigkeit zur Änderung der kommunalen Planung besteht, um auch Sámi-Werte und -Traditionen mit einzubeziehen. Die Stadt sucht nun nach alternativen Planungsansätzen, die die Landwirtschaft und die überreiche Vielfalt lokaler Initiativen mit einschließen.

94

Sápmi umfasst Teile von Norwegen, Schweden, Finnland und Russland. Guovdageaidnu liegt zwar am Rande Norwegens, ist jedoch ein bedeutendes Zentrum des zirkumpolaren Gebietes und Sápmi. Guovdageaidnu ist eine Hochburg von Sámi-Tradition und -Sprache – eine Sprache, die das Wissen und die Praxis umfasst, die für die Rentierhaltung unerlässlich sind. Kommt man in Guovdageaidnu an, bemerkt man, dass es sich bei der Stadt Márkan um eine Siedlung handelt, die gewissermaßen in die flache Landschaft der Tundra eingelassen ist, wie eine „Schüssel". Das Stadtzentrum erscheint als lose verteilte Ansammlung von Gebäuden entlang eines zwei Kilometer langen Teilstücks der Straße E 45. Das Untersuchungsgebiet muss als Feld für Entdeckungen und neue Verbindungen betrachtet werden. Wie kann die Landschaft neue Leitprinzipien für die Planung in Guovdageaidnu begründen?

In diesem Kontext sucht die Gemeinde nun nach neuen Wegen, um eine Basis für die Zukunft neuer Unternehmen und Technologien in Márkan, dem Zentrum von Guovdageaidnu, zu schaffen. Für dieses Vorhaben setzt die Gemeinde sechs Impulse: 1) industrielle und kommerzielle Umstrukturierung, 2) eine neue, eben entstehende Tourismusagenda, 3) kreative Netzwerke und Aktivitäten, 4) öffentliche Dienste und Bildung, 5) eine neue Strategie für attraktiven Wohnbau, 6) die Stärkung von Sámi-Kultur und -Welterbe. Europan nimmt Guovdageaidnu zu einem Zeitpunkt auf, an dem sich gerade alle diese Impulse entwickeln. Kann der Wettbewerb Ideen für eine Serie kleinerer Interventionen und größerer Projekte visualisieren, die zusammen die wirtschaftliche und soziale Produktivität in Guovdageaidnu erneuern können?

Guovdageaidnu is a small town in Northern Norway with a strong Sámi indigenous identity. It is located along the Guovdageaineatnu River. The main industry in Guovdageaidnu is Sámi reindeer. From these embedded practices, a new scene is evolving, with 1,000 individual entrepreneurs entering into cooperation with one another. Guovdageaidnu is at the forefront of Norwegian education, on all levels from kindergarten to secondary school. How can the community capitalize on traditional knowhow and self-reliance combined with advanced education, ICTs, and high-tech solutions?

The municipality of Guovdageaidnu has recently joined a state-run program for industrial and commercial restructuring in the municipality. In 2017, the municipality adopted a plan for the Márkan, the town centre. This plan has proved to be difficult to use as a tool for restructuring industry and commerce. This is partly because the plan does not offer attractive plots for new business initiatives. The municipality acknowledges that there is a need to change local planning approaches to include Sámi values and traditions and encompass new readings of the landscape and the abundant diversity of local initiatives. Sápmi crosses the borders of Norway, Sweden, Finland, and Russia. Guovdageaidnu is on the periphery of Norway but is an important centre in the circumpolar area and Sápmi, and a world centre for reindeer herders. Guovdageaidnu is a stronghold for Sámi tradition and language, a language that incorporates the knowledge and practices necessary to managing reindeer husbandry.

When one arrives in Guovdageaidnu, the Márkan initially appears as a settlement recessed in the 'bowl-like' flat tundra landscape. The buildings in the centre of the town are distributed in an unstructured way along a two-kilometre-long segment of the road E45. The study area must be seen as a field of discoveries and new connections. How can the landscape constitute new guiding principles for planning in Guovdageaidnu?

The municipality is now looking for ways to reinvigorate and shape the future for new businesses and technologies in the Márkan, the centre of Guovdageaidnu. With this scheme, the municipality has introduced six measures: 1) industrial and commercial restructuring; 2) a new tourism agenda in the making; 3) creative networks and activities; 4) public services and education; 5) a new strategy for attractive housing; 6) strengthening Sámi culture and world heritage. Europan has come to Guovdageaidnu at a time when all these measures are emerging. Can the competition visualize ideas for a series of smaller interventions and larger projects that, together, can reinvigorate economic and social productiveness in Guovdageaidnu?

Catalogue of Ideas

Teresa Timm (DE) Architektin / Architect
Merle Jelitto (DE) Architektin / Architect
Paul Raphael Schaegner (DE) Architekt / Architect

Guovdageaidnus Urbanität spiegelt seine Vergangenheit und seine Gegenwart wider, es ist eine hybride Manifestation uralten Nomadentums und des Einzugs der Moderne. Wir verfolgen fünf Strategien aus seiner Geschichte, um seine Zukunft weiterzuentwickeln und bestehende Eigenschaften zu gestalten. Diese fünf Schritte und Strategien lassen sich in Gilles Deleuzes bipolarem System als „glatte" und „gekerbte" Räume einordnen. Den glatten Raum repräsentiert die unberührte und grenzenlose Tundra. Den gekerbten Raum wiederum stellt der definierte Raum moderner städtebaulicher Planung dar.

1. Im Hinblick auf die „glatte Tundra" werden wir Multifunktionalität im öffentlichen Raum propagieren. Wir werden die Tundra aktivieren und multifunktionale städtische Räume und Gebäude definieren. Die Mischnutzung von Raum ist sowohl typisch für das Nomadentum als auch für die Produktive Stadt.

2. Das bestehende Netzwerk an Verbindungen wird erweitert, um das Wegenetz zu optimieren. Wege verbinden städtische und natürliche Orte von Interesse. Sie gestalten eine moderne nomadische Urbanität mit einfachem Zugang zur Natur und intuitiver Orientierung.

3. Wie die erste Einführung lokaler Funktionen in der Tundra wird die Strategie der „funktionalen Akupunktur" die Schaffung von sozialen Orten mit Stadtmöblierung, gewachsenen Strukturen und geplanten Gebäuden ankurbeln.

4. Eine Polarität städtischer Eigenschaften und der Tundra als Umgebung ist charakteristisch für Gebäudegruppierungen in Guovdageaidnu. Um diese Polarität zu verstärken, und damit in der Folge auch die städtischen Eigenschaften, werden Plätze und als Katalysatoren dienende Gemeinschaftsgebäude in öffentliche Gruppierungen eingefügt.

5. Guovdageaidnus Status quo wurde durch Zersiedlung geprägt. Stattdessen benötigt es jedoch inneres Wachstum und das richtige Maß an städtischer Verdichtung und Intensivierung. In den Weiten der Tundra bilden Inseln der Urbanität die fünf verdichteten städtischen Cluster des „gekerbten Guovdageaidnu".

Guovdageaidnu's urbanity reflects both its past and its present. It is a hybrid manifestation of ancient nomadism and the introduction of modernity. We traced five strategies from its history in order to develop its future and elaborate existing qualities. These five steps and strategies incorporate Gilles Deleuze's bipolar system of 'smooth' and 'striated' space. Smooth space is represented by the unspoilt and borderless tundra. Striated space, on the other hand, is represented by the defined spaces of modern urban planning.

1. In connection with the 'smooth tundra', our aim is to promote multi-functionality in public space. We will activate the tundra and define multi-functional urban spaces and buildings. A mixed use of space is characteristic of nomadism as well as the productive city.

2. The existing network of connectivity will be augmented so as to improve the network of paths connecting urban and natural points of interest. They structure a modern nomadic urbanity, with easy access to nature and intuitive orientation.

3. Like the initial introduction of sedentary functions into the tundra, 'functional acupuncture' will stimulate social spaces with street furniture, landmark structures, and programmed buildings.

4. A polarity of urban quality on the inside and the tundra on the outside is characteristic for clusters of buildings in Guovdageaidnu. To enhance this polarity and hence the urban qualities, squares and catalysing community buildings are inserted within public clusters.

5. Guovdageaidnu's status quo has been shaped by urban sprawl. This must now be replaced by inner growth and the right amount of urban densification and intensification. In the vast tundra, urban islands form the five densified urban clusters of a 'striated Guovdageaidnu'.

Teresa Timm, Merle Jelitto und Paul R. Schaegner sind drei Architektur-Nerds, Humanisten und städtische Nomadinnen und Nomaden. Sie haben zusammen an der Bauhaus-Universität Weimar und an der ETSAM Madrid studiert. Danach verschlug es sie in alle Himmelsrichtungen, ehe sie ihre Kräfte für Guovdageaidnus Europan in Hamburg wieder vereinten.

Gemeinsam ist ihnen eine große Neugierde und die Freude am Diskutieren und Umsetzen von Architektur unter Einsatz verschiedener Instrumente und Theorien. Sie verfolgen einen an Benutzerinnen und Benutzer ausgerichteten Ansatz – sowohl empirisch als auch a priori. In Zusammenarbeit mit interdisziplinären Partnerinnen und Partnern erstreckt sich ihr Arbeitsbereich über den gesamten Erdball und alle Bereiche der Architektur.

teresa.timm@gmx.de
info@prsch.ne
merle.jelitto@googlemail.com

Teresa Timm, Merle Jelitto and Paul R. Schaegner are three architecture nerds, humanists, and urban nomads. They studied together at the Bauhaus University in Weimar and at ETSAM Madrid, but then went their own ways before joining forces for the Guovdageaidnu site in Europan 15. They share great curiosity and enjoy discussing and designing architecture through making use of various tools and theories. They pursue a user-centred design approach, both empirical and a priori. Collaborating with interdisciplinary partners, their field of work extends across the globe and the realm of architecture.

teresa.timm@gmx.de
info@prsch.net
merle.jelitto@googlemail.com

CATALOGUE OF IDEAS

Smooth Nomad Space

"Smooth space" is the space of the nomad. It is characterized by a form of free flowing occupation. The desert, the steppe or in this case the tundra is free from codifications which determine behavior, functionality, ownership and other political restrictions.

Smooth space is without human intervention attempting appropriation.

Because they have no borders, smooth spaces sometimes overlap and blend into a smooth experience.

The architectural qualities and identities blur.

"Smooth space is open-ended, nonlinear, intensive, haptic, nomad space".
*Gilles Deleuze

Striated Space of Modernity

"The striated is that which intertwines fixed and variable elements, produces an order and succession of distinct forms". * Gilles Deleuze

Striated space is shaped by the forces of institutionalization and political restrictions in a city. It is gridded, linear, metric, state space. Spatial definition results from architectural elements such as walls, curbs, fences or roofs.

These articulate and clearly mark off spaces with a certain architectural quality and functional identity.

Even though these fundamentally opposing spatial characters exist only in mixture, a delineation of striated from smooth space clearly happened during the development of Guovdageaidnu's urbanity. This polarity reflects Guovdageaidnu's urban hybridity between the ancient nomadic culture and the introduction of a modern lifestyle.

Sámi Urbanism

How smooth became striated

In Guovdageaidnu, all the stages of the development from a smooth nomad space to a striated modern urbanity are still visible.

This polarity has produced a unique composition of features.

Smooth Tundra

The open tundra as the ultimate smooth space is the starting point of Guovdageaidnu and serves as central element to the municipality nowadays.

Connectivity

A network of informal pathways always led through the vast tundra. It still exists in Guovdageaidnu today.

Introduction of functions

The injection of first sedentary urban functions into the tundra was the starting point of the development of Márkkan and Guovdageaidnu as it is today.

Polarity of clusters

Clusters of buildings intuitively define a multifunctional space in between. The polarity of urban quality on the inside and the tundra on the outside originates naturally from the small size of the settlement.

Striated Guovdageaidnu

More and more islands of striated urban space spread out across the tundra. This urban sprawl shaped Guovdageaidnu's urban status quo.

Sámi Strategies

Guovdageaidnu's specialties

Each aspect of Guovdageaidnu's development bears a specific spatial quality that we propose to strengthen and improve by a set of strategies.

Push multifunctionality

All smooth space is multifunctional. The mixed use of spaces is characteristic of a nomad lifestyle and a vibrant productive city. Functional openness is strengthened in Guovdageaidnu's green network as well as in urban plazas.

Improve the path network

Important urban connections and recreational loops are enhanced to encourage walking, cycling and the immersion into smooth space and activities. The path network connects points of public interest in the bowl and on the plateau and provides access to nature.

Functional acupuncture

Along the path network functional acupunctures are injected to activate smooth spaces and enrich Guovdageaidnu's public areas. Public furniture, landmark structures and programmed buildings will form social places and activate the multifunctional space.

Urbanize clusters

Buildings form clusters in which each building faces the tundra on one side and the urban realm on the other. To enhance this polarity and consequently the urban qualities, plazas and catalyst community buildings are inserted in public clusters

Densify Guovdageaidnu

Instead of sprawl, Guovdageaidnu needs inner growth and urban densification. Spatial proximity of important public programs and community spaces will create urban focal points. This will intensify social interaction and encourage economic collaboration.

The path network

A system of connecting and recreational loop pathways is improved within the existing path network.

These will be the axes of community life and functional enrichment without fragmenting the multifunctional smooth space in the geographical center of Guovdageaidnu.

The path network will provide intuitive orientation and unify the polycentric town with its public focal points changing over the seasons through a modern nomadic organisation of urbanity.

Bathing in Nature
13.6km
A relaxing hike through the tundra brings you to a refuge hut, to the northern river and recreational areas. That is where you will find peace within pure nature and within yourself.

Art Walk
11.7km
The Art Walk passes Juhl's Silver Gallery and the Sámi Film Institute as well as various spaces of temporary art installations. It offers resting places on the mountain with a view over Guovdageaidnu as well as at the lake.

The Triangle
3.6km
The Triangle connects all important public clusters to form one cohesive urbanity. One can discover the diversity of Guovdageaidnu, meet people at the Creative Cluster and Dáiddadállu, join events at the Active Cluster and the youth club, learn at the intergenerational Education Cluster or immerse into the public life of the Civic Cluster.

River Round
6.6km
For an overview of Guovdageaidnu's nature and history the River Round will guide you through the most scenic riverside spots like the beach or the bathhouse and to the historic rebellion site and other monuments.

1_25000

Densification

Instead of urban sprawl, Guovdageaidnu should densify its center to create mixed-use urban focal points, a walkable city, an intensified socio-economic interaction and easy access to the tundra.

We propose to enhance and densify the existing clusters of public importance. Therefore two challenges are faced:
* Centrally located attractive landplots are family owned and not accessible.
* Some vacant plots, buildings or venues do not fit the specific demands of projects in planning.

To regain control of urban densification, we propose the foundation of an urban land trust. Due to tight municipal budgets, the city transfers all of its land into the trust.

Its development will finance further action of the trust.

Private land owners either develop their plots or transfer them to the trust to receive repayment over 25 years and the opportunity to buy back the plot or one in similar quality for development. Thereby the landowner is ensured a financial return. The central management of plots will ensure the right plot for the right urban activity to develop symbiotic urban clusters and social mixture.

Pieces of land are given out for a heritable long term lease (99 years) for private development and non profit organisations. The land trust can also be the guarantor for bank loans to empower visionary individuals to lead development.

Guovdageaidnu Urban land trust

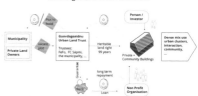

Temporary Lease

Even though Guovdageaidnu needs new spaces, empty venues do exist. They are a potential laboratory for urban innovation and community incubator.

We propose that vacant venues are given to a non-profit organization for 5 or 10 year terms. With a few helping hands or little money the building maintenance is ensured. The erosion of vacant buildings is stopped. The community gains extra social spaces.

Guovdageaidnu

Preis

98

Winner

europan 15

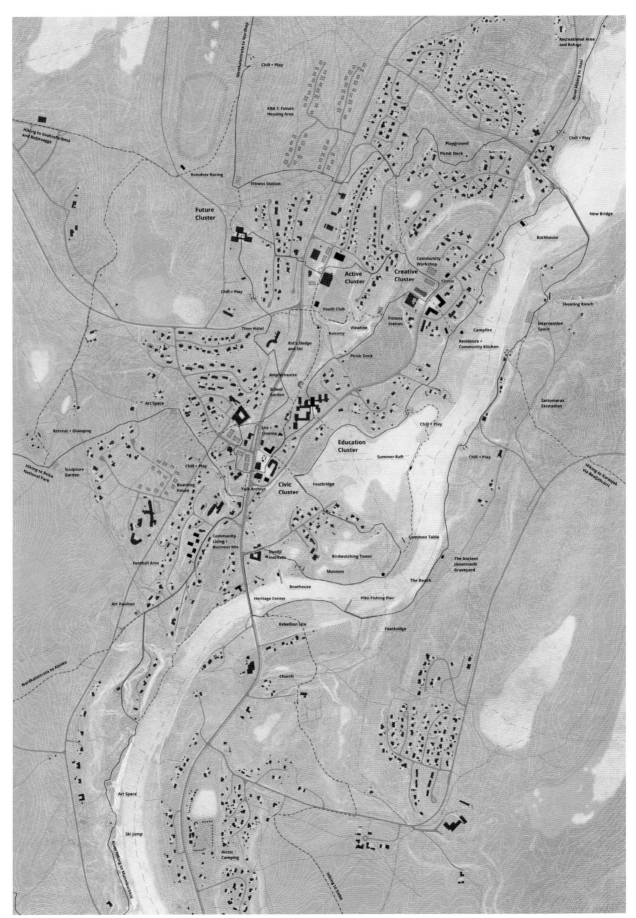

Nordkalottruta to Nordkap

Chill + Play

KBA 1: Future
Housing Area

Recreational Area
and Refuge

River Hiking to Idesi

Reindeer Racing

Hiking to Soahtefielbma
and Bidjovagge

Playground
Picnic Deck

Chill + Play

Fitness Station

New Bridge

Future
Cluster

Bathhouse

Community
Workshop

Active
Cluster

Creative
Cluster

Circus

Chill + Play

Shooting Ranch

Youth Club

Fitness
Station

Intervention
Space

Thon Hotel

Balcony

Viewline

Campfire

Residence +
Community Kitchen

Kid's Sledge
and Ski

Picnic Deck

Art Space

Amphitheatre

School
Garden

Sattomaras
Skistadion

Retreat + Glamping

Uni +
Cinema

Chill + Play

Education
Cluster

Chill + Play

Summer Raft

Hiking to Reisa
National Park

Sculpture
Garden

Chill + Play

Chill + Play

Hiking to Karasjok
Via Madjastuvra

Boarding
House

Yoik Archive

Civic
Cluster

Footbridge

Community
Living +
Business Mix

Common Table

Duodji
Institute

Birdwatching Tower

The Ancient
Jämetmielli
Graveyard

Football Area

Museum

The Beach

Boathouse

Art Pavilion

Heritage Center

Pike Fishing Pier

Rebellion Site

Footbridge

Nordkalottruta to Abisko

Church

Art Space

Ski Jump

Arctic
Camping

River Hiking to Mannhusbrua

Hiking to Sida

1_5000

CATALOGUE OF IDEAS

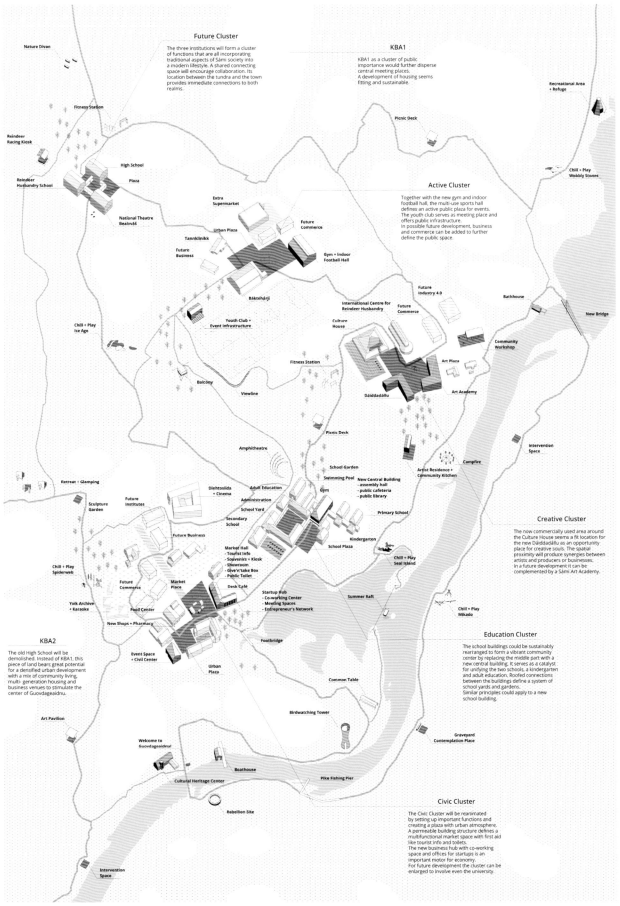

Future Cluster

The three institutions will form a cluster of functions that are all incorporating traditional aspects of Sámi society into a modern lifestyle. A shared connecting space will encourage collaboration. Its location between the tundra and the town provides immediate connections to both realms.

KBA1

KBA1 as a cluster of public importance would further disperse central meeting places.
A development of housing seems fitting and sustainable.

Active Cluster

Together with the new gym and indoor football hall, the multi-use sports hall defines an active public plaza for events. The youth club serves as meeting place and offers public infrastructure.
In possible future development, business and commerce can be added to further define the public space.

Creative Cluster

The now commercially used area around the Culture House seems a fit location for the new Dáiddadállu as an opportunity place for creative souls. The spatial proximity will produce synergies between artists and producers or businesses.
In a future development it can be complemented by a Sámi Art Academy.

Education Cluster

The school buildings could be sustainably rearranged to form a vibrant community center by replacing the middle part with a new central building. It serves as a catalyst for unifying the two schools, a kindergarten and adult education. Roofed connections between the buildings define a system of school yards and gardens.
Similar principles could apply to a new school building.

KBA2

The old High School will be demolished. Instead of KBA1, this piece of land bears great potential for a densified urban development with a mix of community living, multi-generation housing and business venues to stimulate the center of Guovdageaidnu.

Civic Cluster

The Civic Cluster will be reanimated by setting up important functions and creating a plaza with urban atmosphere. A permeable building structure defines a multifunctional market space with first aid like tourist info and toilets.
The new business hub with co-working space and offices for startups is an important motor for economy.
For future development the cluster can be enlarged to involve even the university.

Nature Divan

Fitness Station

Reindeer
Racing Kiosk

Reindeer
Husbandry School

High School

Plaza

National Theatre
Beaivváš

Extra
Supermarket

Urban Plaza

Future
Commerce

Future
Business

Tannklinikk

Gym + Indoor
Football Hall

Báktehárji

Youth Club +
Event Infrastructure

International Centre for
Reindeer Husbandry

Future
Commerce

Future
Industry 4.0

Culture
House

Art Plaza

Dáiddadállu

Art Academy

Chill + Play
Ice Age

Balcony

Viewline

Picnic Deck

Recreational Area
+ Refuge

Chill + Play
Wobbly Stones

Bathhouse

New Bridge

Community
Workshop

Intervention
Space

Campfire

Artist Residence +
Community Kitchen

Amphitheatre

Retreat + Glamping

Sculpture
Garden

Future
Institutes

Future Business

Diehtosiida
+ Cinema

Adult Education

Administration

School Yard

Secondary
School

Market Hall
- Tourist Info
- Souvenirs + Kiosk
- Showroom
- Give'n'take Box
- Public Toilet

School Garden

Swimming Pool

Gym

New Central Building
- assembly hall
- public cafeteria
- public library

Primary School

Kindergarten

School Plaza

Chill + Play
Seal Island

Chill + Play
Spiderweb

Yoik Archive
+ Karaoke

Future
Commerce

Food Center

New Shops + Pharmacy

Market
Place

Desk Café

Startup Hub
- Co-working Center
- Meeting Spaces
- Entrepreneur's Network

Summer Raft

Chill + Play
Mikado

Event Space
+ Civil Center

Urban
Plaza

Footbridge

Common Table

Birdwatching Tower

Graveyard
Contemplation Place

Art Pavilion

Welcome to
Guovdageaidnu!

Boathouse

Cultural Heritage Center

Rebellion Site

Pike Fishing Pier

Intervention
Space

Picnic Deck

Borås (SE)

Borås Standort / Location
110.000 Bevölkerung / Inhabitants
720 ha Betrachtungsraum / Study Site
58 ha Projektgebiet / Project Site

100

Gässlösa verwandelt sich in einen wesentlichen Teil des städtischen Gefüges mit Häusern und Wohnungen, Arbeitsplätzen, Kultur und Dienstleistungen. Aufgabe ist die Planung eines nachhaltigen Stadtviertels, das entlang des Flusses Viskan, unter Nutzung von Fluss, Parks und nahe gelegenen Erholungsgebieten, wachsen kann. Das Gebiet bietet eine gute Gelegenheit, um bestehende alte Gebäude, Räume und Unternehmen mit neuen Entwicklungen und nachhaltigen Lebensweisen zu verbinden und eine neue Art der transformativen Stadt zu erschaffen. Der Standort ist einfach zu erreichen und nur einen Kilometer von Bahnhof, Stadtzentrum und neuen Straßenverbindungen entfernt. Gässlösa soll mit seiner Umgebung sozial verbunden werden, unter Einsatz blau-grüner Infrastruktur, um das neue Gebiet mit dem bestehenden Stadtgefüge zu verbinden und dabei auch die Menschen zusammenzubringen. Der Kontakt mit Vielfalt, verschiedenen kulturellen Ausdrucksformen und Lebensweisen wird neue Ideen, Perspektiven und eine erhöhte Toleranz fördern. Zugang zu Bildung, Gemeinschaft, Sicherheit, Gesundheit, Gleichberechtigung, Integration und Kultur sollte zu den Prioritäten zählen.

Gässlösa befindet sich einen Kilometer südlich des Stadtzentrums von Borås und ist Standort der Textilindustrie der Stadt. Es handelt sich um ein Gebiet in der Nähe des Stadtzentrums, das jetzt dank der Umsiedlung des Klärwerkes gestaltet werden kann. Heute besteht das Gebiet aus einer niedrigen Siedlung aus gemischten Unternehmen, Handel und Kleingewerbe im Gebäude- und Bauwesen. Gässlösa befindet sich im Tal des Flusses Viskan, einer offenen Landschaft, die von bewaldeten Hügeln umgeben ist, und auf denen sich Fitnessparcours und weitere Erholungsmöglichkeiten finden. Über das gesamte Gebiet schafft der Fluss Viskan einen grünen und blauen Pfad, und südwestlich des Areals liegen die St. Sigfrids-Kapelle und der parkähnliche Friedhof.

In städtischen Umgebungen werden zukünftige Orte für Studium und Arbeit geplant. Die Verbindung zwischen Bildung, Forschung, Innovation und Arbeit wird höchstwahrscheinlich an Bedeutung zunehmen. Mehr Arbeit wird IT-basiert sein. Diese Entwicklung wird durch eine dichte und urbane Umgebung gefördert, aber auch zu dieser beitragen. Eine urbane Umgebung ist sowohl nachhaltig als auch produktiv. Hier treffen Menschen zusammen, werden Innovationen entwickelt und wachsen Geschäftsideen. Rund um Viskan ist historisch die Textilproduktion angesiedelt, und hier wächst Borås weiterhin als dichte und gemischte Stadt. Neben Viskan und Gässlösa kann die Urbanisierung in Harmonie mit historischen Siedlungen entwickelt werden. In den alten Gebäuden können kreative Aktivitäten stattfinden; Ideen und Stadt fördern einander. Die lokale Wirtschaft wird breit gefächert und widerstandsfähig gegenüber Konjunkturschwankungen. Die urbane Umgebung wird lebendig, inklusiv und gut an Umweltveränderungen angepasst.

Gässlösa is becoming an integrated part of the urban fabric, with homes, workplaces, culture, and services. The task is to plan a sustainable neighbourhood that can develop along the Viskan River and make good use of the river, parks, and nearby recreational areas. The area offers a good opportunity to combine existing old buildings, spaces, and businesses with new developments and sustainable ways of living so as to create a new type of transformative city. The site is easily accessible, located just one kilometre from the railway station, city centre, and new road connections. Gässlösa is to be socially linked with its surroundings by using green and blue elements to link the new area with the existing urban fabric, and thereby connect people. Exposure to diversity, different cultural expressions and lifestyles will inspire new ideas, perspectives, and greater tolerance. Access to education, community, security, health, equality, integration, and culture should all be priorities.

Gässlösa is located one kilometre to the south of the centre of Borås and is part of the city's textile history. It is an area near the city centre that can now be developed as a result of the relocating of the sewage plant to. Today, the area consists of a low-rise settlement of mixed businesses, commerce, and small industries in the building and construction sector. Gässlösa is located in the valley of Viskan, which is an open landscape surrounded by forested hills. On the hills, there are exercise trails and other recreational opportunities. The Viskan River creates a green and blue path through the area, and St. Sigfrid's Chapel and a park-like cemetery are located to the southwest.

Future places for study and work will be developed in urban environments. The link between education, research, innovation, and work is likely to be significant, especially because work is becoming more information-based. This development will be promoted by (and contribute to) a dense and urban environment. An urban environment is both sustainable and more productive. It is here that people meet, innovations develop, and business ideas grow. Textile production has historically been centred around Viskan, and is where Borås is continuing to grow as a dense and mixed city. Along the Viskan River and Gässlösa, new urbanization can be developed in harmony with historic settlements. Creative activities can take place in the old buildings, with ideas and city nurturing one another. The local economy will become diversified and resilient to cyclical fluctuations. The urban environment will be lively, inclusive, and well adapted to environmental change.

P2P – Plugin 2 Produce

Alexandra Kashina (RU) Architektin, Urbanistin / Architect, Urbanist
Johan Nilsson (SE) Stadtplaner / Urban Planner
Husain Vaghjipurwala (IN) Architektin, Urbanistin / Architect, Urbanist
Mitarbeit / Cooperation:
Franziska Dehm (DE) Urbane Designerin / Urban Designer

Die Produktive Stadt

Die Produktive Stadt demonstriert ungefiltert, wie eine lebendige Stadt konsumiert, bewohnt und geformt wird. Welche Komponenten werden an den Rand gedrängt, außerhalb unseres Blickfeldes, sodass wir einfach das moderne Leben auf uns wirken lassen können? Gässlösa versteckt die zugrunde liegenden Arbeiten nicht, die zum Bestehen und zur Erschaffung einer lebendigen Stadtlandschaft mit Mischnutzung nötig sind, sondern tritt diesen gegenüber. Ressourcen werden abgesichert, Elektrizität produziert, wo immer es möglich ist, Produkte erzeugt, Lebensmittel verarbeitet, alte Materialien wiederverwertet und lokal recycelt, Einwohnerinnen und Einwohner engagieren sich über soziale Grenzen hinweg. Das Ziel eines „lebendigen" städtischen Umfeldes umfasst eine Reihe starker Kontraste: zwischen dem Ruhigen und Weichen (öffentlicher Raum, Wald, Wasser, Hügel, kulturelle Aktivitäten) und dem Lauten und Harten (Altstoffsammelzentrum, Metall- und Holzfertigung, industrielles Erbe, politische Organisation). Den Klimawandel und die soziale Ungleichheit zu bekämpfen, bedeutet Gleichberechtigung, auf soziale Veränderungen vorbereitet zu sein, indem man sich mit den dringlichsten Fragen beschäftigt.

Vision für Gässlösa

Eine resiliente Gemeinschaft verlangt nach Zeit, Fokus und Zielen, die geformt werden, indem man über traditionelle Lebensmodelle, Arbeit und deren Interaktion mit der natürlichen und gebauten Umwelt hinausgeht. Plugin 2 Produce (P2P) ist eine Typologie, die die Produktivität in einem Stadtviertel erhöhen soll. P2P wird an einen Stadtblock angeschlossen und besteht aus drei Teilen: einem reproduktiven, einem sozialen und einem wirtschaftlichen Kern. Es verfügt über keine fixe Form oder Funktion, da es dazu dient, die sozialen und wirtschaftlichen Bedürfnisse der unmittelbaren Nachbarschaft auszugleichen und gleichzeitig Wasser und Energie zu reproduzieren und zu bewahren. P2P ist bestrebt, eine Mischung aus Nutzungen und Nutzerinnen und Nutzern zu erhalten und dafür zu sorgen, dass sich die Bürgerinnen und Bürger auf positive Art und Weise engagieren, um zur Entwicklung von Gässlösa beizutragen.

The Productive City

The productive city showcases how a lively city is consumed, inhabited, and shaped in an unfiltered way. Which components are pushed to the fringes, out of our sight, so that we are able to simply take in modern life? Gässlösa does not hide away, but instead highlights the work that underlies the existence and creation of a lively, mixed-used cityscape. Natural resources are safeguarded, electricity produced where possible, products manufactured, food processed, old materials re-used and recycled locally, and residents engage with one another across social lines. The goal of a 'vibrant' urban environment involves a number of strong contrasts: between the calm and the soft (public spaces, forest, water, hills, cultural activities), and the loud and the hard (recycling yard, metal- and woodworking workshops, industrial heritage, political organization). Fighting climate change and social inequality also means preparing for societal changes by engaging with the most urgent questions.

Vision for Gässlösa

A resilient community requires time, focus, and goals that are shaped by going beyond traditional modes of living and working, and their interaction with the natural and built environment. The Plugin 2 Produce (P2P) is a typology that is added to a district in order to increase productivity. The P2P is plugged into an urban block, and comprises three parts: a reproductive, a social, and an economic core. It has no set form or function, since it serves to balance the social and economic needs of the nearby neighbourhood while reproducing and preserving water and energy with a high density. The P2P aims to safeguard a mix of uses and users, and to enable the citizens to positively engage in helping realize the development of Gässlösa.

102

Mit einem Hintergrund in Architektur und Städtebau liegen unsere Interessen an der Schnittstelle zwischen der gebauten Form und sozialen sowie politischen Themen. Städtischer Raum ist ein beziehungsorientiertes Produkt, in dem sich Praktiken und Ressourcen permanent verändern. Unsere Planungsstrategie folgt einer offenen Form. Mit dieser Position wird die Gestaltung in Gässlösa lediglich zu einem Instrument, um Prozesse zu formen, die Produktivität sowie Berücksichtigung von Metabolismus fördern und die Stadtplanung in das alltägliche Leben der Bürgerinnen und Bürger bringen.

mail.omni@tutanota.com

With backgrounds in architecture and urbanism, our interest lies in the intersection between built form and social and political issues. Urban space is a relational product in which practices and resources are constantly changing. Our planning strategy adheres to an open form. Based on this stance, design in Gässlösa becomes merely a tool for shaping processes that foster productivity and considerations of metabolism and for bringing city planning into the everyday life of citizens.

mail.omni@tutanota.com

P2P - PLUGIN 2 PRODUCE

PRODUCTIVITY

The productive city showcases unfiltered, how a lively city is being consumed, inhabited and made. Which components are pushed to the fringes, out of our sight so we can simply take in modern life? Gässlösa does not hide away, but rather confronts the underlying work for the existence and the making of a mixed-used, lively cityscape.

Natural resources are safe-guarded, electricity is produced where possible, products are manufactured, food processed, old materials re-used and recycled locally, inhabitants engage across social lines. The goal of a 'vibrant' urban environment contains a set of strong contrasts: between the calm and soft (public spaces, forest, water, hills, cultural activities), and the loud and hard (recycling yard, metal- wood workshops, industrial heritage, political organisation). Inhabitants, actors and visitors are exposed to the work and effort it takes to produce balanced high-living standards - and everyone are invited to seek their place in this creation.

To fight climate change and social inequality, real means being prepared for societal changes by engaging in the questions that are most urgent. The planning of Gässlösa is shaped from the start together with those that seek to inhabit it, for their goals and needs in symbiosis with the municipality and private sphere.

The post-industrialist city does not rely on one or a few linear actors or systems. It does not dry out its resources or land for exploitation in order to maximise short-term goals. To balance the metabolisms between natural- and material flows, the city must be organised in a way so we can eat food, consume energy, buy our products and use services in close proximity to where we foremost live, learn and act. This city takes with joy the responsibility for its own production - not only of classic (materialistic oriented) value production but of social and knowledge based exchanges.

VISION

A resilient community demands time, focus and goals that are shaped by going beyond traditional modes of living, working and its interaction with the natural and built environment. The Plugin 2 Produce (P2P) is a typology which is added to a quarter in order to increase productivity. The P2P is plugged into an urban block, containing three parts: A reproductive-, a social- and an economic core. It has no set out form or function, as it serves to balance the social and economic needs of the close neighbourhood while reproducing and preserving water and energy - with a high built density. The P2P aims to safeguard a mix of uses and users, and for the citizens to positively engage in helping realise the development of Gässlösa.

Plugins are spread out in a larger network, housing a broad knowledge base, diversity of skill levels, age and experience, will and capacity to contribute to a urban environment that connects to a larger purpose than the individual, a household or a district.

Small Scale Environment   Biodiversity   Large Scale Volumes

CONTEXT

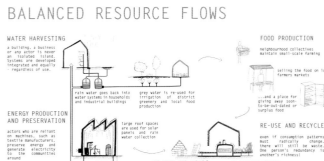

RESOURCES
How to minimize consumption and contamination (water, soil, energy)? How can we better share resources?

MOBILITY
How can we integrate mobility and accessibility into productive territories?

EQUITY
How can we connect social and spatial elements? How can we create productive balance between territories?

BALANCED RESOURCE FLOWS

WATER HARVESTING
a building, a business or any actor is never an isolated island. Systems are developed integrated and equally - regardless of use.

rain water goes back into water systems in households and industrial buildings

grey water is re-used for irrigation of district greenery and local food production

FOOD PRODUCTION
neighbourhood collectives maintain small-scale farming

selling the food on local farmers markets

...and a place for giving away soon-to-be-out-dated or surplus food

ENERGY PRODUCTION AND PRESERVATION
actors who are reliant on machines, such as textile manufacturers, preserve energy and generate electricity to the communities around

waste heat is treated as a recyclable resource, reducing the reliability on other energy systems

large roof spaces are used for solar panels and rain water collection

RE-USE AND RECYCLE
even if consumption patterns must radically change, there will still be waste. One person's redundancy is another's richness!

out comes rest material which can be reassembled into new forms. Un-used fabrics can be turned into new products.

in comes old fabrics, tools, hard plastics, bricks and old building materials

SCALES OF >METABOLISM<

XL

Productivity for Growth
Productivity is combined of three "sub-metabolisms"; Resource-, Social- and Economic production. Any productive community and space derives its strengths from the synergy of these three metabolisms. Local growth is sustained and optimised by the everyday social and resource reproduction. This in turn increases the economic productivity for a Global exchange.

← Productive Network
The post-industrial city has enabled the rethinking of Urban economic production. In the case of manufacturing, a decentralised set-up grants a multitude of actors. Smaller entities form together a larger network in the production process, replacing the reliability on traditional, large industrial compounds. The textile industry becomes a distributed network of small yarn spinners, weavers and designers. The distributed manufacturing allows the city to be more vibrant, mixed, personal and brings the Global economy to the neighbourhood.

Resilient Communities
The productive neighbourhood network sets up the process for its collectivisation, which also seeks to support the local growth. The fusion of the three "sub-metabolisms" of production; Social, Resource and Economic, creates vibrant neighbourhoods whose citizens are 'acting in the Local while effecting the Global'.

L

Industrial Heritage
The prominence they occupy in the site owing to the large volumes avails them to be ideally reused as collectivised spaces for public use. These structures become the physical manifestation of history of the site and thereby provide an umbilical link to the productivity embedded in its future.

Green Heritage
The river bank is foremost used as a neglected backyard for the current industries. But the natural fauna around the river is robust and lively. As important as the built heritage is the greenery sustaining high biodiversity for insect and animal life. Transformed from a backyard to a backbone, the riverbank and its surroundings must be preserved and furthered.

Water
Lying in a small valley forming a basin, Gässlösa is almost entirely a flood-risk zone. By simulating the storm water runoff and the flooding zones, areas with major water logging landforms can be identified. These regions can act as natural reservoirs with great capacity for water retention, water conservation schemes and safe-guarding human habitation around.

Resilient Green Blue Network
The site creates an optimised grid of water and green spaces, both inherited and developed ones for efficient resource management. The water grid contains the large public reservoirs and the distributed rain water harvesting system. The green grid contains the sensitive river ecology, its wetlands and forests and a network of urban farms.

M

Reproductive core
The ability of the area to conserve and re-use its local resources is the first step towards global productivity. The 'reproductive core' contains the technical reproduction and conservation systems like harvesting rain water, grey water reuse, composting and storage of solar power. A monitoring centre in each core provides information on the consumption and production.

Social Reproduction
While resource reproduction is carried out by the community, 'Social reproduction' makes the place for the community. For example day care centres, community kitchens and communal living rooms grant space for inclusion and engagement. These allow for the decrease in consumption of 'private spaces' (e.g. from 35-25sqm per person), thereby reducing construction and increasing density.

CO-Production
Co-working spaces among these users allow early stage professionals and new businesses to set up their work structure. They can benefit from the community as well as vice versa. Such new work spaces usually bring in an added economic advantage in the form of retail and services that follow.

Economic Production
The final essential cog in creating productive environments is the production for economic exchange. Small retail-, co-working- and service spaces spring up on the exterior edge of the typology. The mix allows an overall increased productivity, serving a resourceful cohabitation in the urban environment.

    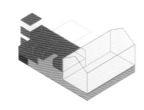

E15
BORÅS

URBAN DESIGN CONCEPT

BUILDING STRUCTURE
- ■ New buildings
- ▦ Preserved buildings

MOBILITY
- ▦ Main roads
- ▦ Fast bike-lanes (w. pathways)
- ⌐ Local pathways pedestrian

FUNCTIONAL MIX
- □ Public
- □ Manufacturing
- □ Social institutions & services
- □ Commercial
- □ Office
- □ Housing

EQUITY
- □ Public
- □ Collective
- □ Private

GREEN STRUCTURE
- ▦ Urban greenery
- Wild nature/recreational
- ⤴ Green connections

WATER CONSERVATION
- ▦ River Viskan
- ▦ Riparian Barrier
- ▦ Water retention and basins
- ⤵ Rain and water flow

CONCEPTUAL PLAN

- ▦ Food Production
- ▦ open water collectors

FOOD PRODUCTION AND WATER COLLECTION

- ▦ electricity producers
- ▦ plugins

ENERGY NETWORK

- ▦ productive buildings
- ▦ social services
- ▦ existing buildings
- ▦ plugins

CLOSENESS BETWEEN PRODUCTIVITY

Nodes
Four heritage buildings are occupied with public functions, serving the neighbourhood and the inhabitants with various essential services. They are the catalysts for further developments.

Convention Centre
Bureau for "Commoning urban design". A link between the city, the private sphere and the future inhabitants. Focus groups are set up with carpenters, plant-enthusiasts, architects, sausage-kiosk owners etc – everyone who wants to actively take part in city-building. From large to small scale.

Incubators for new productive businesses within various fields; textile, agriculture tech-industries, retail, gastronomy, etc.

Exhibition Hall
Bureau for collective city design. Incubators for new productive businesses within various fields; textile, tech-industries, agriculture, retail, gastronomy, etc.

Speculations Fair
An old building becomes the arena for total openness. The wall towards the courtyard is taken out, leaving a hollow structure for user's speculation and appropriation. Large board-game events, concerts, rain-cover on bad days, book fairs or open lectures.

Gässlösa's Energy Transition Association
A pioneering Borås organisation focusing on "a new city in balance with nature". How to fight climate change on a collective basis? Counselling, workshops, field trips and practical tips with inhabitants and actors! Focus on how to balance consumer patterns with production of various resources locally.

Community Centre
Neighbours can meet regarding local initiatives, events or other developments in the area. A public, co-operatively run library and community hall act as an open space for knowledge exchange, parties, tourist information, meetings.

1:4000 N↑

PHASES OF GROWTH

Developing a new area demands us to raise awareness of its costs (consumption) and its what it could give back (production).

	Average Svensson Today	Svensson 2040
🌳	23 tonnes	1 tonnes
⚡	7.4 MwH	3.5 MwH
🍴	230 Kg	2 kg/5qmt
💧	110 lpcd	70 lpcd

Phase 1 - Initiation
The site takes hold through the re-use of its industrial heritage and opens up to the future. These nodes act as early catalysts for further building developments. With establishing Public buildings in the south and economic engines north of the river, Gässlösa enables the right mix of functions for its first 1000 residents. The River is sensitively opened up and its Ecology takes a renewed shape with introduction of green-blue corridors into the area.

Phase 2 - Densification
From the elementary re-production for local growth, the residents advance the productivity through regular monitoring of the local consumption and production. New production and small scale manufacturing units are added with a goal to offset local consumption as well as global economic exchange. The residents have and embodied Gässlösa as their home. As a part of the planning process, the city and its shapers have laid the ground for future collaborations and have become an integral cog in the machine.

Phase 3 - Intensification
Local energy grids, food production and resources have well found their balance and are increasing productivity. As the old and new have synergised their existence in the district, it finds itself well in place for second generation of residents. The last of the old Gässlösa has moved out and makes way for an enclosure of Gässlösa. before it grows further south. The local community can now be focused on the re-alignment of their visions and goals and further inclusion in the district.

materials (tons)
energy (MwH)
food (kg)
water (litres)

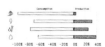
-100% -80% -60% -40% -20% 0% 20% 40%

materials (tons)
energy (MwH)
food (kg)
water (litres)

-100% -80% -60% -40% -20% 0% 20% 40%

materials (tons)
energy (MwH)
food (kg)
water (litres)

-100% -80% -60% -40% -20% 0% 20% 40%

PLUGINS FOR PRODUCTION

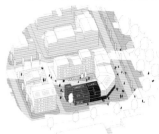

A_ HOUSING SOUTH

B_ ATELIERS AND WORKSHOPS

C_ PERFORMANCE/TECH HALL

D_ HOUSING NORTH

USE MIX

A_Housing south

- communal   - day care   - retail shops
kitchens   centre   - small service
- communal   - elderly care   - yoga & dance
living rooms   - co-working
- co-working

B_Ateliers/Workshops

- communal   - art workshops- repair shops
kitchens   - program for   - workshops
- co-hotel   children with   - ateliers
- artist in   art
residence   - bike help

C_Performance/Tech

- Auditorium   - industrial   - tech service
- Exhibition   re-use advisory- co-working
hall   - hacking labs   - offices

D_Housing north

- communal   - youth centre   - retail shop
kitchens   - urban garden   - small service
- communal   - office
living rooms

E_ MULTIFUNCTIONAL AMPHITHEATRE AND RETENTION POND

F_ INNER COURTYARD ATELIERS

RE:MEDIATE

Alice Lemaire (FR) Architektin, Stadtplanerin / Architect, Urban Designer
Anna Nötzel (DE) Stadtplanerin, Stadtdesignerin / Urban Planner, Urban Designer
Dominika Misterka (PL) Stadtplanerin, Stadtdesignerin / Urban Planner, Urban Designer
Emeline Lex (CA) Stadtplanerin, Stadtdesignerin / Urban Planner, Urban Designer
Fernando Gonzalez-Camino (ES) Landschafsarchitekt, Stadtdesigner / Landscape Architect, Urban Designer
Marcin Zebrowski (PL) Stadtplaner, Stadtdesigner / Urban Planner, Urban Designer
Martin Näf (BR) Architekt, Stadtdesigner / Architect, Urban Designer
Teresa Arana Aristi (MX) Architektin, Stadtdesignerin / Architect, Urban Designer
Tony Nielsen (SE) Stadtplaner, Stadtdesigner / Urban Planner, Urban Designer
Victor Ohlsson (SE) Stadtplaner, Stadtdesigner / Urban Planner, Urban Designer

Das Viertel Gässlösa in Borås wird zu einem eigenen Ökosystem, in dem eine Symbiose zwischen Grünflächen, bebauter Umwelt und Wohngebieten in der Lage ist, die Bedürfnisse von Natur und Menschen auf gleichem Niveau zu unterstützen. Dieses Ökosystem wird einen Funktionskreislauf in Gang setzen, in dem alles, was Eingang in dieses findet, wechselseitig etwas anderes definieren, beeinflussen und unterstützen wird. Die Synthese zwischen Leben, Arbeiten, Natur und Freizeit ist die Haupttriebkraft für die Gestaltungspläne.

Das Ökosystem Gässlösa folgt der grundlegenden Vorstellung einer produktiven „Cradle-to-Cradle"-Umgebung. Das neue und im Laufe der Zeit entwickelte Gebiet wird räumliche Planungssensibilität mit Funktions-Clustern verbinden. Schlussendlich soll so eine produktive Umgebung entstehen, die über verschiedene Phasen hinweg sorgfältig entwickelt ist und Ökosystemdienstleistungen, aber auch unterschiedliche Bedürfnisse der Benutzerinnen und Benutzer unterstützt. Die Ökosystemstrategie mit ihrem „Cradle-to-Cradle"-Prinzip und dem Ansatz der produktiven Stadt wird die Anleitung für räumliche Lösungen bieten. Das System befasst sich mit Fragen der Konnektivität und fördert Lösungen für ein florierendes und nachhaltiges Viertel auf verschiedenen Maßstabsebenen, ohne das Erbe von Ort und Landschaft außer Acht zu lassen.

Innerhalb eines Blockes, eines Clusters oder eines Viertels werden Nachhaltigkeitsthemen wie Abfallwirtschaft, Energieproduktion und -konsum oder Wasseraufbereitung auf innovative und zukunftsorientierte Art und Weise reguliert. Dies soll unter Schaffung einer Umgebung mit Mischnutzung geschehen, die schlussendlich nachhaltig innerhalb ihrer grünen und bebauten Form und was wirtschaftliche und ökologische Veränderungen angeht, widerstandsfähig ist, die sich aber auch mit dem bestehenden städtischen Gewebe und den landschaftlichen Gegebenheiten verbindet. Mit besseren regionalen Verbindungen, erweiterten Landschaftsqualitäten, Funktions-Clustern und verschiedenen Ankerpunkten soll eine lebendige, produktive und flexible Umgebung geschaffen werden.

The Gässlösa neighbourhood of Borås will become its own kind of ecosystem, in which a symbiosis between the green, the built, and the living is able to support the needs of nature and people on an equal level. This ecosystem will create a cycle of functions in which everything that is put into it will mutually define, impact, and support something else. The synthesis between living, working, nature, and recreation is the main driver for the design proposal.

The Gässlösa ecosystem adheres to the fundamental idea of a cradle-to-cradle productive neighbourhood. The new area developed over time will bring together spatial planning sensitivity and clusters of functions, and thus ultimately create a productive neighbourhood that is cautiously developed over different phases and which supports ecosystem services as well as the different needs of users. The ecosystem strategy, with its cradle-to-cradle and productive city approach, will provide guidance for finding spatial solutions. The system addresses connectivity questions and promotes solutions for a thriving and sustainable district on varying levels of scale, without disregarding the heritage of the location and the landscape.

Within a block, a cluster, or the neighbourhood, sustainability issues such as waste management, energy production and consumption, or water treatment will be regulated innovatively and in a future-oriented way. This will give rise to a mixed-use environment that is ultimately sustainable within its green and built form and resilient to economic and environmental challenges, but also connected with the existing urban fabric and landscape assets. With improved regional connections, enhanced landscape assets, functionality clusters, and various anchor points, a vibrant, productive, and flexible neighbourhood will be created.

Das Team besteht aus einer Gruppe von zehn Kolleginnen und Kollegen des Masterprogramms Nachhaltige Stadtplanung an der Universität Lund in Schweden. Während unseres Masterstudiums sammelten wir im Zuge etlicher gemeinsamer Studioprojekte Erfahrungen. In unserem letzten Semester erkannten wir das Potenzial der Fähigkeiten der jeweils anderen sowie den Nutzen unseres jeweiligen unterschiedlichen beruflichen und wissenschaftlichen Hintergrundes, aber auch unserer internationalen Erkenntnisse, die uns dazu brachten, am Europan 15-Wettbewerb teilzunehmen, bei dem wir dank unserer unterschiedlichen Erfahrungen und Expertise eine Gemeinschaftsarbeit schaffen konnten.

urban10.contact@gmail.com

The team consists of a group of ten colleagues from the Sustainable Urban Design master's program at Lund University in Sweden. During our Master's studies, we gained experience working together during several of our studio projects. During our final semester, we saw potential in each others' abilities and found value in our diverse professional and academic backgrounds as well as our international knowledge. This led us to participate in the Europan 15 competition and to create a joint work based on our diverse experience and expertise.

urban10.contact@gmail.com

BORÅS (SE)

RE:MEDIATE

INTRODUCING AN ADAPTIVE URBAN ECOSYSTEM IN GÄSSLÖSA

ALWAYS CLOSE TO NATURE

ACCESSIBLE RIVERFRONT

NATURE/URBAN JUXTAPOSITION

VARIED WORKLIFE SETTINGS

ST SIGFRID CHAPEL SIGHTLINE

1

USES

Gässlöse will become a mixed use neighborhood, in which residential, cultural, and business functions can coexist. Larger scale business typologies will only be concentrated along Gässlösavägen.

STREET NETWORK

Parts of the existing street network will be implemented into the design. Newly proposed streets will be pedestrian and bike oriented, yet allow for emergency cars to enter and residents to drive through.

PUBLIC SPACE SEQUENCE

The inner loop connects public and cultural buildings with educational facilities. Furthermore it is the network of public spaces that connects the green and business spine with neighborhood uses.

GREEN AND BLUE

The landscape becomes an important element in the site's development. Contributing majorly to ecosystem services and biodiversity through phytoremediation, urban agriculture, bioswales, wetlands, and courtyard green.

WITHIN THE LARGER BORÅS

The design will be part of a larger context. Materials, collected from the site's waste management stations, is planned to be delivered to the research facilities in the University and Textile Fashion Centre, and through new technology, the recycled materials may be turned into new textiles. Furthermore, biomass gathered from the site's phytoremediated plants will be delivered to Sobacken power plant and in return, supply Borås with heat and electricity. The design is part of a larger municipal strategy to connect surrounding landscape together with urban green areas in a north-south axis.

INTRODUCING AN ADAPTIVE URBAN ECOSYSTEM

The synthesis between living, working, nature, and recreation are the main drivers for the design proposal. Ultimately creating a productive cradle-to-cradle neighborhood. The vision is that Gässlösa will become its own kind of ecosystem, in which a symbiosis between the green, built, and the living is able to support the needs of people and nature on the same level. This will create a cycle of functions in which everything that is put into it, will mutually define, impact, and support something else. The existing fabric will be incorporated into the design during different phases of implementation, which allows a sensitive design approach that is flexible in functionality and with highly adaptable typologies giving freedom to react according to the needs of the inhabitants, businesses, and other actors, through different forms, sizes, and combinations of housing and business spaces. The over-time developed quarters will create a mixed-use environment that also includes clusters of functionality that contributes to a vibrant public realm and that ultimately is sustainable within its green and build form, and resilient towards economical and environmental challenges, and also connects to the existing urban fabric and landscape assets.

1 CONNECT

Through different activated and productive natural assets, the site becomes an important green value connector in Borås. A diversity in natural assets will be resilient and reactive under changing environmental circumstances, forming the heart and foundation of the site's development.

2 RELATE

The flexible grid development follows various given circumstances on site, such as topography levels or views towards the Viskan river and the mountainous surroundings. The new network sensitively incorporates the heritage of landscape and built structure into the new design.

3 EDUCATE

The inner loop ties together various urban and green fabrics of the site and its surroundings. Educational, public, and cultural facilities follow this network of public spaces as different anchor points within the area, creating an accessible public realm that is not only exclusively commercially used.

4 PRODUCE

Different sized businesses have the opportunity to (re-)settle in various large, medium, or small scale business typologies on site. Furthermore will short term rental, between 2-5 years, be facilitated in order to ensure a renewal of the businesses in certain party of the site.

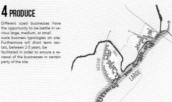

FROM JÖSSAGATAN TO THE GREEN HEART
SECTION AA'
SCALE 1/1000

FROM THE UPCYCLING AREA TO THE SCHOOL
SECTION BB'
SCALE 1/1000

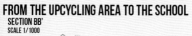

2

BORÅS (SE) / RE:MEDIATE

MASTERPLAN

The overall plan reveals a well-integrated landscape and urban structure that offers variations and a wide range of atmospheres. The goal is to celebrate the site's assets and connect the new programs forming the ecosystem.

A green productive spine connects the site from North to South and supports part of the local ecosystem. Connecting from Sta Birgitta griftegård, it merges with the river. A green heart articulates the two sides of the site where greenhouses and outdoor cultivation create a productive heart. The spine then crosses over to the Viskatorget, under the community center, through the new elementary school and continues South into the forest towards the Mediatek. A panoramic view over the site and a scenic calm meeting area allow for a stop in the forest-scape and then connects to the sports field area South of the site.

A large number of adaptive blocks welcome the new residents. They provide a flexible structure for small to medium businesses and housing, always adapting to changes through a well-though phasing plan. The built structure creates an inner loop that strengthens the connectivity within the site by tying the education center together with public spaces, playgrounds, schools and a variety of landscape settings. Sightlines and anchor points that relate to the existing fabric give the proposal clear visual connections to key urban and landscape assets.

A series of productive and public buildings are located along Gässlösavägen, which becomes an urban connector across the site. Productive activities that require larger square footage are located in the South, which improves transportation access and decreases car traffic into the neighborhoods.

By using phytoremediation, the polluted soils and water can be cleaned overtime, and be used for urban farming and other recreational use. By activisting and opening the riverfront, the river can be celebrated once more and ensure a connection to the city center.

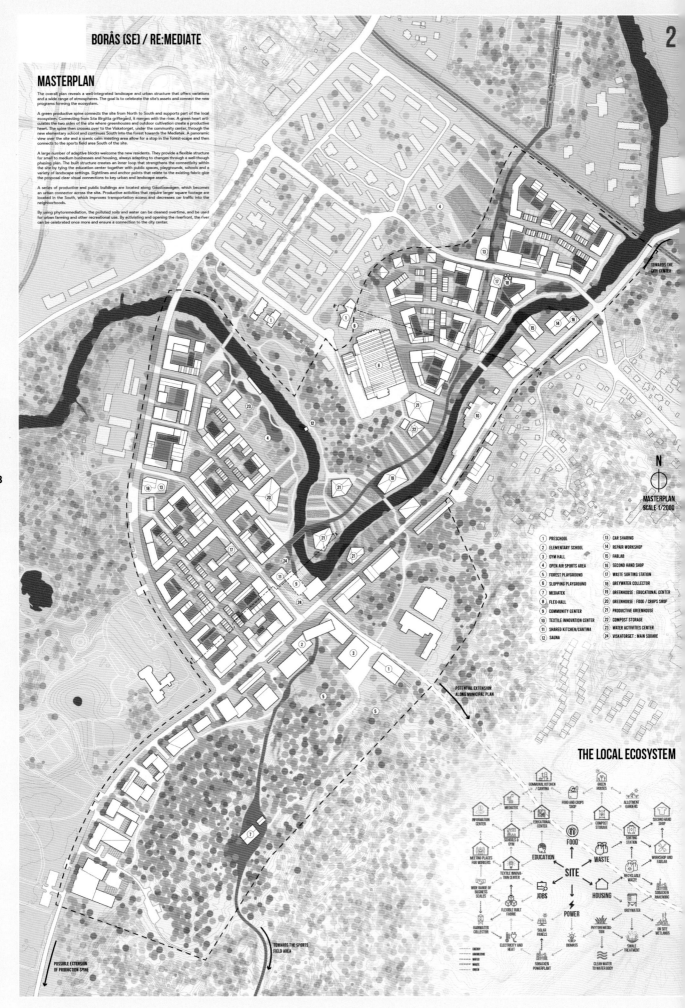

TOWARDS THE CITY CENTER

N

MASTERPLAN
SCALE 1/2000

1 PRESCHOOL
2 ELEMENTARY SCHOOL
3 GYM HALL
4 OPEN AIR SPORTS AREA
5 FOREST PLAYGROUND
6 SLOPPING PLAYGROUND
7 MEDIATEK
8 FLEX-HALL
9 COMMUNITY CENTER
10 TEXTILE INNOVATION CENTER
11 SHARED KITCHEN/CANTINA
12 SAUNA

13 CAR SHARING
14 REPAIR WORKSHOP
15 FABLAB
16 SECOND HAND SHOP
17 WASTE SORTING STATION
18 GREYWATER COLLECTOR
19 GREENHOUSE : EDUCATIONAL CENTER
20 GREENHOUSE : FOOD / CROPS SHOP
21 PRODUCTIVE GREENHOUSE
22 COMPOST STORAGE
23 WATER ACTIVITIES CENTER
24 VISKATORGET : MAIN SQUARE

POTENTIAL EXTENSION
ALONG MUNICIPAL PLAN

POSSIBLE EXTENSION
OF PRODUCTION SPINE

TOWARDS THE SPORTS
FIELD AREA

THE LOCAL ECOSYSTEM

BORÅS (SE) / RE:MEDIATE

3

PHASE 1

In preparation of the first construction of buildings, the demolition of buildings mainly focuses on the sewage treatment plant in the heart of the site, as well as a building complexes to the North and the South of the site. Along the riverbank, plants for phytoremediation purposes will be planted.

PHASE 2

The school complex at the heart of the site will start the construction process. The development of business buildings along the Southern half of Gässlösavägen and the neighborhood area along Jössagatan happens simultaneously. Divided green fabrics will be connected through this development.

PHASE 3

Along Jössagatan, Gässlösavägen and the Viskan River, the construction development continues. The green heart will extend towards the North and create a green spine that connects green assets. Urban agriculture and green houses will be introduced in the green heart.

PHASE 4

The final construction phase starts, remaining gaps will be filled South of Viskan River and South of Kärngatan. The green spine and heart continue to be activated through recreational and productive purposes, as they continue to increase the connection towards existing green assets.

PHASE 5

The finished development creates a balanced area in which the green development is regarded equally to the housing and business development. A variety of uses and sequences of spaces establish a coherent and interconnected site within its boundaries, but also beyond.

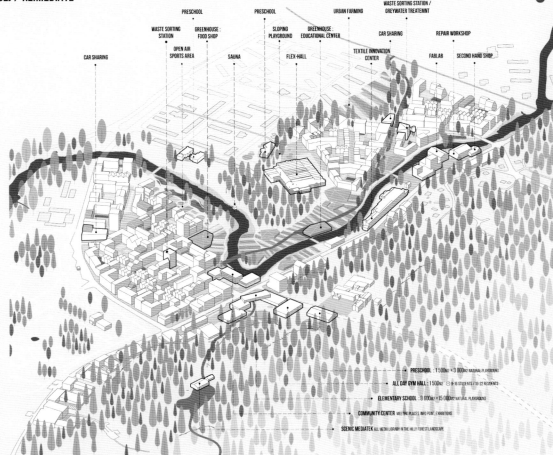

CAR SHARING · PRESCHOOL · WASTE SORTING STATION · OPEN AIR SPORTS AREA · GREENHOUSE : FOOD SHOP · SAUNA · PRESCHOOL · SLOPING PLAYGROUND · FLEX-HALL · GREENHOUSE : EDUCATIONAL CENTER · URBAN FARMING · TEXTILE INNOVATION CENTER · CAR SHARING · WASTE SORTING STATION / GREYWATER TREATEMINT · REPAIR WORKSHOP · FABLAB · SECOND HAND SHOP

PRESCHOOL : 1 500M2 + 3 000M2 NATURAL PLAYGROUND

ALL DAY GYM HALL : 1 500M2 · 9-16 STUDENTS / 15-22 RESIDENTS

ELEMENTARY SCHOOL : 8 600M2 + 15 000M2 NATURAL PLAYGROUND

COMMUNITY CENTER MEETING PLACES, INFO POINT, EXHIBITIONS

SCENIC MEDIATEK ALL MEDIA LIBRARY IN THE HILLY FOREST LANDSCAPE

ADAPTIVE AND PRODUCTIVE BLOCKS

A RESPECTFUL PHASING

TODAY

0 - 10 YEARS

10 - 15 YEARS

15 - 25 YEARS

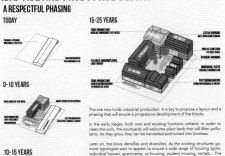

The site now holds industrial production. It is key to propose a layout and a phasing that will ensure a progressive development of the blocks.

In the early stages, both new and existing functions cohabit. In order to clean the soils, the courtyards will welcome plant beds that will filter pollutants. As they grow, they can be harvested and turned into biomass.

Later on, the block densifies and diversifies. As the existing structures go, more typologies start to appear to ensure a wide range of housing types: individual houses, apartments, co-housing, student housing, rentals... The phytoremediation beds can be moved to newly cleared areas. The cleaned soil can be turned into production urban farming, working together with the roof greenhouses. Trees planted in the early phases have now reached a decent size and participate in the cleaning process of the soil and air.

Finally, underground parking is proposed. As the whole site develops, public transportation, bike and pedestrian paths aim to support the daily commutes. The goal is to provide food as locally as the block, limiting heavy car-orientedh movements. Therefore, underground spaces can also welcome production through aquaponics.

FOR WHO ?

By 2020, nearly 45% of workers will be freelancers. Who should the site aim to welcome in order to adapt to the rapid changing worklife ?

FUTURE WORKLIFE PROFILES

WORK FROM HOME

INDEPENDENT ENTREPRENEURS

L/XL COLLECTIVES

L/XL COLLECTIVES

5 TO L BUSINESSES

BUSINESS FLEXIBILITY WITHIN THE BLOCK

Large office buildings are becoming outdated. Sweden ranks 7th in Europe as one of the best countries for remote working. The design offers a built structure that not only welcomes a large diversity of working profiles but is highly flexible. By introducing an ever-changing framework and allowing for short term rentals, the workspace is always adapting to needs. If a business needs to grow, it no longer needs to move outside of the city. The Block together with the Business Spine provide work environments, production and research spaces for all.

XS	S	M	L	XL
30M2	40 - 600M2	55 - 300M2	100 - 800M2	400 - 1200M2

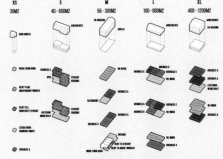

PRODUCTIVE GREEN HEART

WEEPING WILLOW TREES · YEARLY SUNFLOWER EVENT · INDIAN GRASS · PRODUCTIVE GREENHOUSE · OUTDOOR SEASONAL FARMING

Halmstad (SE)

Halmstad Standort / Location
100.000 Bevölkerung / Inhabitants
180 ha Betrachtungsraum / Study Site
14 ha Projektgebiet / Project Site

Die Gemeinde Halmstad erstreckt sich entlang einer Bahnlinie an der Westküste, in einer geografisch begünstigten Lage, zwischen zweien der drei größten Städte Schwedens. Halmstad ist bestrebt, zu einem Kerngebiet innerhalb dieser dynamischen Wachstumslinie zu werden. Die Entwicklung des Bahnhofsareals ist eine wesentliche Komponente bei der Verwirklichung dieses Zieles.

Die Aufgabe des Wettbewerbes besteht darin, den Hauptbahnhof Halmstad in einen neuen Knotenpunkt der Stadt zu verwandeln, durch den die Verbindungen zwischen national und regional, Leben und Arbeiten, Pendeln und Besuchen als Impulsgeber für die urbane Entwicklung des Gebietes dienen sollen. Ziel ist es, das Stadtzentrum nach Osten hin zu erweitern, um dieses neue produktive Gebiet mit einzuschließen, und die abgesonderten Areale in den östlichen und westlichen Teilen der Stadt anzubinden. Der Hauptbahnhof Halmstad wird ein in die Stadt integriertes Element sein, mit neuen Funktionen und verstärkter Anbindung an wichtige Brennpunkte in der Umgebung. Aufgabe ist es, die städtischen Eigenschaften des Gebietes zu stärken, die Abgrenzungen von Eisenbahn, Hauptstraße und Fluss zu überbrücken, und Volumina und Funktionen für ein Reisezentrum und weitere Bauwerke vorzuschlagen. Gesucht werden innovative technische Lösungen für Erschütterungen, Verkehrslärm und Regenwasserspeicherung.

Die Lage zwischen zwei bedeutenden Wachstumsgebieten – der Region Göteborg und der Region Öresund – sowie (aus Unternehmensperspektive) die Nähe zu Nordeuropa macht die Stadt attraktiv für neue Unternehmensgründungen. Halmstad ist ein bekannter Sommerurlaubsort, der wunderschöne Strände mit einer städtischen Umgebung verbindet.

Die Entwicklung des Hauptbahnhofes Halmstad wird einen neuen Cluster der Fortbewegung mit einem Schwerpunkt auf Fußgängerinnen und Fußgänger, Radfahrerinnen und Radfahrer und öffentlichen Verkehr begründen. Durch die Stärkung der urbanen Werte des Gebietes wird eine neue Dynamik entstehen, die Wohnbereiche mit wichtigen Knotenpunkten verbinden wird, etwa verschiedene Handelsdrehscheiben (Stadtzentrum, Nyhem), Kultur (Österskans) und Innovation (Universität Halmstad). Bedeutende Arbeitgeber in der Umgebung sind das Militär, das Krankenhaus, der Hafen und das Industriegebiet Lars Frid. Die Einbindung des Gebietes in die Stadt, aber auch die Verbindung zwischen wichtigen städtischen Knotenpunkten werden nach Fertigstellung verstärkt und intensiviert.

Der Hauptbahnhof Halmstad wird zu einem wichtigen Ankunftsort in der Stadt und wird für die meisten Besucherinnen und Besucher den ersten Eindruck der Stadt ausmachen. Erst einmal ausgebaut, wird das Areal die Identität der Stadt stärken und zu einem einprägsamen Reiseziel werden.

The municipality of Halmstad is located along the West Coast railway line, a geographically favourable location between two of Sweden's three major cities. The municipality strives to become a regional core in this dynamic line of growth. The development of the station area is an essential component in realizing this goal.

The competition task is to transform the Halmstad Central Station area into the new hub in the city, through which the connections between the national and the regional, living and working, and commuting and visiting serve as a catalyst for the urban development of the area. The aim is to expand the city centre eastwards to include this new productive area and to link the segregated areas in the eastern and the western parts of the city. The Halmstad Central Station area will be an integrated part of the city with new functions and improved connections to important focal points in the surroundings. The task is to strengthen the area's urban qualities, to bridge the barriers presented by the railway, the main road, and the river, and to propose volumes and functions for a travel centre and other built structures. Innovative technical solutions for vibrations, traffic noise, and rainwater harvesting are sought as well.

Its location between two major growth areas, the Gothenburg region and the Öresund region, and its proximity to – from a business perspective – Northern Europe makes the city attractive for the establishment of new business. Halmstad is a famous summer resort, which combines beautiful beaches with an urban environment.

Its development of the Halmstad Central station area will establish a new cluster of movement focusing on pedestrians, bicyclists, and public transport. The strengthening of the area's urban qualities will create a new dynamic in the area that links residential areas to important focal points, such as different hubs of commerce (city centre, Nyhem), culture (Österskans), and innovation (Halmstad University). Important workplaces in the surrounding area are the military, the hospital, the harbour and the Lars Frid industrial area. The integration of the site within the city, as well as the connection between important urban focal points, will be strengthened and intensified when redevelopment has been completed.

The Halmstad Central Station area will become an important destination for arriving in the city and be the first impression of the city for most visitors. Fully developed, the area will strengthen the municipality's identity and become a memorable destination.

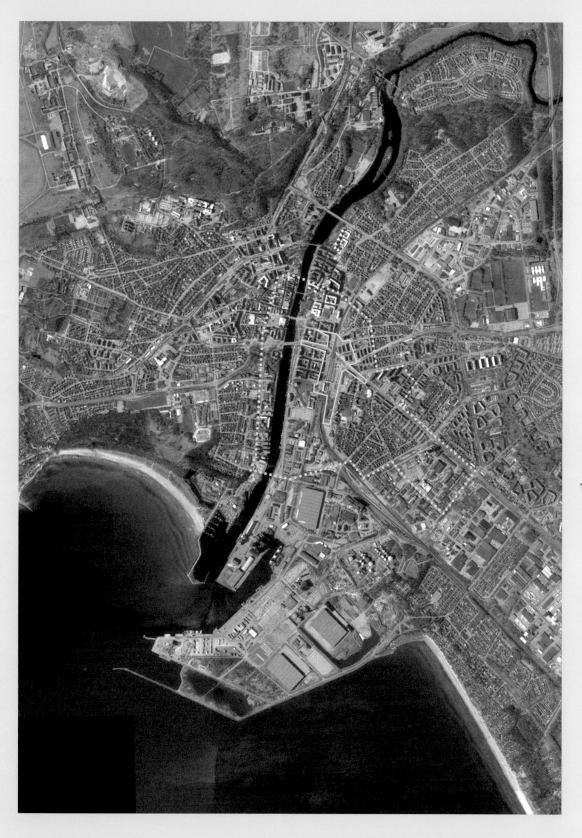

Walking Halmstad

Piotr Wisniowski (PL) Architekt / Architect
Joachim Heinz (DE) Ingenieur, Architekturstudent / Engineer, Architecture student
Karl Fredrik Bengtsson (SE) Architekturstudent / Architecture student
Soheil Shahnazari (IR) Architekturstudent / Architecture student

Augenblicklich scheint es sich bei Halmstad um eine geteilte Stadt zu handeln, mit einer Trennung in Nord-Süd-Richtung, verursacht durch den Fluss Nissan und die benachbarten Bahngleise, die sich von Norden nach Süden erstrecken. Das städtische Gefüge des Projektstandortes selbst ist ebenfalls zergliedert, öffentlicher Raum und wichtige Orte werden vom Verkehr unterbrochen.

Das Projekt „Walking Halmstad" entwirft einen effizienten Verkehrsknotenpunkt, der zugleich zahlreiche neue und attraktive Plätze für die Einwohnerinnen und Einwohner von Halmstad schafft und es diesen ermöglicht, sich ganz einfach fortzubewegen, sich zusammenzufinden und ihre Unternehmen zu führen. Eine Vielzahl von Eingriffen hat ein durchgehendes und in weiten Teilen barrierefreies städtisches Gefüge zur Folge. Dies umfasst auch das alte Stadtzentrum am Stora torget, eine ausgedehnte Einkaufs-straße entlang der Fredsgatan mit einem neuen Platz und einem Bahnübergang, eine Promenade entlang eines neuen Mischgebäudes, das Parken mit Mietflächen für lokale Geschäfte verbindet, eine Markthalle im alten Stationsgebäude und schließlich das neue Reisezentrum auf der anderen Seite der Schienen, mit Zugang zum neu aktivierten Studierendenpark.

Das Projekt schlägt ein Verkehrskonzept mit einer starken Priorisierung von Fahrrädern und Fußgängerinnen und Fußgängern vor. Der Hauptradweg entlang der Viktoria-gatan wird von zwei zusätzlichen Fahrstreifen begleitet, die den Osten mit dem Westen verbinden. Im Süden bieten zwei neue Brücken eine wichtige Verbindung zur Uni-versität Halmstad. Ein weiterer neuer Radweg führt durch die ebenfalls neue Unterführung an der Fredsgatan. Vor dem alten Bahnhof wird die Stationsgatan für den Auto-verkehr geschlossen. Nur Taxis und Busse werden pas-sieren dürfen. Die gleichen Beschränkungen gelten für das Gebiet um die neue Unterführung an der Fredsgatan. Der gesamte vom neuen Reisezentrum verursachte Kraft-fahrzeugverkehr wird auf die westliche Seite der Gleise umgeleitet, die östliche Seite soll lediglich dem lokalen Verkehr des angeschlossenen Viertels dienen.

Halmstad currently seems to be a divided city, with the main divisions extending from north to south as a result of the Nissan River and the nearby railroad tracks. The urban fabric of the project site itself is fragmented as well, and public spaces and points of interest are inter-rupted by traffic.

The proposal 'Walking Halmstad' creates an efficient transportation hub that simultaneously provides plenty of new and attractive spaces for the people of Halmstad, which thus enable them to easily move, gather, and run their businesses. A variety of interventions give rise to a continuous and largely barrier-free urban fabric. They include the old city centre at Stora Torget, a long shop-ping street along Fredsgatan with a new square and railway crossing, a promenade along a new hybrid build-ing that combines parking with rentable spaces for local businesses, a market hall in the old railway station build-ing, and finally a new travel centre on the opposite side of the tracks, with access to the newly activated student park.

The project proposes a traffic concept with a strong priority for bikes and pedestrians. The major bike lane along Viktoriagatan will be supplemented with two additional lanes connecting the east with the west. In the south, two new bridges provide a valuable connection with Halmstad University. Another new bike lane leads through the new underpass at Fredsgatan. In front of the old train station, Stationsgatan will be closed to private car transport, with access only for taxis and busses. The same restrictions apply to the area close to the new underpass at Fredsgatan. All car traffic related to the new travel centre will be directed to the western side of the tracks, while the eastern side will only be used by local traffic for the connected district.

Wir sind ein internationales Team, das aus Fredrik aus Schweden, Piotr aus Polen, Soheil aus dem Iran und Joachim aus Deutschland besteht. Wir haben einander im schwedischen Lund kennengelernt, wo wir während eines Studienprojektes miteinander gearbeitet haben. Joachim kam 2006 nach Skandinavien und verfügt über ein Doktorat in Maschinenbau. Dann beschloss er, Architektur zu studieren und verfasst im Augenblick seine Masterthesis bei Ramböll in Kopenhagen. Während Fredrik, So-heil und Joachim Architektur studie-ren, ist Piotr bereits als Architekt bei Jakobsson Pusterla tätig.

info@jakobssonpusterla.com

We are an international team con-sisting of Fredrik from Sweden, Piotr from Poland, Soheil from Iran, and Joachim from Germany. We got to know each other in Lund, Sweden, where we worked together during a study project. Joachim came to Scandinavia in 2006 and had a doc-torate in mechanical engineering. He then decided to study architecture and is currently writing his master thesis at Ramböll in Copenhagen. While Fredrik, Soheil, and Joachim are still studying architecture, Piotr already works as an architect at Jakobsson Pusterla.

info@jakobssonpusterla.com

WALKING HALMSTAD

Halmstad appears to be a divided city. The main divisions of the city drag from north to south due to the river Nissan and the railroad tracks parallel to it. However, also the urban fabric at the project site itself - east of river Nissan - is tattered in pieces. Public spaces and points of interests are interrupted by traffic.

The proposal of 'Walking Halmstad' aims to provide a variety of interventions that create a unified, continuous and mostly barrierfree urban tissue for the people of Halmstad. By foot or bike, the new walkable area encloses the old city center at Stora Torget, an extended shopping street along Fredsgatan, a new square with underpass and amphitheater at the railway crossing, the promenade along a new building that combines both parking and rentable spaces for local businesses, Stationparken and its market in the old station building, and the new travel center on the other side of the tracks with access to the newly activated Studentparken. Apart from a general gain to the city, the newly patched urban tissue facilitates various possibilities to access and switch between the various means of transportation and thereby fulfills the requirements of an effective transportation hub.

In order to reach the objective of a continous and walkable urban tissue, the project suggests a new and better defined traffic concept with particular priority to bikes and pedestrians.

The major bike lane along Viktoriagatan and Laholmsvagen will be accompanied by two additional lanes that connect the east with the west. In the south of the project area, two new bridges over river Nissan and the railway tracks provide a valuable connection towards Halmstad university. A second bike lane is introduced at the new underpass at Fredsgatan. The project area exhibits three bike parkings with direct access to the train tracks, one of them close to the local and regional bus stops.

In front of the old train station, Stationsgatan will be closed for cars and only taxis and busses are allowed to pass. The same counts for the area close to the new underpass at Fredsgatan. In both areas, the street exhibits pedestrian friendly pavement. The one-way street at Fredrik Stromsgata is paved in the same way, giving high priority to pedestrians and low priority to cars. Traffic on the east side of the tracks is not supposed to be related with the new travel center; only local traffic of the connected quarter is expected.

The local and regional bus lines are kept as they are, the regional bus terminal stays at its current position.

In the following we will put focus on the four main interventions in the 'Walking Halmstad' project site, which are

1. Square at Fredsgatan with underpass and amphitheater
2. Building Hybrid that combines local parking with spaces for local businesses
3. The old station building as a market hall and activation for Stationsparken
4. The new travel center and activation of Studentparken

Elements in the Project Area

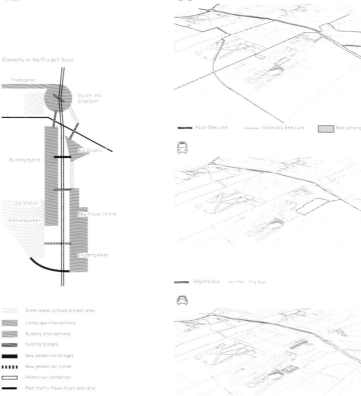

Green areas outside project area
Landscape interventions
Building interventions
Existing bridges
New pedestrian bridges
New pedestrian tunnel
Pedestrian connection
Main traffic flows (train and cars)

Major Bike Lane — Secondary Bike Lane — Bike parking

Regional bus — City bus

Low traffic — Medium traffic — High traffic — Park & ride
Cars one way — Taxi — Local parking

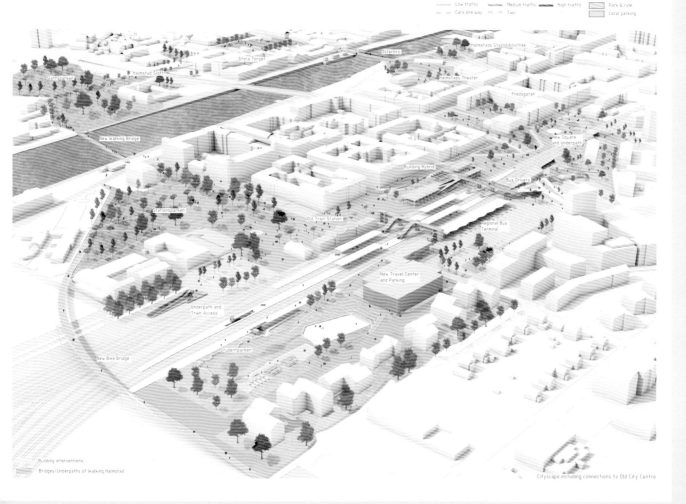

Building interventions
Bridges/Underpaths of Walking Halmstad

Cityscape including connections to Old City Centre

The crossing in the north of the project site is accomplished as an barrier-free underpass. It constitutes a major new connection between the western and eastern part of the city. The circular lines form an underpass in an S-shape that minimizes the needed space to create an accessible crossing with maximum 6% slope.

Staircases provide access from the directions that are not in favour of the ramp orientation. On each side of the tracks, terraces are formed to an amphitheater with a small stage area, which is protected from the major taffic line of the underpass.

The underpass can also be read as a diagonal separator that separates the car traffic and parking in the north-eastern end from a newly created square in the south-western area. This square is oriented to the south west and provides a high amenity value with fountain, café and food trucks.

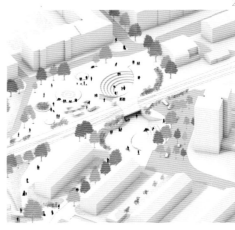

In the eastern part of the railway tracks, along Stationsgatan, we introduce a new building, that will transform and adapt over time.

Primarily starting as a parking garage for the local traffic in the area, it will gradually change into a place that artists and local businesses inhabitate. The decreasing demand for car parkings will gradually increase the available space for the new inhabitants. Workshops and connected small dwelling units can also be rented temporarily.

The building also serves as a further entrance to the eastern side of Halmstad by utilizing the bridge that lies on top of the building. On the other side a landscaped roof-structure leads to the existing pedestrian bridge over Laholmsvägen as well as down to street level.
The triangle shaped building hosts a 2-storey bike parking, a kiosk, and a recreation lounge with restrooms and showers for bus drivers.

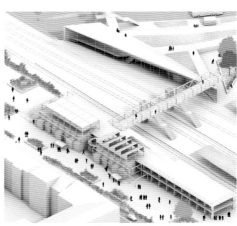

The old train station building will be transformed into a market hall, with permanent food stands inside, and a weekly market outside on the square facing Stationsparken.

In front of the old train station, Stationsgatan will be closed for car traffic and provide a continous urban fabric for pedestrians. The Grand Hotel on the other side of the square will also profit from this closing. A public café facing the square could attract both, hotel guests and passing by visitors.

Stationsparken will not only gain from the new market hall, but also from the new pedestrian bridge over the Nissan, connecting with the park of Halmstad slot and thereby closing the circle of 'Walking Halmstad'.

The new travel center is located on the east side of the railway tracks, directly behind the old train station.

Due to the vincinity to the old train station, the historical building from the late 19th century can serve as an entrance gate to the new travel center, f.ex when approaching the center from the new walking bridge over river Nissan. With its location next to the Studentparken, both the traffic center and Studentparken will benefit. While travellers have the freedom to enjoy their waiting time in the park, landscape interventions and added possibilities for recreational activities will make the park a more attractive public space for both locals, students and travellers. The rain water management function is maintained by keeping some of the ponds as well as introducing a rainwater basin which can hold water during sudden cloudbursts, and can else be used for recreational activities and events.

The location in the south also provides space for a bigger park&ride parking garage for travellers.

M1 1000

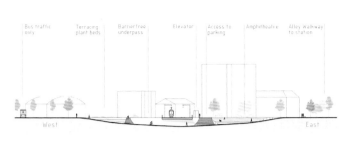

Bus traffic only | Terracing plant beds | Barrierfree underpass | Elevator | Access to parking | Amphitheatre | Alley walkway to station

West — East

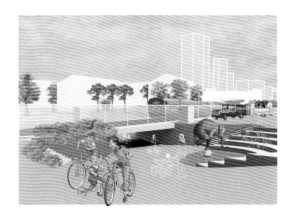

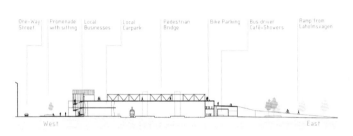

One-Way Street | Promenade with sitting | Local Businesses | Local Carpark | Pedestrian Bridge | Bike Parking | Bus driver Café+Showers | Ramp from Laholmsvägen

West — East

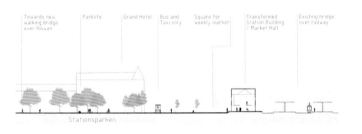

Towards new walking bridge over Nissan | Parklife | Grand Hotel | Bus and Taxi only | Square for weekly market | Transformed Station Building / Market Hall | Existing bridge over railway

Stationsparken

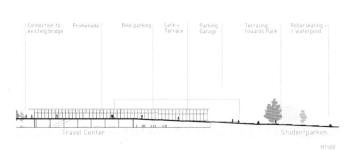

Connection to existing bridge | Promenade | Bike parking | Café + Terrace | Parking Garage | Terracing towards Park | Rollerskating + / Waterpond

Travel Center — Studentparken

M1:500

Uddevalla (SE)

Dalaberg, Hovhult und Bulid Standort / Location
35.000 Bevölkerung / Inhabitants
474 ha Betrachtungsraum / Study Site
233 ha Projektgebiet / Project Site

Die Stadt Uddevalla liegt im Zentrum der historischen Region Bohuslän und konnte sich ihr kulturelles Erbe, das so typisch für das Gebiet ist, bis heute erhalten. Die Strategie von Uddevalla legt den Schwerpunkt auf drei Bereiche: Leben, Leidenschaft und Lage, die zu einer besseren Lebensqualität führen sollen. Die Bürgerinnen und Bürger von Uddevalla sollen sich respektiert und stolz fühlen und das Selbstvertrauen und das Verlangen verspüren, sich selbst sowie ihre Umgebung weiterzuentwickeln. Die Stadt weist eine ganze Menge an Treffpunkten auf, die Kreativität erzeugen und fördern. Uddevalla ist Teil der Wachstumsregionen von Oslo und Göteborg. Die Stadt kann auf ein großes Potenzial verweisen, was in erster Linie auf ihre industrielle Geschichte und die attraktive Lage im Herzen von Bohuslän, mit der einmaligen Kombination von Meer, Wald, Bergen und Fjord, zurückzuführen ist.

Der Wettbewerbsstandort umfasst Wohngebiete, die typisch für das soziale Wohnbauprogramm der 1970er Jahre sind, Einfamilienhäuser am Stadtrand, aber auch reichlich Landschaft, in der man der Natur nahe ist. Die urbane Gestaltung von Hovhult wird von einem Bautypus dominiert. Das Gebiet Dalaberg wiederum umfasst eine größere Vielfalt an sozialen Wohnbauten, mit Gebäuden, die bis zu sieben Stockwerke hoch sind. Bulid ist heute eine ungenutzte Landschaft, in der die Natur sich selbst überlassen wurde. Obwohl die Wettbewerbsstandorte abgegrenzt sind, kann das Gebiet nicht als eine separate Einheit betrachtet werden. Stattdessen muss es im Kontext der urbanen Entwicklung der gesamten Stadt gesehen werden.

Uddevalla, das strategisch an der schwedischen Westküste liegt, war von Anfang an als Handelsknotenpunkt konzipiert. Seit der Industriellen Revolution siedelten sich hier immer mehr industrielle Produktionsstandorte an. Mit der Gründung einer der größten schwedischen Werften kurz nach dem Ende des Zweiten Weltkrieges erfuhr die Stadt einen weiteren wirtschaftlichen Aufschwung. Dies erhöhte den Bedarf an Wohnungen und führte in der Folge zum sozialen Wohnbauprogramm. Bald darauf fand eine Expansion Uddevallas, besonders an der Peripherie, statt, was auch die Bezirke Dalaberg und Hovhult umfasste. Ab Mitte der 1980er Jahre zeichnete sich jedoch in vielen europäischen Städten allmählich ein weltweiter wirtschaftlicher Wandel ab, und selbst die Werft in Uddevalla musste, zusammen mit vielen weiteren Wirtschaftszweigen, schließen. Während dieser Zeit stieg die Arbeitslosigkeit und viele Menschen verließen Uddevalla. Als eine Folge davon nahm die Segregation zu, vor allem in Gebieten, in denen sozialer Wohnbau weit verbreitet war. Nach einer gewissen Zeit wurden bekannte soziale Probleme tragend, wie steigende Arbeitslosigkeit und Exklusion.

Um diese negativen Trends umzukehren, möchte die Stadt das Potenzial aufgreifen, das in der kulturellen Vielfalt liegt, und eine gut integrierte Umgebung schaffen, die zur Entwicklung der gesamten Stadt Uddevalla beiträgt.

The city of Uddevalla lies in the centre of the historic Bohuslän region and maintains a cultural heritage particular to the region to this day. Uddevalla's strategy focuses on three areas: life, passion, and location so as to lead to a better quality of life. Diversity and tolerance stimulate development. The idea is that the citizens of Uddevalla should feel respected and proud and have the confidence and desire to develop themselves and their surroundings. The city has an abundance of meeting places that inspire and develop creativity. Uddevalla is part of the growth regions of Oslo and Gothenburg. The potential of the city is strong largely due to its industrial history and its attractive location in the heart of Bohuslän region, with its unique combination of sea, forests, mountains, and fjords.

The competition site includes residential areas typical for the social housing program of the 1970s, suburban family houses as well as a large rural landscape where one can come close to nature. The district of Hovhult is dominated by one building type. The Dalaberg area on the other hand includes more varied forms of social housing, with buildings of up to seven storeys. Bulid today is an unused landscape where nature has been left to own. Although the competition sites are demarcated, the area cannot be seen as a separate entity. It must instead be considered within the context of the urban development of the city as a whole.

Strategically located on the west coast of Sweden, Uddevalla developed as a trading hub from its very beginnings. After the industrial revolution, more and more industrial production sites were established here. With the founding of one of Sweden's biggest shipyards shortly after the end of the Second World War, the city experienced another commercial boost. This created a need for more accommodations, which led to the social housing program. Soon afterwards, Uddevalla expanded, especially on its outskirts, including the districts of Dalaberg and Hovhult. Starting in the mid-1980s, however, global economic transformation gradually took hold in many European cities; even the shipyard in Uddevalla was shut down at this time, along with many other industries. During this period, many people became unemployed and moved away from Uddevalla. One consequence was that segregation increased, especially in areas where social housing is prevalent. After a time, well-known social problems emerged, such as increased unemployment and exclusion.

In order to reverse these negative trends, the municipality wants to tap into the potential of cultural diversity and realize a well-integrated environment that contributes to the development of the entire city of Uddevalla.

Wake „BU-HOV-BERG" up!

Elena Golub (DE) Architektin / Architect
Xi Wu (CHN) Architekt, Stadtplaner / Architect, Uraben Planner
Nan Liu (CHN) Architektin, Stadtplanerin / Architect, Urban Planner
Rocío Miranda Barreda (ES) Architektin / Architect

„BU-HOV-BERG" ist der neue Name einer gut integrierten und produktiven urbanen Umgebung, dem „Million Program", zu dem neben Hovult und Dallaberg auch das benachbarte ländliche Gebiet Bulid gehört.

Dieses Projekt beabsichtigt, neue Arten von urbanen Infrastrukturen auf der Grundlage vorhandener Ressourcen vor Ort zu erkunden, um so eine attraktive städtische Einbindung in das am stärksten voneinander getrennte Viertel der Stadt zu gestalten und schließlich die Entwicklung der gesamten Stadt Uddevalla auf produktive Weise anzuregen.

Nach einer intensiven Analyse der vorhandenen Ressourcen vor Ort konzentriert sich unser Projekt auf drei Potenziale: natürliche Ressourcen in Bulid „BU", Million-Program-Wohnungen und ihre soziale, demografische Vielfalt in Hovhult „HOV" und den Architekturkomplex Lillbräckan in Dalaberg „BERG". Ein neues aktives lineares Band dient nicht nur als Verbindung zwischen den drei neu entwickelten Gebieten mit ihren unterschiedlichen Stadtteilen, sondern auch als Anziehungskraft für die umliegenden Bewohnerinnen und Bewohner, Touristinnen und Touristen und neue Wirtschaftszweige. Auch bietet es Möglichkeiten für Beschäftigungen, kulturelle Angebote und Freizeitaktivitäten.

In der Folge entsteht eine positive Beziehung zwischen dem sanierten Stadtteil „BU-HOV-BERG" und der Stadt selbst. Die umgebende Landschaft ist nicht mehr nur das Umland für Ernährung oder Energieversorgung. Die bisherige Vorstadt wird zu einem urbanen Magnet, der die städtischen Ströme nach Norden zieht und eine neue Entwicklungsdynamik der gesamten Stadt Uddevalla prägt.

'BU-HOV-BERG' is the name chosen for a well-integrated and productive urban environment consisting of the 'Million Program' areas of Hovhult and Dalaberg as well as Bulid, an adjacent nature area.

This project aims to explore new types of urban infrastructures based on the existing local resources in order to shape attractive urban integration in the city's most segregated district, and, ultimately, to foster the development of the entire town of Uddevalla in a productive way.

After analysing existing resources on site, this project focused on the following three points: natural resources in Bulid (BU), Million Programme housing and its social, demographic diversity in Hovhult (HOV), and the architecture complex Lillbräckan in Dalaberg (BERG). A new, active linear band is created as a connection running through the three areas being redeveloped with their districts of different characters and as an attraction for surrounding residents, tourists and new economies. It also offers new employment possibilities, plus cultural and recreational activities.

A positive relationship between the 'BU-HOV-BERG' districts undergoing redevelopment and the city of Uddevalla is thus created. Greenery is no longer merely a hinterland for food or energy supply. The previously suburban area will instead be an urban magnet, drawing urban flows to the north and shaping a new dynamic of development in Uddevalla as a whole.

Wir kennen uns durch unsere Arbeitsstelle. Schnell haben wir festgestellt, dass wir viele gleiche Interessen und vor allem gleiche Ansichten in der Architektur haben. So kam der Wunsch relativ früh auf, neben unserem Beruf gemeinsam an unterschiedlichen Wettbewerben teilzunehmen.

opa711@gmx.de

We got to know each other through our jobs, and soon recognized that we have various common interests and perspectives in the field of architecture and urban design. We therefore decided to take part in an exciting competition together as a team in our free time.

opa711@gmx.de

Uddevalla(SE)

Wake "Bu-Hov-Berg" up!

Wake "BU-HOV-BERG" up !

"BU-HOV-BERG" is the new name of a well-integrated and productive urban environment, which consists of "Million Programme" areas Hovhult and Dalaberg, as well as the adjacent natural area **Bulid**.
This project aims at exploring new types of urban infrastructures based on the existing **resources** on site, in order to shape an attractive **urban integration** in the city's most segregated district, eventually to motivate the development of the whole Uddevalla in a productive way.

The City Uddevalla and its Hinterland – between urban and green

Where to accommodate the increasing amount of residents and new, innovative businesses?
How to make the whole Uddevalla attractive and productive again?
The vast green area in northern part of Uddevalla could be an alternative answer. This project starts with a green finger structure, leading the natural landscape into urban spaces to the south, and spreading the current urban environment into hinterland in the north, in order to shape a new relationship between the city and its hinterland, and create synergies between urban and green.
In consequence, a new positive relation between redeveloped district "BU-HOV-BERG" and the city Uddevalla is created. Green is not only the hinterland for food or energy supply anymore, instead, the previous suburban area will be an urban magnet, attracting the urban flows to the north, and shaping a new dynamic of development of the whole Uddevalla.

Resourcing the site:

"BU"– green, "HOV"–Million Programme, "BERG"– Dalaberg-Lillbräckan
This projects focused on the following three of them : **natural resources** in Bulid, **Million Programme Housing** and its social, demographic diversity in Hovhult, and the **architecture complex Lillbräckan** in Dalaberg.
A new active linear band is created as a connection through three neighborhoods, and new cultural and economic functions would be implanted into this linear link.

Bulid – Activation of natural resources

Bulid is nowadays relatively unutilized, despite of its proximity to forest and land. In the green finger structure, five zones with four different uses are defined : **recreational area, multi-family dwellings** with urban farming, **horticulture and craft workshop**, and **sport facilities**. Those new functional zones in green would attract residents and small businesses from both "BU-HOV-BERG" and Uddevalla.

Hovhult – "Do-It-Yourself" Million Programme

The Renewal project of Million Programme focuses on the typical three-storey, low rise apartment type in Hovhult. A renewal proposal is created based on the **existing structure** of Million Programme and the social, **demographic diversity** of existing residents.
The Million Programme is frequently perceived as cheap and small rental apartment and stringent, monotonous urban atmosphere. **The key question is** : How to create a new architectural diversity in terms of **family structure** and apartment typology ?
The well-built structures of Million Programme are preserved as a **basic infrastructure** : the old staircases are replaced by a **new circulation system**; one more storey is partly added up together with **roof garden**. In this way, the whole system of Million Programme would be opened up to a freedom for each tenant or owner to have an **individual design** by himself. All the other architectural elements, such as floor plate, facade, interior staircase and balcony would be flexible according to the **wish** of tenants.
Block filled-in buildings will offer more communal spaces for the entire block, providing migrants good chance to integrate into society, local residents a meeting spot to exchange their working experience and social background, new residents a productive atmosphere to bring in alternative economies.

Dalaberg - Renewal of Lillbräckan

The existing architectural feather of Lillbräckan is well preserved as a **new icon** of the whole area, with a **spatial rearrangement** and a **functional update**. On the top of garage and supermarket, the previous abandoned courtyard is redesigned into an active **public platform**, with a good pedestrian connection with the band and a great proximity to the main entrance of the whole area," Bridge Fjällvägen".
On the level of courtyard, lie all the public functions, such as commercial spaces and workshops. On the upper levels, a diversified range of apartments are provided, from single person apartment, Duplex for home offices and new start-ups, to the penthouse with roof garden.

The center of this region would be **relocated** from current Dalaberg Center to Lillbräckan, where the diversity of new housing alternatives, spacious rental areas for new start-ups and businesses, and the active public space on the courtyard, could promote the **establishment of a new icon** on site in the future.

An active band going through "BU", "HOV" and "BERG"

The active band is a link going through all the three redeveloped areas, serving as a **connection** with the different characterized districts and an **attraction** to the surrounding residents, tourists and new economies. Four different functional zones are defined : **commercial area** in Lillbräckan, **event area** around the main entrance to the site, productive and **communal zone** in-between two major Million Programme areas, and **playgrounds** with educational functions.

A series of **synergy effect** would happen on this active band, in the way of interacting with surrounding urban environment: With a good proximity to the existing communities, the band will provide the current communal buildings a series of new **public spaces** and recreational areas.
Entrepreneurship and creativity will be encourages, and new Start-ups, co-working and three sector industry will have a far reaching influence on Million Programme residential area, with the supply of new employment opportunities and communication chances.

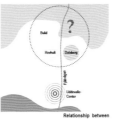

Relationship between urban and green

discover the Resources

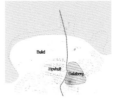

current Situation

lead Green into Urban

Spread Urban into Green

New Street Networks and Connections

Densification

Implanting Urban Catalyst

New Street Networks

→ main Vehicle Connection
→ main pedestrian Connection
— existing Street
— new Street
○ existing Bus Station
○ new Bus Station

Functions

Dwelling | Mixed Use - flexible using in GroundFloor +
Education | residential
Sports | Mixed Use- flexible
Culture | using in all floors
Industry | Band
Car Park

New Uses into Band

3D Playground
productive and Community Zone
Event Area
Commercial+ New Center

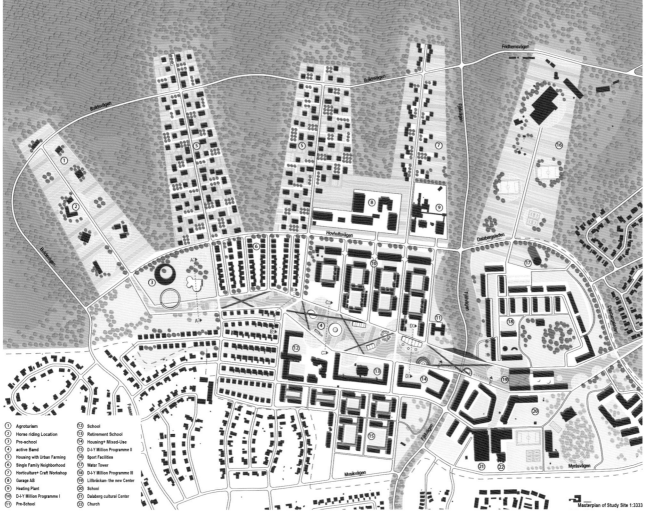

① Agroturism
② Horse riding Location
③ Pre-school
④ active Band
⑤ Housing with Urban Farming
⑥ Single Family Neighborhood
⑦ Horticulture+ Craft Workshop
⑧ Garage AB
⑨ Heating Plant
⑩ D-I-Y Million Programme I
⑪ Pre-School
⑫ School
⑬ Retirement School
⑭ Housing+ Mixed-Use
⑮ D-I-Y Million Programme II
⑯ Sport Facilities
⑰ Water Tower
⑱ D-I-Y Million Programme III
⑲ Lillbräckan- the new Center
⑳ School
㉑ Dalaberg cultural Center
㉒ Church

Masterplan of Study Site 1:3333

Uddevalla(SE)

Wake "Bu-Hov-Berg" up!

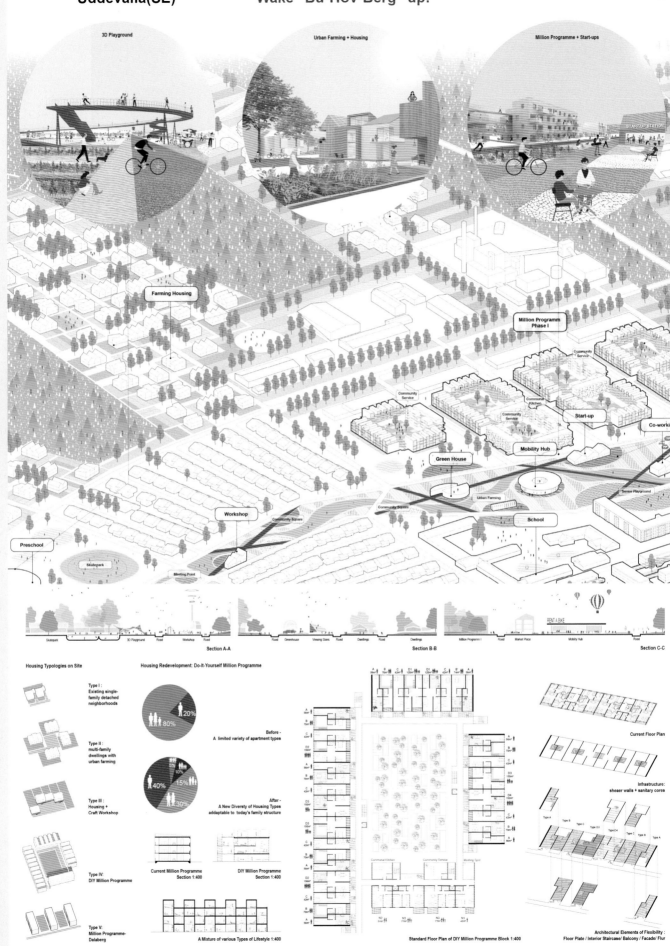

3D Playground

Urban Farming + Housing

Million Programme + Start-ups

START-UP STATION

Farming Housing

Million Programm Phase I

Community Service

Community Service

Communal Kitchen

Community Service

Start-up

Co-working

Green House

Mobility Hub

Urban Farming

Community Square

Senior Playground

Workshop

Community Square

School

Preschool

Skatepark

Meeting Point

Skatepark   3D Playground   Road   Workshop   Road   Section A-A

Road   Greenhouse   Viewing Stairs   Road   Dwellings   Road   Dwellings   Section B-B

RENT A BIKE

Million Programm I   Road   Market Place   Mobility Hub   Road   Section C-C

Housing Typologies on Site

Type I :
Existing single-
family detached
neighborhoods

Type II :
multi-family
dwellings with
urban farming

Type III :
Housing +
Craft Workshop

Type IV:
DIY Million Programme

Type V:
Million Programme-
Dalaberg

Housing Redevelopment: Do-It-Yourself Million Programme

20%
80%

Before -
A limited variety of apartment types

5%
10%
40%   15%
30%

After -
A New Diversty of Housing Types
addaptable to today's family structure

Current Million Programme
Section 1:400

DIY Million Programme
Section 1:400

A Mixture of various Types of Lifestyle 1:400

Standard Floor Plan of DIY Million Programme Block 1:400

Current Floor Plan

Infrastructure:
shener walls + sanitary cores

Type A   Type B   Type C   Type D3   Type D4   Type C   Type B   Type A

Architectural Elements of Flexibility :
Floor Plate / Interior Staircase/ Balcony / Facade/ Flur

Uddevalla(SE)

Wake "Bu-Hov-Berg" up!

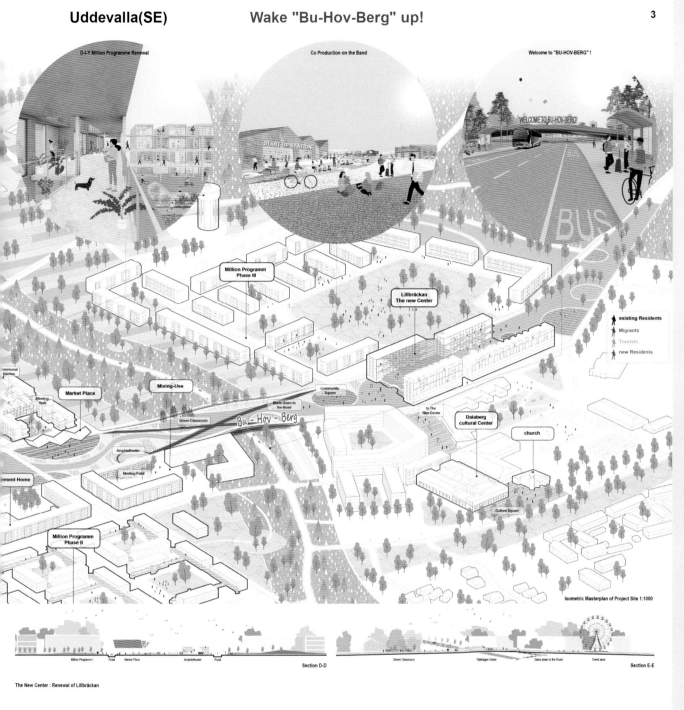

D-I-Y Million Programme Renewal

Co Production on the Band

Welcome to "BU-HOV-BERG" !

WELCOME TO BU-HOV-BERG!

Million Programm Phase III

Lillbräckan The new Center

existing Residents
Migrants
Tourists
new Residents

Market Place

Mixing-Use

Community Square

Stairs down to the Road

Green Classroom

Bu-Hov-Berg

to The New Center

Dalaberg cultural Center

church

Amphitheater

Meeting Point

Meeting Point

ement Home

Culture Square

Million Programm Phase II

Isometric Masterplan of Project Site 1:1000

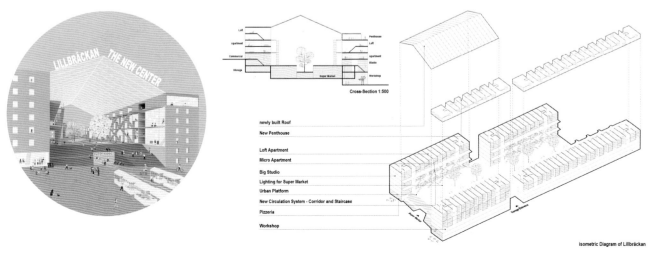

Million Programm I | Road | Market Place | Amphietheater | Road

Section D-D

Green Classroom | Fjälbägen Street | Stairs down to the Road | Event area

Section E-E

The New Center : Renewal of Lillbräckan

LILLBRÄCKAN THE NEW CENTER

Loft
Apartment
Commercial
storage

Penthouse
Loft
apartment
Studio
Worskhop

Super Market

Cross-Section 1:500

newly built Roof

New Penthouse

Loft Apartment

Micro Apartment

Big Studio

Lighting for Super Market

Urban Platform

New Circulation System - Corridor and Staircase

Pizzeria

Workshop

isometric Diagram of Lillbräckan

Appendix

Jurys
Juries

Deutsch-polnische Jury / German-Polish Jury
Prof. Christa Reicher (Vorsitz / chairperson)
Annette Friedrich
Anne Keßler
Alessandro delli Ponti
Peter Stubbe
Hubert Trammer
Prof. Mario Tvrtkovic
Dr. Irene Wiese-von Ofen

Stellvertreterin / Substitute
Karin Sandeck

Lokale Jury Bergische Kooperation / Local jury Bergische Kooperation
Prof. Kunibert Wachten (Vorsitz / chairperson)
Christof Gemeiner
Jochen Kral
OB Tim Kurzbach
Dr. Claudia Panke
Uta Schneider
Peter Stuhlträger
Prof. Rolf Westerheide
Dr. Irene Wiese-von Ofen

Stellvertreter / Substitutes
Frank Boberg
Lutz Groll
Hartmut Hoferichter
Dr. Stefan Holl

125

Lokale Jury Selb / Local jury Selb
Prof. Angela Mensing-de Jong (Vorsitz / chairperson)
Carsten Hentschel
Prof. Janna Hohn
Rudolf Kirschneck
Helmut Resch
Dr. Klaus von Stetten
Prof. Mario Tvrtkovic

Stellvertreter / Substitute
Stefan Manthey

Lokale Jury Warszawa / Local jury Warszawa
Sławomir Gzell
Marek Kempa
Karol Kobos
Monika Konrad
Michał Tatjewski
Hubert Trammer
Karin Sandeck
Wojciech Wagner
Tomasz Zemła

Bildnachweis
Credits

28
Die produktive Stadt
Werksviertel, München
(Foto: Stefan Werrer)

29
Themenfeld Arbeits- und
Wissenschaftsstadt, Masterplan
Darmstadt 2030+ (Abb.: Labor für
urbane Orte und Prozesse)

29
Bürgerforum, Masterplan
Darmstadt 2030+ (Abb.: Labor für
urbane Orte und Prozesse)

30
Quartierskonzept Thales-Areal,
Rahmenplan Oststadt/Nordoststadt
Pforzheim (Abb.: Labor für urbane
Orte und Prozesse)

35
Luftbilder der Städte Hilden,
Ratingen, Solingen, Wülfrath-Düssel

37–39
Bergisch Plugin
Nikolai Werner, Daniel Branchereau,
Moritz Scharwächter, Vassilissa
Airaudo

41–43
The Productive Region
Marc Rieser

45
Luftbild Selb
Archiv Stadt Selb

47–49
Scherben bringen Glück
Simon Gehrmann, Roderich Eßmann,
Margarita Vollmer, Robin Thomae

51–53
Selbstgemacht
Alberto Montiel Lozano, Pedro de la
Torre Prieto

55
Luftbild Warschau
Archiv Stadt Warschau

57–59
Feedback Placemaking
Ada Jaśkowiec, Michał Strupiński

61–63
NEW neighborHUT
Edyta Nieciecka, Stanislaw
Tomaszewski

65–67
Volcano
Michał Purski

77
Luftbild Hyvinkää
Archiv Stadt Hyvinkää

79–81
The Green Ring
Radostina Radulova-Stahmer,
Deniza Horländer, Viktorija Yeretska

83
Luftbild Tuusula
Archiv Stadt Tuusula

85–87
60°North
Natalia Vera Vigaray, Patxi Martin
Dominguez, Josep Garriga Tarrés,
Emmanuel Laux, Agnes Jacquin,
Alexandra Jansen

89
Luftbild Romainville
Archiv Stadt Romainville

91–93
Bridging Productivities
Sascha Bauer, Jonas Mattes,
Jannis Haueise, Ender Cicek

95
Luftbild Govdageaidnu
Archiv Stadt Govdageaidnu

97–99
Catalouge of Ideas
Teresa Timm, Merle Jelitto, Paul
Raphael Schaegner

101
Luftbild Borås
Archiv Stadt Borås

103–105
P2P – Plugin 2 Produce
Alexandra Kashina, Johan Nilsson,
Husain Vaghjipurwala

107–109
RE:MEDIATE
Alice Lemaire, Anna Nötzel,
Dominika Misterka, Emeline Lex,
Fernando Gonzalez-Camino,
Marcin Zebrowski, Martin Näf,
Teresa Arana Aristi, Tony Nielsen,
Victor Ohlsson

111
Luftbild Halmstadt
Archiv Stadt Halmstadt

113–115
Walking Halmstad
Piotr Wisniowski, Joachim Heinz,
Karl Fredrik Bengtsson, Soheil
Shahnazari

117
Luftbild Uddevalla
Archiv Stadt Uddevalla

119–121
Wake „BU-HOV-BERG" up!
Elena Golub, Xi Wu, Nan Liu,
Rocío Miranda Barreda

Impressum
Imprint

© 2020 by jovis Verlag GmbH

Herausgeber / Editor
Europan
Deutsche Gesellschaft zur Förderung von
Architektur, Wohnungs- und Städtebau e.V.
Vesta Nele Zareh
Friedrichstraße 23 A
10969 Berlin
www.europan.de

Redaktionsteam / Editorial staff
Kaye Geipel, Saskia Hebert, Sven Kröger, Jens Metz,
Michael Rudolph, Vesta Nele Zareh

Englische Übersetzung / English translation
Amy Klement

Deutsche Übersetzung / German translation
Alexandra Titze-Grabec

Gestaltung / Graphic design
Rolf Eusterschulte, Berlin

Druck / Print
Gutenberg Beuys Feindruckerei,
Hannover Langenhagen

Auflage 700

Bibliografische Information der Deutschen Nationalbibliothek
Die Deutsche Nationalbibliothek verzeichnet diese Publikation in
der Deutschen Nationalbibliografie; detaillierte bibliografische
Daten sind im Internet über http://dnb.d-nb.de abrufbar.

Bibliographic information published by the Deutsche
Nationalbibliothek
The Deutsche Nationalbibliothek lists this publication in the Deutsche
Nationalbibliografie; detailed bibliographic data are available on the
Internet at http://dnb.d-nb.de

jovis Verlag GmbH
Lützowstraße 33
10785 Berlin
www.jovis.de

jovis-Bücher sind weltweit im ausgewählten Buchhandel erhältlich.
Informationen zu unserem internationalen Vertrieb erhalten Sie von
Ihrem Buchhändler oder unter www.jovis.de.

jovis books are available worldwide in select bookstores. Please
contact your nearest bookseller or visit www.jovis.de for information
concerning your local distribution.

ISBN 978-3-86859-642-7

Mediapartner

german-architects.com
Profiles of Selected Architects